HEAD GAMES:
THE GLOBAL CONCUSSION CRISIS

Christopher Nowinski

Head Games The Film, LLC

The information and suggestions found in this book are designed to provide a resource that may be useful in making informed choices about participation in sporting activities. The book is not intended to, and does not, provide medical advice, nor substitute for evaluation and treatment of any specific medical symptoms or conditions by a medical professional and should not be relied upon in any form or to any extent for that purpose. The author is not licensed to practice medicine nor physical rehabilitation therapy of any form. Except as otherwise noted, the views expressed in the book are those of the author based upon his personal experiences, interviews of athletes, medical and therapeutic professionals and others connected to the topic, and his lay analysis of various medical studies and available data on the topics presented in the book. Each of the author and the publisher specifically disclaim any liability or responsibility to any person for any decisions or actions taken in reliance on the information provided, or the views expressed, herein. Any person who has questions regarding a particular medical condition or symptoms similar to those described in this book is urged to consult a licensed physician expert in the field.

*Dedicated to my wife Nicole, and to the players, young and old,
and their families, whose lives have been changed
forever by brain injuries.*

CONTENTS

Foreword

BY ISAIAH KACYVENSKI

I am deeply honored to be writing this introduction for my best friend, my college roommate, and someone who has taught me a lot about experiencing life and pursuing the truth. From the vantage point of my eight-year NFL career, I have watched his interest in concussions evolve from a simple idea to an unstoppable movement. When Chris first started talking about concussions and potential long-term impact on the brain, I thought he was out of his mind. Now I realize he's saved a lot of minds, and just by reading this book, you will have the power to do so as well.

I first met Chris Nowinski in the summer of 1995. We reported to preseason football camp two weeks before the rest of our freshman class at Harvard University. I noticed him while I was in the dining hall lunch line and distinctly remember thinking that Chris looked like he didn't quite fit in. And this is saying plenty, considering I showed up at Harvard with my red hair cut in a reverse mullet and scooted around campus on a broken-down, undersized ten-speed bike I bought at a garage sale for $10; it shot sparks from the front rim because I popped the front tire and couldn't afford to fix it.

After having difficulty sizing up Chris—physically he was gawky to the point of not yet having grown into his body and lanky to the point of being almost freakish—I was still curious enough to sit down with him for lunch. I quickly learned that Chris didn't fit into any easy stereotypes. He was big, but he was not dumb. In fact, he was extremely well-spoken, to the point where I felt self-conscious with how I sounded. Chris could talk, and he could sing—in the first hour I met him he told me all about his role in his high school production of *West Side Story* (and even sang a few lines). I also found out that

v

he had been the captain of his football and basketball teams in high school. When he was done talking, I was finally able to ask him the question I originally came over to ask, so I could neatly bucket him in my head: "So, what position do you play?"

As I've come to learn since then, Chris is one of a kind, and he continues to surprise me, just as much as he did that first day I met him. After college, Chris and I were poised to go our separate ways. As a kid growing up in poverty in an abusive home, and at times homeless, I dreamed of playing in the National Football League. Football was my source of power from the age of nine. It was the platform that gave me the self-esteem and confidence to do anything I wanted to do. At Harvard, I refused to give up on that dream and worked hard enough that I was picked up by the Seattle Seahawks in the fourth round of the 2000 NFL draft. My Harvard education was my backup plan: I graduated pre-med and planned to be a doctor if I couldn't be a linebacker.

Chris and I both found success that was built upon our work ethic. Chris became the youngest male Hardcore Champion in the history of World Wrestling Entertainment, and I enjoyed tuning in on Monday nights to watch him antagonize the crowd—and then inevitably get his butt kicked. I, in turn, ended up grinding out eight years in the violent work environment that is the NFL and helped lead the Seattle Seahawks to the Super Bowl in 2006 as one of their player-appointed captains.

I'd always appreciated the physical nature of professional wrestling. Although it was performance, with the speed those giants were moving at I knew that a miscalculation of even a fraction of an inch could be devastating. So I wasn't surprised that Chris got a concussion in 2003. Yet I was surprised by the stark changes that took place in almost every facet of his life over the next five years as he recovered from post-concussion syndrome. The loud, energetic, well-spoken person I had come to know transformed into something much different. These were dark times for Chris. He no longer wanted to talk to anyone, even to me, his closest friend. He just wanted to be left alone, where he hoped he would heal, and he would go back to normal life—or whatever you call life in the WWE.

Chris's life never did return to his old version of normal. But when Chris decided to write *Head Games: Football's Concussion Crisis*, I knew I had a portion of him back. This was the Chris I knew, a guy who would take on writing a book on head trauma in sports because *he thought it should be done*— not what it looked like to anyone on the outside—and because he thought it would be a disservice to a massive number of people if it were not done. Never mind that he never published anything before this. Never mind that he started without even the slightest clue of how to write a book.

And, to be honest, at first I thought Chris had lost his mind entirely. Here was a really talented guy—one of the smartest I'd known during my entire time at Harvard—and he was going to write a book on concussions because he took a bad blow? Chris had already proven he could have success in whatever he wanted, yet now he was choosing to be an advocate for change in how brain trauma was viewed?

I have loved football deeply my whole life, and I was in debt to everything it had given me. I also knew that I had several diagnosed concussions in the NFL—seven, to be exact—and those were the ones I simply could not hide from trainers and doctors. Although I was sympathetic to Chris's plight, it was hard not to question everything about his plan. I had taken hundreds, if not thousands, of those same blows, and I'd gotten up and back into the game and the next play every time. And now he was going to write a book because he couldn't get back in there? And attack the game I love, which had given me so much? In my opinion, it just wasn't possible that football could have purposefully ignored, or even misrepresented, such a life-threatening risk to its players.

As usual, Chris didn't care what I thought, because he was following his convictions. He wasn't following fame or prestige or money—not surprisingly, there is very little income to be made in the head trauma field—he was following his heart and mind in his search for the truth. And he still is to this day.

Chris asked me to read his final draft of the first edition of *Head Games* before it came out in 2006. I not only refused to help him, I told him not to mention my name in the book or in any conversation surrounding the concussion controversy. I refused to let him use our relationship or connect me with his inside knowledge of what was really happening on NFL sidelines. Even though he was my best friend, I distanced myself from him.

After the book came out, I realized that I'd had such a strong reaction because I was scared. I was scared to be associated with him for fear of how his book would reverberate throughout the NFL. I was scared that I would lose my job, and my edge. If I knew the truth, I may not be able to attack my competitors without fear. I knew I could hurt my knee, or my shoulder, which had been reconstructed twice, so what I didn't know about my brain couldn't hurt me—or so I thought at the time. This game of football had been my dream, my life, and I never wanted it to end. When it did end, I wanted it to be on my own terms, and not because I was labeled as a "concussion guy." Frankly, this is the same exact fear that a lot of guys in the NFL have, day in and day out. Each player who makes the NFL just does not want to let it go. A lot of players subscribe to the old adage—whether conscious or not—that "ignorance is bliss." I subscribed to this same way of thinking, even though I was a Harvard graduate with the insight of a former pre-med student and knew what Chris was writing about.

I knew I was wrong, even then. Now I can say that, because I see the world through a different lens. I retired from the NFL after eight years—and eight surgeries—in 2008. I entered Harvard Business School in 2009 to obtain an MBA, and I attacked that as I did anything on the football field. But while I was preparing for entrance exams, I quickly realized that I was not the same person who was able to grind through pre-med courses with a full football and study schedule during my undergraduate years. Chris has told me he feels the same way as he begins his third year of a Ph.D. program in Behavioral Neuroscience at Boston University School of Medicine.

I now realize how important this issue is, and thanks to Chris and his immense ability and leadership in the head trauma field, I have embraced the idea of making contact sports safer for the generations to come. Chris has forever changed the world, and I am grateful to him for that, especially as a father. I have a young son, Isaiah Jr., and I want him to enjoy and learn and love the sport of football the way that I did. Yet now I realize the game has to change fundamentally; in fact, all sports need to change. I cannot with a good conscience send my son out to play football the same way I played. My son will play a type of football that is a much safer game—or he will not play at all.

Chris has once again showed me the meaning of perseverance in search of what is right and meaningful while using all of his God-given talent. In the face of immense odds and scrutiny he went looking for an answer to something that is highly complex, on so many levels. The world owes him a debt of gratitude for the work he has done to push sports-related concussions to the forefront.

Head Games is an eye-opening and intense journey that is a must-read for parents and athletes alike. This amazing story tells each of us what we still have to do to ensure the safety of our kids.

Introduction

I am pleased to provide some opening words for this outstanding work by Christopher Nowinski on a topic of long personal interest and research. The human head is unique in that its content, the brain, is largely incapable of regeneration. Thus, a brain injury takes on a singular importance. While today many parts of the body can be replaced either by artificial hardware or transplantation, the brain cannot be replaced.

Interest in and the published medical literature about a concussion, which is the most common sports-related brain injury, has increased exponentially over the last decade. Once thought of as a transient impairment of brain function, we are now aware that concussion may involve a structural injury to the brain, lead to permanent neurological deficits, and can end a sports career. The media has devoted extensive coverage to a number of prominent athletes who were forced to retire due to enduring symptoms following multiple cerebral concussions.

The National Football League, and to a lesser extent the National Hockey League, are devoting time and money towards studying this problem. It is obvious, given the potential serious consequences of multiple cerebral concussions including post-concussion syndrome and the dreaded later life neurodegenerative disease, Chronic Traumatic Encephalopathy, that prevention is paramount. Yet in many sports, even when played with proper technique, a cerebral concussion is an inherent risk. Furthermore, and compounding the problem, in especially the helmeted sports, most mild concussions go unrecognized by sideline medical personnel.

In this book, Chris Nowinski in a personal, provocative, compelling, and authoritative manner gives the lay public a comprehensive insight into sports-related concussion. I recommend this book ardently to every athlete playing contact/collision sports, as well as their parents and family. Chris has compiled an encyclopedic resource on this topic that will not only enhance informed decisions by athletes and their families but also afford safer participation. I hope and expect it will continue to stimulate the still ever-increasing interest and needed critical study on this currently hotly debated topic.

ROBERT C. CANTU, M.A., M.D., F.A.C.S., F.A.C.S.M.

Author of *Concussion and Our Kids*, Houghton Mifflin

Clinical Professor of Neurosurgery and Co Director Center for the Study of Traumatic Encephalopathy, Boston University Medical Center

Co-Director, Neurological Sports Injury Center Brigham and Women's Hospital, Boston, MA

Senior Advisor NFL Head Neck and Spine Committee

Member and section co-chair Mackey White Traumatic Brain Injury Committee NFLPA

Adjunct Professor, Exercise and Sport Science University of North Carolina, Chapel Hill;

Medical Director, National Center for Catastrophic Sports Injury Research Chapel Hill, North Carolina.

Chairman, Department of Surgery; Chief, Neurosurgery Service; and Director, Service Sports Medicine; Emerson Hospital, Concord, Massachusetts.

Author's Preface

When I wrote *Head Games: Football's Concussion Crisis*, first published in October, 2006, my goal was to raise awareness of the hidden epidemic of brain injury and its related diseases in American football and to lay out a plan for reform. The experience taught me an important lesson: books don't create change, people do.

After the book came out, I got off the sideline and got in the game. I became an activist, a researcher, and a vocal advocate. I co-founded the non-profit Sports Legacy Institute and the Center for the Study of Traumatic Encephalopathy at Boston University School of Medicine. Some have given me credit for playing a leading role, along with many others, in initiating the dramatic cultural change we have seen in sports ever since.

The book has inspired two documentaries. *Head Games,* released in 2012 and directed by the legendary Steve James, focused on North American sports and *Head Games: the Global Concussion Crisis,* released in 2014 for the international market. The second documentary focuses on soccer (football), rugby, and Australian rules football. To coincide with the release of the documentary, I was invited to update the book each time. Both times I accepted, because the story of how we changed the world is worth telling, and the rapidly changing recommendations are worth knowing for every athlete, former athlete, parent, coach, medical professional, and for anyone that cares about someone who is at risk for brain trauma.

A word on how the book is structured: In Part One, I have stayed true to the original 2006 text as much as possible. Keep in mind it was written in 2006, and I didn't know everything I know now. Part Two chronicles the battle from 2006 to today. Part Three provides practical updates on the research and recommendations for safer sports.

I am excited about the changes that have occurred since 2006. However, based on what we've learned, I'm also more scared than I was back then. While I am confident future generations of athletes will be safer, I have grave concerns for the guys I played with and those who came before me. It is now crystal clear that the old way of dealing with concussions has destroyed brains and has torn apart families, and we have a lot of brains to fix and families to mend.

Few people know the truth about head injuries in sports. Someday I hope to have a son, and I bet he'll want to play contact sports. On the one hand, I'll want him to play so he can have the same fun I had and face the same challenges I faced. Today, at 35 years-old, my brain is still functional. Yet knowing what I now know about what might be in store for me and the guys I played with, I'm not sure what sport I'll be able to give him my blessing to play. There are still too many unanswered questions. But I have the luxury of having a theoretical kid. You may have a real one who needs real answers to real questions. I hope this book provides those answers.

QR code description

Throughout this book you will see QR scan codes. Scan these codes with your mobile device or tablet with QR scanning capabilities to link to online video of more detailed interviews and experiences.

Prologue

The last six years had been building to this moment. It was October 28, 2009, and at 9:45 A.M. I entered the room 2141 of the Rayburn House Office Building in Washington, D.C. as an invited witness for a hearing called by the House Judiciary Committee on "Legal Issues Relating to Football Head Injuries." Surrounded by members of Congress, doctors, former National Football League (NFL) players, and the commissioner of the NFL, Roger Goodell, I was the one who probably seemed out of place.

As a football player who reached his peak as a second-team All-Ivy player at Harvard University, and a former World Wrestling Federation (WWE) Superstar, which was my actual job title, I had no medical qualifications, no legal qualifications, and few football qualifications. But that hearing would have never happened without me, and the committee invited me to share the message I had been shouting for years because they were finally ready to hear it. That message? Football needed to change. The evidence had become overwhelming that it was destroying the brains of too many of its participants, and the NFL was refusing to believe it.

The first iteration of the NFL began in 1920, and in nearly one hundred years, the NFL had never admitted that brain trauma in football could cause later-life problems like depression, memory problems, or dementia in football players. That is despite the fact that a disease common to boxers, caused by blows to the head had been named "punch drunk" all the way back in 1928. Today, around four million children a year, about one in eight boys in America, put on a helmet and take to the gridiron confident that no problem had ever been found from all those thousands of hits to the head.

In front of Congress and the world, I hoped that this would be the day that we finally turned the tide. The room was a who's who of football, but I still saw things through the eyes of a boxer. In my corner I had a team I'd been slowly building over the last six years. I walked in with my doctor and mentor, the neurosurgeon Dr. Robert Cantu. When I recognized his brilliance, his passion, and his ethics, I got right behind him and had been trying to push him and his message out to bigger and bigger audiences ever since. Now in his early seventies, he was fit and full of energy; still practicing medicine and playing tennis twice a week. He'd been banging the drum on concussions for four decades before finally getting the attention he deserved.

I was also joined by the neuropathologist Dr. Ann McKee. Blond and striking, she ran a Brain Bank back in Boston with over 2,000 specimens. When I started bringing her the brains of football players in 2008 she was shocked by their state of ruin, and she vowed to commit herself to the study of "punch drunk" disease, now called Chronic Traumatic Encephalopathy (CTE). An artist and Green Bay Packers fan at heart, she had been reluctantly pulled in front of the cameras, and stayed there out of a sense of duty.

Seated behind her was Dr. Bob Stern. Though not testifying that day, when we first met and he learned about the true scope of the concussion crisis, the former rugby player never looked back, rallying Boston University School of Medicine to open the first center in the world dedicated to the study of this little-known brain disease with Dr. Cantu, Dr. McKee, Dr. Stern and me serving as co-directors. The evidence that had been created in the last year from the center was the reason we were all there that day.

Dr. Eleanor Perfetto, one of the original members of the board of directors of the Sports Legacy Institute, a non-profit Dr. Cantu and I launched in 2007, was already seated when I arrived. An epidemiologist and public health expert, she was really there to share the experience as an NFL wife who had watched her husband, Ralph Wenzel, mentally decline starting in his early fifties. He was

xvi

now sixty-seven and living up the road in a dementia facility. An unstoppable advocate, Eleanor felt an obligation to speak for Ralph because he could no longer speak for himself. To my left sat Dick Benson, whose son Will suffered a head injury in a game on September 17, 2002. He spent six days in a coma before passing. An investigation found that he likely suffered from Second-Impact Syndrome, meaning that he died because he hadn't fully recovered from a concussion he received two weeks earlier.

The room was brimming with reporters, led by the journalist who had almost single-handedly carried the torch on this issue, Alan Schwarz of the *New York Times*. As a reporter Alan was not in anyone's huddle, instead acting as a referee, but I was proud that I had made the phone call that finally found us someone to enforce the rules.

Across the ring I saw the opposition. There were a total of sixteen people invited to testify that day, including multiple NFL medical experts, but the person everyone was there to hear from was NFL Commissioner Roger Goodell. Roger was an NFL lifer. The son of a Senator, his dream job was to work for the NFL, and through an extensive letter-writing campaign he was hired in 1982 as an intern. He was promoted through the ranks and named commissioner in 2006, just as the concussion issue was about to break through in the mainstream press.

He had stayed true to the NFL company line, which stated that there was not yet enough evidence to definitively conclude that concussions and repeated brain trauma had any ill effects. But Roger seemed smarter than his predecessors, and we all hoped that this was the day that he would make a clean break from the ignorance of the past. Our team had been making it harder and harder for the NFL to claim there were no consequences, as by this time I had secured the brains of thirteen former NFL and college football players, and every single one was diagnosed by Dr. McKee with CTE, the degenerative brain disease that has only been linked to trauma.

I worked with the media to let people know each of those players' stories, so that Andre Waters, John Grimsley, Tom McHale, Mike Borich, Wally Hilgenberg, Lou Creekmur, and Justin Strzelczyk were again household names but this time not for their football play. They were now remembered for how terrible their lives became before they died, either by suicide, a gun accident caused by an impaired memory, a drug overdose, another drug overdose, Lou Gehrig's disease, dementia, and being thrown through the windshield at 88 miles per hour in a high-speed chase with police, respectively.

With all the cameras and the congressmen and the pressure, I knew that today was our best chance to force the NFL to change so I came out swinging hard. My submitted testimony was not written to make any friends:

> Some parents still see the NFL as something romantic, rather than simply another business owned by billionaires. Therefore, they still believe the NFL when [the NFL] doubts the research on CTE, and they still sign up their kids with the dream of them becoming NFL stars, blind to the risks of the game.

> As someone who showed up to class in college, I can tell you that when NFL spokespersons refute the risk of CTE by saying to the *New York Times*, "There are a great many people who have played football and other contact sports for many years and at high levels who do not appear to have suffered these types of deficits," they are being intellectually dishonest. People smoke and don't get lung cancer, but enough people do that if I lit up a cigarette in this room right now people would get angry and I'd be fined. Those at the NFL who give those quotes are not stupid, so belittling this important research with such pithy comments is something sinister, a choice to intentionally mislead the public about the risk that playing football has to their

health. As someone who really could have used that information when choosing to play the game, it makes me more than a little upset.

So much of this battle has mirrored the Big Tobacco problem of the last 50 years. I ask you, if you were able to create all the smoking laws and awareness we have today back in the 1950's, when the first conclusive pathological research was done linking smoking to lung cancer and cardiovascular disease, would you choose to save those millions of people who did not understand the risks of smoking?

I was thirty years old and fearless. I was also angry. I had been one of those boys who wanted to impress, who wanted to be tough, and I never admitted to having a concussion my entire football career. I also never realized I'd had one until years later because I had never been properly educated that when my head hurt, it was a bad thing. After all, it was football – everything always hurt. Pain was weakness leaving the body!

That attitude had cost me my career with WWE, and had cost me my mid-twenties while I struggled through post-concussion syndrome. Now I faced an uncertain neurological future and a high risk of CTE, and while my brain still worked I was going to use it to make sure others didn't follow in my footsteps.

The Commissioner was given the first opportunity to provide remarks on my testimony. I was intrigued by what was coming, because in his submitted remarks (which are usually much longer than the five-minute oral remarks), he'd come close to admitting a link between football and CTE, writing:

Recently, a number of media stories have been published about a condition known as CTE – chronic traumatic encephalopathy. As you may hear from other witnesses today, this condition has been seen in the brains of several former NFL players, in athletes in other sports, and even in an athlete who was only eighteen years old. How susceptible athletes and others are to this condition, and the precise causes and contributing factors, are issues for scientists and doctors to study and decide. It is fair to assume that head trauma may play a role.

"Fair" to "assume" that head trauma "may" play a role was far from an admission, but it sounded reasonable enough to create hope. Goodell's testimony also drew attention to, perhaps unintentionally, the crux of the issue, writing:

The NFL Youth Football Fund has distributed more than $150 million to the development of our sport on the youth and high school level since it was started by our office and the NFLPA in 1998.

This hearing was partially about the NFL lying to their players and the public about the consequences of concussions. But what took it to a whole new level of depravity was the NFL was admitting to pumping $15 million a year into helping kids play football. If they were lying about consequences *and* paying to hook kids early, then they were no better than the cigarette companies advertising to children while denying the links to lung cancer. They were dangerously close to that line, with an NFL employee telling The New Yorker, "It's all about getting a football, this unusual-looking object, into a kid's hands as soon as you can. Six years old, if possible."[1]

The real show came after the oral testimony when Chairman John Conyers held the floor for questions. He did not call for the hearing to let the NFL hide behind doctors and half-truths. His first question went right to the heart of the issue.

Chairman John Conyers: Commissioner Goodell, is there a link between playing professional football and the likelihood of contracting a brain-related injury such as dementia, Alzheimer's, depression, or CTE?

Commissioner Goodell: You are obviously seeing a lot of data and a lot of information that our committees and others have presented, with respect to the linkage. And the medical experts should be the one to be able to continue that debate. But our bottom line is, we are not waiting for that debate to continue...

Goodell then went into over a minute of specific things the NFL had done. Conyers wasn't having it.

Commissioner Goodell: ...It is a very important responsibility to set the right----(interrupted)

Chairman John Conyers: Well, you have testified to that. But I just asked you a simple question. What is the answer?

Commissioner Goodell: The answer is, the medical experts would know better than I would with respect to that. But we are not treating that in any way in delaying anything that we do. We are re-enforcing our commitment to make sure we make the safest possible deal for our----(interrupted)

Mr. Conyers. All right. Okay. I have heard it...

Chairman Conyers let out an audible sigh. Commissioner Goodell eyes darted around the room. He held up under tense questioning, and it looks like he escaped without admitting the connection. That raised the ire of other members of the committee, who decided to try to threaten and embarrass Commissioner Goodell into rethinking his stance.

Congresswoman Maxine Waters, whose husband is a former NFL player, went right at Goodell. She said, "We have heard from the NFL time and time again. You are always studying, you are always trying, you are hopeful.... I know my time is drawing to a close, but let me just say this to Mr. Goodell and everybody who is here today, that I think it is time for the Congress of the United States to take a look at your antitrust exemption. I think that you are a, what, $8 billion organization who have not taken seriously your responsibility to the players.

"The fact of the matter is, yes, people want to play. The fact of the matter is they are going to be injured. And we know, no matter what kind of helmet you build, no matter what kind of equipment that you have, it is a dangerous sport and people are going to be injured.

"The only question is, what are you going to do? Are you going to pay for it? Are you going to pay the injured players and their families for the injuries that they have received in helping you to be a multibillion-dollar operation? That is the only question.

"And I know that you do everything that you possibly can to hold on to those profits. But I think the responsibility of this Congress is to take a look at that antitrust exemption that you have and, in my estimation, take it away."

Congresswoman Linda Sanchez played the Big Tobacco card, saying, "The NFL sort of has this kind of blanket denial or minimizing of the fact that there may be this, you know, link. And it sort of reminds me of the tobacco companies pre-1990s when they kept saying no, there is no link between smoking and damage to your health or ill health effects. And they were forced to admit that that was incorrect through a spate of litigation in the 1990s."

No matter what punches were thrown at him that day, Commissioner Goodell took the hits and managed to stay on his feet, never admitting a thing. When the hearing concluded, my teammates and I all looked at each other, searching each other's eyes to try to process the events of the day. What happened? Were we winning? Losing? Did we just squander our greatest opportunity? Or were we one more punch from knocking them out?

Before I tell you the answer to that question, let me take you back to why I was going toe-to-toe with the NFL in the first place.

Part 1: 2003-2006

Chapter 1: The Concussion Crisis Revealed

My journey into the world of concussions began with a kick to the head. "Holy shit, kid! You okay?" was the first thing I heard.

The referee, Nick Patrick, leaned in, trying to figure out if I'd survived. Moments before, Bubba Ray Dudley's boot had met my chin with enough force to make the Hartford Civic Center explode. Or that's what it looked like to me as I lay on my back in the middle of the ring. Something was wrong with my vision. I didn't know where I was, what was happening around me, or why I was staring up at fuzzy-looking lights on the distant ceiling of a gigantic arena— I only knew that something was terribly wrong. I looked to the side, and saw thousands of people staring back at me. I gazed back up at Nick. I didn't want to move. My head felt like it was in a vice.

A three-hundred-pound man with a crew cut and army fatigues appeared out of the fog—ready to squash me. I braced myself for the impact. Crash! My head hurt more. Instead of rolling off me, he hooked my leg, and the referee started counting.

"One! Two!"

Why is he counting? It starts coming back to me: I'm a professional wrestler for Vince McMahon's World Wrestling Entertainment, and I'm in the middle of a tag-team match. My partner Rodney Mack is in my corner with our manager Theodore Long. This isn't a real fight. Then why am I injured? Isn't this stuff scripted?

I can't remember the script.

1

"Kick out, kid!" Nick whispers to me. I jerk the militant off me before the ref reaches the count of three. I felt like a panicked child lost in a crowd—a crowd of thousands of pumped-up WWE fans all staring at me. I still couldn't answer the most important question: What comes next? I know I have to do *something*, but what?

I never figured that out. I was able to finish the match against the Dudleys because they were professionals and made up a new finish. I stayed down at the right time for the three count because I had no choice—they really pinned me. I stumbled backstage, dazed, and lay down on the cold cement floor trying to compose myself. I was coherent and aware of my surroundings, but I couldn't get past an odd, throbbing headache. After a half hour or so, as the headache dissipated but did not go away, I became concerned about performing in the show the next night. On the way out, the doctor WWE had hired for the night took a look at me and said, "You *might* have a concussion. Let's see how you feel when you get to the arena tomorrow."

I drove two hours to the next town and grabbed a hotel. I entered the Pepsi Center in Albany, New York at about 5:00 p.m. the next day. I felt strange, but I wasn't in "pain." Feeling strange didn't meet my criteria to take the night off, so I told everyone I felt fine and started to get ready for my "tables match" with the Dudley Boyz. If you've watched wrestling, you know that for this type of match to end, somebody has to go through a table. Guess who that was going to be? That's right, me.

I crept into the ring apprehensively. I opened up the match, locking up with Bubba Ray Dudley. He attacked me with a forearm to the back. I barely felt it— on my back. But for some reason, my head went fuzzy again, the blood pounding so fiercely that I thought my head would explode.

Twenty minutes later, after a Dudley Death Drop (or "3D") sent me smashing through the table to the great joy of the crowd, I crawled backstage and found another place to lie down. The headache was much, much worse. I saw the

2

doctor again, and I was told that I *might* have suffered a concussion the day before, and that may be why my head hurt so much tonight. The doctor said he couldn't be sure because he hadn't been there the night before. The intense pain went away after another hour or so, and I felt well enough to leave the building.

After the match, I headed to New York City. I was scheduled to wrestle on *Monday Night RAW* at Madison Square Garden the next night, in front of millions of people. I looked so sluggish when I arrived at the arena that two WWE agents, Fit Finlay and Dean Malenko, who were aware of my head problems, changed my match, over my objection, into something quick and simple—with no chance of head trauma. I survived the match without incident and went home to Boston.

▼▼▼

For five straight weeks I continued to have symptoms, but I ignored them. Nobody told me not to work out, so I went to the gym nearly every day. A few minutes into each workout, my head would pound like never before. Being bullheaded, I tried to ignore it, but each day it eventually became overwhelming and forced me to quit the session early.

It was the strangest sensation. I could be in the middle of a set of bench presses, and after a few repetitions I would feel so odd, both physically and emotionally, that I would lose my desire to lift the weights off my chest. My trainer would have to rack the weight for me. It wasn't pain, it was more like intense apathy. At that moment, I wouldn't have cared if somebody had dropped a weight on my face.

But I had the mentality that this was an injury I had to overcome, that I had to work through. If I only lasted ten minutes at the gym, my goal the next day was to go fifteen. I also continued to wrestle when asked.

3

Everything changed after "The Incident" that occurred five weeks after the concussion. I was on the road. I'd had a match the night before. We were performing *Monday Night RAW* the next morning, and I went to sleep in a hotel room in Indianapolis, Indiana. I was with my girlfriend at the time.

At some point during the night I woke up to her screaming. As I began to orient myself I recognized that I was no longer in bed. I was on my elbows and knees on the ground, staring at the carpet. My girlfriend was yelling my name. "Chris! Chris!" "What?" I answered. "Are you okay?" Feeling no pain, and having no idea of what she'd just witnessed, I yelled back, "I'm fine. Why?"

I looked to my right and saw shards of glass. I saw a table lamp on its side on the ground, casting angled light. The alarm clock was on the ground, telling me it was 1:30 a.m. The nightstand was broken, its glass and wood surface chipped.

She told me I'd been having a nightmare. My screaming had woken her up, and when she opened her eyes she saw me standing on the bed, clawing at the wall as if I were trying to climb it. I was sweating, and all my muscles were engaged. My girlfriend tried yelling my name to wake me. Then she tried pulling me back down on the bed, but she wasn't strong enough. After a few seconds of standing there, I apparently yelled, "Oh no!" and jumped off the bed and crashed headfirst into the wall as if I were trying to catch something. I bounced off the wall and into the nightstand. After about ten seconds on the ground, I woke up.

I don't remember any of this. I only remember dreaming that she was falling, and that I had tried to "save" her. When she told me what she'd seen, I was officially freaked out. I turned on the TV and stared at it until sunrise, scared to fall asleep again and terrified about what I might have done to my brain.

My love affair with banging things with my head started early. I started playing organized soccer at the age of six, although I don't remember when I started headers on a regular basis. When I moved up to junior high, soccer didn't have the same allure. That was probably because I wasn't very fast or skilled, and therefore not very good. But the other big reason was because my friends were trying out for the football team, and football had a better reputation. That's where the tough guys went, or so it seemed through my twelve-year-old eyes. I first asked my mother if I could play in eighth grade, as there was a youth league in my town. She told me no, because she was worried that I would "get hurt" and she thought my bones needed more time to grow and mature. She asked if I would wait until high school, and I agreed.

So my love affair with football was postponed until 1992, at the tender age of thirteen. Growing up in the Chicago suburb of Arlington Heights, Illinois, I learned to live for Friday-night games under the lights at John Hersey High School. As a 6' 3", 160-pound beanpole, I somehow found success as a middle linebacker, starting on varsity as a sophomore and captaining my team two years later as a 6' 5", 230-pound defensive end.

I was lucky enough to be recruited by Harvard University, where I played for four more years, including the 1997 Ivy League Championship season. That defense, which I was a part of as a member of the defensive tackle rotation, gave up only four touchdowns in seven Ivy League games, and none of them on the ground (the older I get, the more I tell people that). Harvard, like all the Ivy League schools, doesn't offer athletic scholarships, but the educational opportunity was too great to pass up. So were the dining halls: I benefited from Harvard's all-you-can-eat system and bulked up to 295 pounds, earning Honorable Mention All-Ivy League accolades as a junior and making second team All-Ivy as a senior. I also graduated *cum laude* with a degree in sociology.

When I was younger, I thought football was the greatest sport ever invented. It combines intelligence, power, grace, speed, collisions and pure, unadulterated violence. Eleven dedicated men work together on the field, their success dictated by a willingness to sacrifice personal glory for the good of the team. The lessons that football teaches its players and the entertainment it gives its fans are unparalleled in American team sports. There's no doubt that it has surpassed baseball as America's true pastime. Football taught me what I believe to be the simplest and most important maxim for success: In football, and in life, you're guaranteed to get knocked down. What separates us is what happens next. Will you get back up and get in there?

Nowinski Football

After graduating I joined many of my fellow classmates at WWE. Actually, I didn't see any other Harvard graduates at WWE—I was the only one. Vince McMahon loved to have ring announcer Lillian Garcia introduce me as "The only Harvard graduate in the history of WWE, Christopherrrrr NowINski." That probably should have told me something…

Wrestling for the WWE wasn't exactly my dream job growing up, mainly because of my mother. She didn't allow me to watch wrestling on TV because she thought that just watching it would cause brain damage. (Oh, the irony!)

I became hooked on wrestling the summer before my senior year of college, while living on-campus to train for the upcoming football season. I had five roommates. We each weighed over 250 pounds, and were crammed into a two-bedroom apartment with one television. I was on the lower bunk and too close to the guy on the futon. Since the other guys never missed wrestling, I was forced to watch it Monday and Thursday nights. At first I resisted, but I slowly fell in love with the show, tuning in to watch The Rock, Stone Cold Steve Austin, and Kurt Angle battle for supremacy.

Coming out of college, I wasn't one of the lucky few hundred football players who make the pros, so I was forced to give up the game. My first real job after college was a summer internship with the consulting firm Trinity Partners, LLC. I worked for a Harvard football alum, and focused on commercialization strategy in the pharmaceutical and biotech industries. Most of the firm's employees were Ivy League graduates with science and economics degrees, so I was an anomaly with my sociology background. But I guess I learned enough in college and on the job to keep up.

Strangely enough, the owner of Trinity Partners, John Corcoran, was a huge wrestling fan and used to consult for a group that was considering purchasing Vern Gagne's American Wrestling Association (AWA). We started to talk wrestling in the office. One day, as John and I were debating the merits of the Stone Cold Stunner vs. the People's Elbow as finishing maneuvers, he asked me if I'd ever considered becoming a professional wrestler. I had not. Since I'd dabbled in theater, and had had success in athletics, John thought I could make it. I said, "I don't know. I have a good job here."

He said, "Work here part-time and go to wrestling school full-time. Give it a shot and we'll see what happens. If it doesn't work out you can always come back here."

With that kind of golden parachute, how could I say no? I enrolled at Killer Kowalski's Wrestling Institute in November of 2000. I loved it—each practice was more fun than the one before. Three months into my training, MTV and World Wrestling Entertainment announced a casting call for the first season of *Tough Enough.* The toughness and confidence I had learned playing football at Harvard got me through to the end. The trainers discovered that though most of

7

the cast members were crumbling both physically and emotionally, they couldn't break me. I knew how to work through pain and adversity—how to play hurt. For example, after the show I found out I had torn a ligament in my wrist in the first week of training. It had hurt the entire time, but I knew I couldn't stay in the contest with a cast, so I just taped it and didn't tell anyone about it.

Unfortunately, toughness did not equal talent, and when two contestants were awarded contracts with World Wrestling Entertainment at the end of the show, I wasn't one of them.

Still, I wasn't dissuaded. Even if the WWE didn't know it yet, I knew I could become good enough to make it in that business. Six months later my perseverance paid off and the WWE hired me. In 2002, I made my debut in front of five million viewers on *Monday Night RAW* as Christopher Nowinski, a.k.a. Chris "Harvard," the Ivy League snob. I became known for taunting the audience for its lack of intelligence. Sometimes I would recite poetry from the ring. I wrote and recited a poem in Moncton, New Brunswick, Canada. (To understand the rhyming scheme, you need to know that Canadians say "grade 3" instead of "third grade.")

Roses are red, Violets are blue,

The reason I'm talking so slowly,

Is because no one in Moncton has passed grade 2

In Hersey, Pennsylvania, where they make a lot of chocolate, I used *Willy Wonka* as my muse. I spent all afternoon rewriting the Oompa Loompa lyrics, singing before the 5,000-person crowd:

Oompa Loompa, do-ba-dee-doo,

I've got a perfect puzzle for you.

Oompa Loompa, do-ba-dee-dee,

If you are wise you'll listen to me.

What do you get if you don't go to school?

A factory job that a monkey can do.

With good manners you will go far

Like the men from Harvard do-ba-dee do!

I ended with a cartwheel and everything. I'd often play up my purported education during a match. In a Hardcore match in Bridgeport, Connecticut, I assaulted Al Snow with a human skeleton, ripped off the skull, got down on bended knee, and began reciting *Hamlet*:

Alas, poor Yorick! I knew him, Horatio: a fellow
of infinite jest, of most excellent fancy.

Those were good times.

▼▼▼

The "toughness" that had brought me success on the gridiron followed me into wrestling. Five days after I sustained my final concussion, we had a show in Poughkeepsie, New York. I was to team up with Rodney Mack. As I packed for the trip, I was weighed down by the knowledge that I wasn't physically prepared for the show due to my ongoing concussion symptoms, but it never seriously crossed my mind not to wrestle. This was my job, and the fans were expecting me. Besides, the WWE would have had to shuffle the card around me at the last minute, drawing attention to my asking for a night off for a headache and feeling sluggish. I tried to imagine how they would react to that request, considering the kinds of injuries other wrestlers have endured in order to perform:

- Stone Cold Steve Austin was dropped on his head in a 1997 match. He broke his neck, and was a transient quadriplegic for 90 seconds. He said, "By all rights, I should have just laid there and waited for the MDs to come and give me the proper assistance. But I was thinking of the business, I was thinking of the show. I was looking to finish the match. Finally I started getting some movement back. I couldn't crawl on my hands; I could barely crawl on my elbows . . . I rolled up Owen [for the pin to finish the match]."[2]

- Former Olympic Gold Medalist Kurt Angle chose to postpone surgery on his broken neck to wrestle at Wrestlemania XIX. The entire arena knew that if he got hit the wrong way, he could be paralyzed. Angle was also knocked unconscious once in a WWE Heavyweight Championship triple-threat match—where three wrestlers compete in the ring at once. He was carried backstage while the other two wrestlers improvised a new match. When he regained consciousness, he stumbled back down the ramp, got back in the ring, and, despite the fact that he didn't know where he was or what was going on, managed to finish the match with the help of the other wrestlers. He still doesn't remember doing it.

- Former WWE Champion Brock Lesnar, working with Kurt Angle at Wrestlemania XIX, was injured while attempting a "shooting-star press" off the top rope. "I was a good 10, 12 feet off the mat on my jump, and I landed smack on my forehead and face. I weigh 290 pounds, so you can just imagine the force and the momentum of that. When I hit, I don't remember anything because I got a concussion. I won the match, but I couldn't tell you what happened."[3] He was back wrestling within two weeks.

- Former WWE Champion Triple H tore his quadriceps muscle in the middle of a match. Even so, he continued to wrestle for another five minutes because he wanted to finish the match in a way that was best for the story line.

As these heroic performances ran through my mind, I decided there was no way I could ask for the night off. But when I arrived at the arena, I found I didn't have a choice. Apparently, I looked like such a mess that the trainer and doctor refused to let me wrestle. They were onto something. The next day I had to carry my bags up a flight of stairs to get into the arena in Syracuse, and I had to stop every few steps to keep from passing out. I took that night off, too. Sunday I sat out in Elmira, and at *RAW* in Buffalo on Monday I finally got some serious medical attention.

I was experiencing a lot of pain in the back left side of my head, and the doctors were worried that I may have suffered a subdural hematoma, meaning that my brain was bleeding inside my skull, which can be fatal. That afternoon I was sent to get a CT scan on my brain, and it showed no bleeding. I was immediately seen by a neurosurgeon, who told me that I had "probably" suffered a minor concussion the previous week. He asked me if I'd ever had a concussion before. I told him no, because this was before I met Dr. Cantu and learned what one was. Based on the assumption that this was my first concussion, he recommended that I take a few days off, and predicted that I would be fine in a week or two. My frustration at having to wait was growing. This was *not* how I had gotten my job, *not* how I had made it this far, and if this continued, I was certain my dreams would end.

That recommendation got back to the arena, so by the time I got back Vince McMahon had heard about it and told me I had to take the night off from wrestling. That night I accompanied my tag-team partner at ringside for his

11

singles match, and the increase in my blood pressure just from cheering him on nearly knocked me out. I had a throbbing headache when I got backstage.

I went to see a neurologist when I got back home to Boston. He advised me to take a week or two off, and also recommended that I not get back into the ring until I felt better. I missed one weekend of shows and a televised *RAW*. The next week I still wasn't feeling better, but I was getting restless. Since all the doctors had told me that I should have been feeling better by now, I began to doubt myself—I wondered if maybe the symptoms were all psychological. I feared losing my position in the company. Those fears were realized when I received a midweek phone call from my tag-team partner Rodney Mack. He said, "Congrats, glad to hear you are feeling better!"

"Feeling better? What are you talking about?" I asked.

"Your name is on the list for this weekend's shows." Every week we'd receive a list of who was working the next week's shows, and it wasn't often decided until the last minute. It was good to be on the list, because you made more money when you work.

My heart skipped a beat. I hadn't yet received clearance, but now the entire roster had seen the list and assumed I was healthy. I told Rodney that I hadn't been cleared. He advised me that I should figure this out.

Looking back, it was probably an honest miscommunication, but the backstage culture of pro wrestling is hyper-paranoid, and I was knee-deep in that culture. What I concluded was that they had put me on that sheet on purpose, and may have even put Rodney up to calling me, because they were sending me the signal that I'd been out too long with this silly concussion. I booked an appointment with the doctor and asked him to clear me, and I lied and answered the questions the right way to get cleared. Two days later I boarded a plane for our show that weekend in Omaha, Nebraska.

▼▼▼

Rodney Mack and I were scheduled for a tag-team match against Rosey and Tommy Dreamer. As we prepared for the match, I knew that something was wrong. I was having trouble remembering the few prepared sequences of moves that we'd talked over; this had never happened to me before. One of the few things I had going for me in the ring was my memory—I never made mistakes. I was worried about performing our match. I didn't want to embarrass myself in front of my co-workers or the crowd, and I didn't want to make a mistake in the ring that would injure my opponents or me. There is truly very little margin for error in this business.

Fear of embarrassment from backing out just before the match overwhelmed my thoughts of self-preservation.

I told myself, "You felt this way as you got on the plane, rented a car, and drove to the arena. The match is only an hour away. Sorry, pal, but it's way too late to change your mind."

I did the only thing I felt I could do to help myself: I asked the other guys if I could "take it easy" that night, and not take many bumps. As a rookie, I was taking my life in my own hands—the other three guys were older veterans, and would have been justified in ignoring my plea. From the looks on their faces, I thought they were going to beat me up right then and there. But because they were good guys, they didn't, and I survived the match.

The next morning we flew to Green Bay.

Tommy asked, "Do we need to take it easy on you again?"

"Yes, please, sir," I answered, to a pair of rolling eyes. We worked a similar match that night, and again I walked away in a slight daze with only a headache.

But something changed overnight. The next morning I woke up feeling miserable. I met the rest of the wrestlers at the airport and hopped on a plane to Indianapolis, where we were to rent cars to drive to a Sunday afternoon show in

Terre Haute. By the time we landed in Indianapolis, I was having trouble focusing.

At the baggage claim, my tag team's manager, Theodore Long, pleaded with me in his best fatherly voice, "You don't look so hot. Your head's messed up. You shouldn't wrestle."

I was finally starting to agree. I drove to the arena with our head of security, Jimmie Tilles, but didn't talk for most of the ride because I just couldn't keep up with the conversation. By the time we arrived at the arena, Theodore and Rodney had already warned the head road agent, Black Jack Lanza, that something was wrong with me. He saw me in the parking lot and told me that I wasn't wrestling that night. When Jimmie heard that, he exclaimed, "Thank goodness." Part of me was relieved, and part of me was concerned that this would set my career back.

I went back to the hotel, and that's the night I jumped off the bed. My girlfriend escorted me to the arena the next morning. I was met at the door, and told that I wasn't getting in the ring again until they knew what was wrong with me. I was no longer in any mood to argue. Vince McMahon was kind enough to pull me aside and tell me to take as much time as I needed to heal.

He said, "It's not worth it. You only have one brain."

I ran into head agent John Laurinaitis, who scolded, "Ya gotta tell us when you're hurt."

As I continued the long walk to the locker room, I passed Stephanie McMahon, Vince's daughter and the head of the creative department at the time. She repeated Vince's offer to take as much time as I needed. During the conversation, my girlfriend told Stephanie about the incident at the hotel the night before. Stephanie's jaw dropped. I was uncomfortable, so I tried to lighten the mood by pointing out how romantic it was that I yelled my girlfriend's name when I jumped, and that I was trying to save her from falling in my dream. Neither woman was impressed.

14

There was a physician at the show, and he told me that sleep disturbance could be a side effect of a concussion. He asked me if I had a history of concussions.

I said, "I've been dinged here and there, but nothing I would call a concussion."

"Well, without a previous history of concussion problems, you should probably be fine in a week or two."

He handed me a prescription for muscle relaxers. "This should make you sleep more soundly. We don't want you to hurt yourself."

The neurologist I was seeing kept recommending longer and longer periods of rest. We chose not to medicate my headaches with Tylenol, ibuprofen, or prescription drugs because the doctor was concerned that it would mask the pain and I would begin exercising again too quickly.

The stress of not knowing what was wrong with me or how to cure my headaches was devastating, and I became depressed. Concentrating, reading, and carrying on a conversation made my head hurt. I couldn't even pass the time and lift my spirits by hanging out with friends or watching a funny movie because laughing gave me a splitting headache. That was the worst. Laughter is the best medicine, my ass.

On top of the emotional problems, my memory was off. I couldn't remember people's names, socially or professionally. A few months after the injury I was backstage at a WWE show in Chicago with the Brooklyn Brawler, Steve Lombardi. He was giving me a good-natured ribbing me about my concussion, and as a joke he started pointing to people and asking, "Remember his name? Remember her name?" It was funny because the people he pointed to were some of the most recognizable wrestlers in the world—like Triple H and Ric Flair— people I'd worked with for a couple of years and had idolized for even longer. It stopped being funny when I struggled to come up with their names. At one point I paused so long that he stopped walking and said, "You're kidding with me, right?"

15

I put on my biggest grin. "Of course, Brawler."

I wasn't kidding. I was in big trouble.

It was now over two months since the original injury, and it was clear I wasn't getting better. I was reaching the end of my rope. Some days I wouldn't get off the couch. Some days I would try to go to bed at 5 p.m. and self-medicate with alcohol and my sleeping pills because my head hurt and I had nothing to distract me from the pain. But then I would dread waking up 4 a.m.—alone, in the dark, and with the headache. My girlfriend traveled three nights a week for work and wasn't always around, so I mostly suffered alone. My friends tried to be there for me, but after a while their patience for my constant misery grew thin. Football season was starting. At least I could watch that.

But by wintertime, with all that I would learn about concussions that season, I couldn't watch football in the same way. The joy of the big hit was gone for me.

Chapter 2: My Concussion Education

One of the really frightening things was the night following the 1994 NFC championship game between San Francisco and Dallas. Troy Aikman played for Dallas; they beat San Francisco and Aikman got a concussion. I visited him in the hospital room, and he asked me if he'd played in the game. I told him he did. He asked me how he had played. I said, "Well." He then wanted to know if winning that game meant that they were going to the Super Bowl. "Yes," I said. He asked when the Super Bowl would be played and where—I answered him, and he got really excited. His face brightened, and it was great.

Five minutes later, he asked me whether he'd played in the game that day, and if they'd won, and how he'd played, and whether that meant they were in the Super Bowl. I answered. Another ten minutes passed, and he asked me the same questions again. I thought for a while he was joking—but he wasn't. This went on, so I finally wrote down the most commonly asked championship game night questions.

—Leigh Steinberg, sports agent

I always related concussions to boxing. When I played, I didn't know they even existed in the NFL. If they would have sat me in a room and said, "You cannot leave here until you guess the one mystery injury that could end your career," I'd still be in that room. I would never have thought concussions were part of football.

—Merril Hoge, nine-year NFL veteran

Part of my frustration was caused by a sense of vagueness—not just the cloudiness in my mind, but the kinds of answers I was getting from medical authorities. It seemed that there were few ways to accurately diagnose and describe what had happened to me, predict how long symptoms would persist, and chart a recovery course and time frame. That left me to wonder if my symptoms were all in my head. This made the calls from the WWE ever more difficult.

The WWE liaison would call every few days. The conversations grew short and routine: "How are you feeling?" "Terrible." "All right, I'll check back in a few days."

They decided to send me to the "experts." I hopped on a plane and met a new doctor. We talked about how the injury happened, and then he gave me a laptop so I could take a new kind of concussion test—a computerized neurological assessment. Considered superior to a non-computerized test because of its sensitivity to small changes, the program would ask a series of questions that measured things such as memory and reaction time.

In one section, I was asked to remember some black-and-white pictures and graphics. Later I was shown a larger group of pictures that included some from that earlier group. As pictures flashed on the screen, I was asked to press "yes" if I recognized a picture from the earlier group, and "no" if it was a new picture. About ten questions in, I started to panic, as I wasn't recognizing anything. At first, I answered "no" to each question, and after a while it dawned on me that there was no way they could show me ten new images in a row, so there had to be some "yes" answers sprinkled in there somewhere—but I couldn't remember having seen a single one of the pictures. So I began randomly answering "yes."

When the doctor scored the test, he didn't seem worried. I had passed. I was stunned into silence. I asked for more details, and he told me I'd scored very well on most sections. I asked him about the section I guessed on.

"He told me I'd scored in the same range as "your average NFL player." I confessed that I had guessed on those answers. He shrugged it off. Since I was within normal ranges, the test couldn't confirm I was still suffering from the concussion. As we wrapped up the consultation, I heard again that there was no reason to believe that I wouldn't be better in a couple of weeks.

I left the office frustrated. Another doctor, another vague answer. I was starting to think that this whole concussion treatment concept was suspect. In football, when I had broken a bone or tore a ligament, a doctor would touch something and ask, "Does this hurt?" I would say yes or no. Then he'd do something else, and ask, "How about this?" Eventually he'd figure out what was wrong, take an x-ray or MRI, and tell me, "If you can take the pain, you can play," or "You're good to play in three to four weeks."

But a doctor couldn't just touch my head to identify the source of the pain. I was told that MRIs and CT scans were not sensitive enough to detect concussions. And the computerized neuropsychology tests were relatively useless without a baseline score. When a doctor would perform a clinical exam, he'd ask, "Was there a loss of consciousness?" I'd answer, "No." Invariably, the doctor would say, "Hmm," and scratch his chin. He'd ask me to stand up, and then he'd put me through a physical routine much like a drunk-driver test from the television show *Cops*. The doctor would take out the old-school reflex hammer and hit me a few times. I'd flinch. He'd ask me questions to test my mental dexterity. Over time I learned to count backward by 7's from 100. Sometimes I'd get asked about the symptoms I was experiencing. That was especially frustrating, because I didn't know what symptoms were relevant. How could I possibly know what to say?

As the doctors were running out of tests, I was running out of hope. I'd wandered into a medical no-man's-land. I looked normal from the outside and could carry on a conversation, so everyone assumed I was fine. I was the only one who believed that something was wrong.

All I knew was that I had a headache, bright lights bothered me, I hadn't had a good night's sleep in weeks, I could barely remember my appointment dates, I was depressed, and I wasn't getting better. And to top it all off, I didn't know how, or if, I'd ever recover.

My luck was about to change. Through a friend, I learned that one of the world's leading concussion experts worked at a hospital just a half hour from my home. I figured he was my last hope, so I made up my mind not to leave his office until I had some answers.

Dr. Robert Cantu had an impressive résumé. When I saw him in 2003, he was chief of neurosurgery at Emerson Hospital in Concord, Massachusetts, the medical director for the National Center for Catastrophic Sports Injury Research, vice president of the National Operating Committee on Standards for Athletic Equipment (NOCSAE), and a former president of the American College of Sports Medicine. He sat on the editorial board of multiple medical journals, and he had authored over three hundred scientific publications and nineteen books on neurology and sports medicine. He also had the prestigious honor of being the first person to publish return-to-play guidelines for sports concussions, in 1986.

But if I'd learned anything during my ordeal, it was that a good résumé was no guarantee of good doctoring.

To begin the consultation, he asked me the same question I'd heard from everyone else. "How many concussions have you had?" I told him I'd had zero before this one. He paused thoughtfully and asked another question. "Well, how many times after a hit have you experienced symptoms like headaches, confusion, dizziness, double vision, or ringing in your ears?"

I stifled a laugh. "All the time," I answered. "Those are 'dings' and 'bell ringers.'"

Robert Cantu, MD

"Can you describe those occasions?" he asked.

"In April, I was kicked in the head and blacked out for five or six seconds," I said.

Two months prior to my concussion, I was working a match in Louisville, Kentucky, when Mike Bucci (also known as, at various points in his career, Nova, Super Nova, Nova Frehley, "Hollywood" Nova, "Hollywood" Bob Starr, and Simon Dean) threw me into the ropes. I recall running toward the ropes, hitting a wrinkle in time, and then realizing that I was on my back in the middle of the ring. Nova picked me up by my hair, and I struggled to remember what I was supposed to do next. As we continued, I had to ask him, over and over, "What's next? What's next?"

As we recovered in the locker room after the match, Nova asked me why, when he'd kicked me in the back of the head, I fell on my back instead of doing the forward flip that was expected. Chuckling, he said, "It looked weird." He may as well have been speaking a foreign language, because I didn't know what he was talking about. Eager to protect my reputation and shift the blame for the screw up to him, I quickly broke into character and said in the most condescending voice I could muster, "Because you kicked me so hard I blacked out, you jerk." (I didn't really say "jerk.") I had no idea if that was what had actually happened, but it worked because everybody laughed. Two years later I found out it was funny because it was true. When I began tracing my concussion history, I finally convinced Nova to give me his copy of the tape of the match. He knew that I was looking for that kick; he had been in denial for the last two years that the kick was any big deal. But as he handed it to me he confessed, "By the way, I kicked you so hard that I honestly thought I broke my foot." On the tape, I saw that after he kicked me in the head I froze in midair as if I'd slipped on ice, and fell a few feet forward, and somehow a few feet sideways—I guess from the force of the kick that actually went to the side and back of my head.

Dr. Cantu asked if I'd felt anything strange after that match. "Yeah," I said, "but I thought it had to do with my nose." This had been one of my first matches after a complicated surgery to replace the cartilage in my nose with plastic. I needed surgery after my face was smashed in the 2003 Royal Rumble—courtesy of the wrestler Edge.* In addition to kicking me, Nova had fallen on my nose and undone the surgery—which was painful, bloody, and annoying enough to garner my full attention after the match. That made it especially easy to forget about the blackout.

"Yes, the evidence would point to that being a concussion," Dr. Cantu concluded.

Hmm, that means I've had two concussions now, I thought. Wait a minute . . . what if I was involved in a big collision in football, but I don't remember feeling the hit? I do remember that the sky turned orange for a few minutes...

During a preseason inter-squad scrimmage in my sophomore year in college, I was on the kickoff-return team as a blocker. In 95 percent of kickoffs, the kicker sends the ball as far as he can, and a small, fast kickoff-return specialist will catch it and run it back. Unfortunately, our backup kicker was terrible, and kicked it 20 yards short—right to me. Since I was big, dumb, and slow, I just ran straight ahead. When I saw our best headhunter, Clint Kollar, coming at me, I lowered my head and ran straight for him. When I opened my eyes, I noticed that everyone was excited, but I didn't know if they were excited for me or for Clint. I didn't know whether I'd crushed him or he'd crushed me. I never felt anything. I didn't understand why they congratulated both of us until I saw the film the next day. The explosive hit caused us both to fall sideways, and it looked awesome on film. I distinctly remembered staggering to the sideline, taking a knee, and blinking about a thousand times to see if I could get the sky to turn from orange back to blue.

Dr. Cantu remarked, "That definitely fits in the concussion category."

Wow, I've had three concussions, I thought. Then I remembered another one.

"Once during the filming of *Tough Enough,* I got clotheslined in the face, the ceiling turned orange for a few minutes, and I was told that I acted strangely for the rest of the day. What about that?"

I was on a reality show in 2001 called *Tough Enough.* A partnership between WWE and MTV, the show set out to find and train future superstars for the WWE while giving the world a glimpse of what it takes to become a professional wrestler. The show combined elements of *The Real World* and *Survivor.* Thirteen contestants (eight males and five females) would live in a house together, and their lives and WWE training would be taped. One person would be eliminated every week. The thirteen of us were put through grueling six-hour training sessions every day. On the last day of *Tough Enough* practice, when we were down to the final five contestants, the students wrestled the trainers. WWE Superstar Tazz decided to rough me up a little, a common initiation into the business from a veteran to a rookie. Just about every wrestling move is based on a real way to hurt someone. Usually it is impossible to tell as an observer when someone is "shooting" on someone and really attacking them. Tazz started our match with a "shoot clothesline" that chipped my teeth and knocked me silly. I only remember this next part because they aired it on the show; I survived about ten legitimate kicks to the back of the head. I couldn't defend myself. Then I saw myself on my hands and knees. Tazz was standing on top of me, facing the same direction, throwing alternating forearms to my face that were whipping my head a foot to the left, then a foot to the right.

The next thing I saw on the video was me nearly breaking my neck. I was standing but bending over, and Tazz grabbed me by the scruff of my shirt and top of my shorts, turned 90 degrees, and whipped me into the middle turnbuckle. My balance was so poor I couldn't stop myself and if I didn't catch one of the ropes I was going in headfirst. I rolled out under the bottom rope and sat outside the ring, pulling little white grains of sand out of my mouth. It took me a couple minutes to realize that the sand was my teeth. I didn't say a thing. The other trainer, Al Snow, later told me that I had seemed "out of it" for the rest of that day. At the time, I wasn't worried about it. It was the last day of the competition and I still had judges to impress.

Dr. Cantu nodded and said, "Yes, that was probably—"

"What if I was playing football, got 'dinged' when I was blindsided by a hit, and later was told that I called people by the wrong name in the dining hall that night at dinner?" "Yes, that—"

"How about being elbowed in the face during a tag-team match, spending five minutes outside the ring seeing double, and then trying to figure out where I was?" I asked. I got a scar on my cheek that time, so it was easier to verify.

"Could have been," he said.

That added up to about a half-dozen concussions from the age of eighteen on—that I could remember.

"Having had multiple concussions could be the reason why you're not recovering as quickly as we'd like," said Dr. Cantu. "And the bigger problem is that you never took any time off to recover."

Time off to recover? I didn't know what he was talking about.

In the sports I played, when you get knocked down you pick yourself up, dust yourself off, and get back out there. I was told:

If you can walk, you can play.

Pain is weakness leaving the body.

If it ain't bleedin' it ain't hurt.

Suck it up.

Take off your skirt, Sally.

That was the culture I loved. I would never take a day off for a headache. What had that done to me?

Dr. Cantu gave me a piece of paper with a list of symptoms on it. He asked me to mark on a scale of 1 to 5 those symptoms that were bothering me at that moment. The sheer number and range of symptoms was surprising. There were twenty or so symptoms on the list, everything from nausea to irritability. A commonly accepted definition of concussion is a "trauma-induced alteration in mental status that may or may not involve a loss of consciousness."[4] The NFL uses the following definition:

> A traumatically induced alteration in brain function manifested by an alteration of awareness or consciousness, including but not limited to a loss of consciousness, "ding," sensation of being dazed or stunned, sensation of "wooziness" or "fogginess," seizure, or amnesic period, and by symptoms commonly associated with post-concussion syndrome, including persistent headaches, vertigo [dizziness], light-headedness, loss of balance, unsteadiness, syncope [LOC], near-syncope, cognitive dysfunction, memory disturbances, hearing loss, tinnitus [ringing in the ears], blurred vision, diplopia [double vision], visual loss, personality change, drowsiness, lethargy, fatigue, and inability to perform usual daily activities.[5]

I scored a 15 on the symptom test. That meant I wasn't doing horribly, but I wasn't exactly a model of health, either. I worried that Dr. Cantu would tell me,

25

"You're cleared to wrestle when you're a 5 on this test," and then it would be up to me to determine when I was a 5. If that was the case, I knew that ultimately I would lie to myself and on the test so I could go back to work. So I started asking questions.

"Why do I have a score of 15? What's going on in my head?"

During this meeting and the weeks that followed, Dr. Cantu would blow my mind (no pun intended) about concussions. To answer my questions, he started with the basics: A concussion is actually not defined by a physical injury, but by a loss of brain *function* that is induced by trauma. Thinking of the concussion as a brain malfunction or as an alteration in mental status—and not as a mysterious invisible injury inside my head that couldn't be detected by conventional tests— was much easier for me to comprehend.

I immediately thought of a couple of wrestlers I'd worked with who had a concussion and lost brain function. At age eighteen, Renee Dupree was the youngest wrestler ever signed by the WWE. Once we were working a show somewhere in America's heartland (with or without concussions it's hard to keep track of all the places we've been) and word got backstage that Renee was hurt. Security and the trainer helped him out of the ring, and I walked with him to the locker room. He was bleeding above his eye, and totally out of it. The trainer went to get supplies to clean up the cut, and asked me to stay with Renee. Since injuries are so common in wrestling, no one was paying much attention to us. Renee looked up, noticed me there, and asked, "Did I wrestle yet?" "Yes," I answered.

"How was the match? Was it good?"

I told him, "Yes, very good."

"Good, good," he said. For about thirty seconds he stared straight ahead. Then he asked me, "Did I wrestle yet?"

"Uh, yes."

"How was the match? Was it good?"

I told him, "Yep, very good."

"Good," he said again. Thirty seconds later, he asked again. The trainer came back by the fourth go-round. An hour later Renee seemed relatively normal, and the next day he apologized profusely for "whatever he might have said after the match."

Bubba Ray Dudley had a similar but more tragic story. He suffered a concussion during a match just months after his mother had died. Her death had hit him hard, but he had kept his emotions bottled up to stay strong for the rest of his family. When he got backstage after suffering the concussion, his malfunctioning brain was suddenly focused on his mother, but he could only remember that she had been sick, not that she had passed away. He asked Tommy Dreamer and Spike Dudley, "How's my mother?" Although they didn't understand why he was asking the question, they dutifully answered, "She passed away a few months ago." For the first time since his mother died, Bubba Ray began to cry. Then, oddly, he stopped crying and started talking about something else. A few minutes later, he asked another wrestler, "How's my mother?" "She passed away a few months ago," he was told. He began crying again, as if hearing the news for the first time. He stayed in a hotel that night with Dreamer, who was asked to keep an eye on him. Dreamer told me this cycle repeated over thirty times with various people over the course of the evening. Each person thought they were doing the right thing by answering the question honestly. When Tommy finally had Bubba away from everyone, he decided it was too painful to let continue. When Bubba Ray would ask again, Tommy would answer "She's fine." Bubba doesn't remember any of it.

Dr. Doug Smith, director of the Center for Brain Injury and Repair at the University of Pennsylvania, later explained to me what was happening in our brains. "It's called concussion or mild traumatic brain injury. But there's nothing mild about it," he said. "The brain is elastic; it's like a Jell-O mold. And it wiggles around. In a concussion your brain changes shape very quickly. And

27

the really sensitive area of the brain is the white matter where all these nerve fibers travel from one part of your brain to another allowing your brain to communicate. In a concussion, these axons get quickly stretched. And that causes injury in a unique way."

Dr. Smith went on to illustrate the damage to the axon by picking up what looked like Silly Putty. "If I kind of make a cylinder and I pull it apart, it just gets thinner and thinner. The same material, if I apply a very dynamic stretch..." I watched the material snap it two. He continued, "It's how fast I stretched it. And it broke. And that rapid stretch doesn't break these nerve fibers, but it can damage parts of those nerve fibers. They're like a garden hose and inside are railroad tracks called micro-tubules that transport material back and forth throughout the axon. And if you break the railroad tracks, all transport stops. It's like the train car just fell off the tracks there and everything can pile up. If you disconnect these axons they're gone forever. You can function without quite a few axons at a certain point but you're at a disadvantage."

Doug Smith, MD

The physical injury then triggers chemical and metabolic changes that together are often termed the "neurometabolic cascade of concussion."[6] I asked David Hovda, PhD, director of the UCLA Brain Injury Research Center and internationally known for his work on traumatic brain injuries, to explain. He told me, "When the brain gets pushed or pulled or moved violently, all the cells in the brain fire. It's kind of like a small seizure. When that happens, chemicals, called neurotransmitters, are released. These are the chemicals we use in the brain to communicate from one cell to another. When they communicate all at once, they activate receptors, and these receptors spill out ions, which is normally what they do—but not to this degree."

Dr. Hovda explained that the concussion causes potassium ions to rush out of the cells and flood the brain, while calcium ions rush inside the cells. "The cells activate pumps to send one ion—potassium—back in, and another ion—calcium—back out," he said. "This requires energy, and that energy is derived from metabolism, or from utilizing the fuel in the brain. The brain fuel used originally is glucose, so the brain will burn a lot of glucose to get its ions back where they belong." But the calcium impairs the cells, and the brain can't create the energy needed to fire the pumps, Dr. Hovda explained. "When calcium comes in, it messes up the machinery that the cell has to make the energy to drive the pumps. So after a concussion, you have an increased need for energy, but you have a deficiency in the ability to make energy."

Essentially, the brain is now running on low batteries, so it doesn't function as well. "The cells turn off and become quiet," he told me. "When you do a metabolic study, the brain has essentially shut down, so the individual will exhibit symptoms as if the brain is not working well. He has a hard time remembering or learning new things, and he'll feel tired and lethargic for a long period of time." All this activity occurring in the brain then manifests as a wide range of acute symptoms.

Symptom	% Reporting at Time of Injury
Headache	92%
Dizziness	72%
Blurred vision	67%
Disorientation	58%
Confusion	56%
Disequilibrium	44%
Nausea/vomiting	39%
Anterograde amnesia	31%
Neck pain	31%
Photophobia	31%
Sleepiness	28%
Fatigue	25%
Loss of consciousness	19%
Retrograde amnesia	19%
Irritability	17%

SOURCE: K. M.Guskiewicz, S. E. Ross, S. W. Marshall, "Postural Stability and Neuropsychological Deficits After Concussion in Collegiate Athletes," *Journal of Athletic Training* 36/3 (2001): 263–373.

The symptoms will continue for varying periods of time, depending on a person's individual brain chemistry, the severity of the injury, prior concussions, the number and severity of secondary collisions after the first concussion, and other factors.

Thanks to Dr. Cantu, Dr. Smith, and Dr. Hovda, I began to understand what had happened to me and why I was feeling as I did. But I was plagued with symptoms and with questions: How long would my symptoms last? What would the long-term effects be? Would I ever be normal again? Would I be able to get back in the ring?

Chapter 3: The Road to Recovery

It became clear that there was such a thing as a "second concussion syndrome." If a player got a concussion in game A, he was much more susceptible to a concussion if he got hit again in the head soon after. One week Steve Young got a concussion. The doctors asked him if he'd gotten a concussion, and he said, "No." They okayed him to play in the next game, and he got a second concussion. Getting two concussions was exponentially worse than getting one, and was enough to knock him out of the game.

—Leigh Steinberg, sports agent

We're too focused on the "event." In a heart attack, there is an event; in a hip fracture, the broken bone is the event. With brain injury, after the initial impact, the damage is not done—after the initial injury, it can continue. That's what's so challenging about these injuries.

—Dr. Heechin Chae, MD

By now, I had a pretty clear understanding of what had happened inside my head right after the injury in Hartford. But to be honest, I was more concerned with *when* I would get better than *how*. But no matter how much I wanted to feel better and move on with my life, I was stuck in a rut. My instinct told me that *when* I would recover was a function of the number of concussions I'd had.

Dr. Cantu told me how most concussion symptoms are transient, meaning that they don't last very long. The following table makes that point clear. The researchers went back and asked athletes about the same symptoms listed in Chapter 2, but this time wanted to know which symptoms had persisted three days after the injury.

Symptom	% Reporting Symptom at Time of Injury	% of Those Reporting Symptom Three Days Later
Headache	92%	45%
Dizziness	72%	12%
Blurred vision	67%	17%
Disorientation	58%	0%
Confusion	56%	10%
Disequilibrium	44%	0%
Nausea/vomiting	39%	14%
Anterograde amnesia	31%	18%
Neck pain	31%	64%
Photophobia	31%	36%
Sleepiness	28%	60%
Fatigue	25%	33%
LOC	19%	NA
Retrograde amnesia	19%	14%
Irritability	17%	50%

SOURCE: K. M. Guskiewicz, S. E. Ross, S. W. Marshall, "Postural Stability and Neuropsychological Deficits After Concussion in Collegiate Athletes," *Journal of Athletic Training* 36/3 (2001): 263–373.

As the table shows, some of the symptoms (such as disorientation) disappeared, while others (such as irritability and sleepiness) took a few days to appear.

The unique symptoms that each concussion causes can be related to the area of the brain that has been traumatized. Dr. Cantu has written, "Some symptoms relate primarily to the brain stem or dysfunction of its connections, like unconsciousness, tinnitus, light-headedness, unsteadiness, ataxia, headache, nausea, vomiting, and incoordination. Other symptoms result from cerebral cortex dysfunction and occur acutely, including confusion, disorientation, anterograde and retrograde amnesia, decreased information processing, and short-term memory impairment. Still others may be delayed in onset, like depression, fatigue, sleep disturbance, irritability, and feeling 'foggy.'"[7]

Unfortunately, this way of understanding symptoms is murky, because if the injury is "diffuse," many different parts of the brain can be injured in a single concussion.

Thus, in order for Dr. Cantu and me to predict when my specific symptoms would disappear, we had to think at a more basic level. We knew that the malfunction was primarily caused by two processes, physical damage and the neurometabolic cascade. It's easy to understand why we recover from a neurometabolic cascade—eventually the ions in the brain become balanced, and blood flow returns to normal.

However, if there was physical damage, the brain doesn't return to normal in the same way: the damage is permanent.

Dr. Cantu told me, "When we say the brain has healed, the damage is permanent. However, you can return to the functional level you previously had because there are enough spare parts of the brain to take over that function. Although it's more complex than this, one way of looking at it is that we are born with millions of extra nerve cells and neurons. This explains why people can start losing them in their twenties and still be mentally keen in their eighties. Obviously the greater the number of extra cells you are born with, the greater number you can lose before you're down to a critical level— before you start to see neurologic deterioration.

"What happens with multiple head injuries is that in some instances, you lose thousands, if not more, nerve cells. Then you reach a critical limit, where you start not to have enough nerve cells to function at the level that you once did. You now pick up permanent rather than transient neurologic impairment. That's a supply-and-demand way of looking at it."

The brain uses the extra neurons to compensate, and this leads to recovery from physical damage. This is called *plasticity*. However, you eventually run out of spare parts. Using this framework, my lack of recovery could have been an indication that I had reached some sort of "critical point" where I was running low on extra neurons. With that as a possibility, Dr. Cantu attached a medical label to my predicament: "post-concussion syndrome." I was familiar with that syndrome, as it has ended many athletes' careers.

The idea that at a certain point you can no longer recover as quickly or fully from concussions is supported by a multitude of studies that show that after suffering one concussion, athletes are more likely to have a second one.[8] [9] [10] Plus, additional concussions tend to be more severe. People with a history of concussions are between four and seven times more likely to get knocked unconscious.[11] [12] In essence, we chip away at some sort of "brain reserve."

Dr. Cantu decided to perform an MRI to see if there was any physical evidence of brain damage. I told him that I'd already had one, and it was negative.

"While it's a long shot, sometimes the evidence can take a while to appear, and sometimes you just have to know what to look for," he said.

I left the doctor's office with more answers, but even more questions.

A few days later, I drove back to the hospital for my second MRI in two months. The MRI process is always impersonal; you don't know the nurses and technicians, and they don't know anything about you, save for the part of your insides that a doctor wants to see. This encounter was no different. I slipped into the tube with nary a word spoken. Some people find being trapped in that tiny tube with the loud noises and vibrations of the machine claustrophobic. I've had so many MRIs over the years that I usually fall asleep. This particular morning, the technician interrupted my nap. My new habit of acting out my dreams was causing me to squirm, ruining the MRI images. When I left, I felt anxious about the test results. Yet, since I was confident they wouldn't find anything wrong, I figured the only harm done was having wasted the morning.

On my way home from the hospital, I got a phone call from a number I didn't recognize. It was the MRI technician. With a strange tension in her voice, she urged me to return the next morning for another test.

Hesitating, I asked, "Why, did something not work?"

"We'd like to take some more pictures" was all I could get her to say.

I couldn't tell if she was hiding some huge discovery that they would only tell me in person, or if she honestly didn't know why they wanted to see me again. Either way, that's a phone call you don't want to get. I got more worried when I found out that this busy MRI center (I'd had to wait over a week for my first appointment) had cleared an early morning appointment for me the next day.

From the moment I ended the call, I desperately tried to figure out what diagnosis could possibly require such an urgent second test. Scenarios ran through my mind like flash cards. The stack of cards was short, due to my lack of knowledge of the brain and my lack of imagination. I could only think of two legitimate reasons why I had to go back. Either they had made a mistake, and nothing was wrong (this is what I was hoping for) or they had found a brain tumor (this terrified me). What else could be so urgent that I had to go back to the hospital the next day, but not urgent enough that I didn't have to go that very second? I figured that a tumor would explain why my symptoms weren't going away.

I had to stop torturing myself, so I distracted myself by watching a movie, and then tried to go to bed. I figured I'd have plenty of time to make myself crazy on the 45-minute drive to the hospital the next morning. Despite my best efforts, and the usual sleeping pills, I didn't get much rest that night.

When I arrived the next morning, everything seemed eerily normal. The same nurses and technicians were there. No one was acting weird—as far as I could tell. They slid me into the tube again. There was a mirror over my head set at a 45-degree angle so I could see out past my feet—probably there for the claustrophobics. I had a good view of the technician's room, where they watch the live pictures on computer screens. In my experience, there are usually only one or two people in the technician's room. I did a quick head count. One, two, three, four . . .Uh, oh, I thought. That's too many people.

In addition to the two technicians, I saw Dr. Cantu and another man wearing a lab coat. I assumed he was the doctor scrutinizing the pictures on the screens. No one had told me that all those people would be there. I don't think I was supposed to know they were there. It was just my luck that two workmen were installing new blinds over the windows that day, so the doctors were in full view. I felt a wave of nausea and started to sweat. I wanted out of the tube.

After twenty more minutes of agony, the test was over. The doctors had left, and the technicians weren't very talkative. I was told to go up to Dr. Cantu's office on the eighth floor. That hadn't been on the agenda either. Not good. When I arrived, there were four people in the waiting room, but I wasn't even given a chance to sit down. I was whisked right in to see the doc.

By this time, I think I'd stopped breathing. Dr. Cantu must have noticed, because he gave me an overly reassuring smile.

"Don't worry, you're fine."

A wave of relief swept over my body, followed by a wave of confusion. "What did you think was wrong?"

"Well, Chris, you have a few small areas in and on the surface of your brain that show up as white spots on the MRI. Multiple white spots can be early evidence of multiple sclerosis. We had to rule that out, and we did."

"How?" I asked.

"If you had MS, you'd have a lot more of the spots."

He seemed satisfied. I was not. "Okay, then what are these spots?"

"Well, the answer is that we don't know . . . I would venture to guess they're most likely the residual evidence of tissue damage caused by impacts—concussions. But they look like they've been there for a while, so they're probably not from your latest ones."

"Does that confirm that I've had concussions that I didn't know about?"

"More than likely," he answered.

I sat back in my chair and let it all soak in. Sweet. I have dead chunks of brain from all those shots I took over the years. I didn't know that was even possible. By the end of the week, I would receive a physical copy of the MRI report, and would discover that "a few areas" meant five, and "small" meant as big as 4mm x 3mm on some slides. I didn't know what was considered big, but I decided that that was all the dead brain tissue I was comfortable having.

As the evidence that years of abuse had considerably damaged my brain continued to mount, I wasn't so gung-ho about returning to the wrestling ring "a week after the symptoms disappeared." Dr. Cantu had told me that it would be very likely that I would get another concussion, and that it would probably be much worse than my last one. If it was taking me months to get over this concussion, it could take me years to get over the next one. Or maybe I'd have the symptoms forever.

But I soon found out this wasn't the worst of my worries. There was another variable I hadn't yet thought of while planning for my return—the need to take time off between concussions. Having one more concussion would be bad, but having another one before I'd fully recovered from the first could be exponentially worse.

I first learned about this risk when Dr. Cantu sent me to see a headache specialist. From my Cambridge apartment I walked over the Charles River to the Pain Management Clinic at Spaulding Rehabilitation Hospital. This hospital sits behind the sports arena where the Boston Celtics and Boston Bruins play. I had an appointment with Dr. Heechin Chae, the associate medical director for Spaulding's inpatient brain injury rehabilitation program. Dr. Chae was a headache specialist and a licensed acupuncturist, and we bonded immediately. While Dr. Chae inserted the needles each week, I'd ask him questions about concussions, just like I did with Dr. Cantu.

Dr. Chae had so much to say that I got the feeling that he'd been waiting for someone to ask him about his experiences treating these injuries. All that year he'd been treating teenagers with post-concussion syndrome. The worst cases were kids who had received a second concussion before they had recovered from the first. He was clearly frustrated. He saw concussion treatment as a double standard, because most doctors, even neurosurgeons, treat severe brain injuries completely differently than mild brain injuries.

"I don't know how much sense that makes, because we're dealing with the same organ," Dr. Chae told me. "No cardiologist ignores a 'mild' heart attack. He doesn't say to his patient, 'Don't worry about exercise or your diet unless the heart attack is severe.' He still treats every patient as if he has had a heart attack. Yet we don't treat a concussion in the same way as we do a brain injury. For some reason we tell people, 'You're fine,' when we know they aren't."

Dr. Chae felt that his brain-injury treatment mantra was often lost on his colleagues. He stated, "There's nothing you can do about the initial damage from a head injury. The reason that we spend so much time, energy, and money is to *prevent further damage.* A concussion is the same principle—*it's a head injury*—but we do a terrible job preventing secondary or further injury." If the brain receives further impacts before the chemical and metabolic fluctuations that occur after a concussion have returned to normal, the damaged brain cells, in one expert's words, "teeter on the brink," and another impact may kill brain cells that would otherwise recover.[13] The brain is vulnerable to permanent and severe damage during this recovery period, which may take days, weeks, or months. In some ways, it's like the Death Star in the movie *Star Wars* when the deflector shield is down. (Yes, I like science fiction.)

Dr. Chae preferred a different analogy. "Imagine that the brain is a city that experiences an earthquake. The earthquake isn't bad enough to make the buildings fall down, but it does create structural damage in the foundations. If there's an aftershock—even if it's much weaker than the earthquake— the structures are more vulnerable to collapsing.

"Worse, when the second earthquake hits, and it will, there's a risk that the buildings will fall down. I would say that's analogous to the brain. Once you damage the brain, there's some structural damage, and the brain is vulnerable to another impact. In that case, you can actually kill brain cells. Not suffering any further trauma is important because by returning to play too quickly, you expose your brain to the risk of further damage that could have easily been prevented. Sitting out allows the brain to strengthen its structures and withstand other types of injuries. Consistent with my knowledge about brain injuries in general, the second, third, and fourth injuries are a lot more detrimental to the person's long-term outcome than the first."

▼▼▼

I later found out that Dr. Chae had one patient in mind while we were discussing this little-known risk. In the fall of 2003, twelve-year-old Willie Baun was a typical seventh-grader who loved to play football. His father, Whitey, was a coach of his local peewee team, and had been since Willie started playing at the age of seven. Willie's mother, Becky, described Willie as "very friendly, very outgoing, very social, and good at sports. He's a 'ball' kid."

Willie got his first concussion of the season on an onside kick. He and another player went for the ball and collided helmet-to-helmet. Although Whitey was initially concerned, Willie appeared fine, and walked off the field on his own. Whitey asked one of the other coaches to check him out. The coach said that Willie was a little woozy, but okay. Willie went back in the game, but Whitey noticed by the way he was playing that something was wrong.

Whitey pulled him out, and he and Becky took Willie to the hospital after the game. The doctor said Willie had suffered a concussion and that he should take at least three weeks off, depending on when his headache went away. The headache took a full three weeks to go away, and a few days later Willie returned to the team. Whitey remembers, "[Three weeks] seemed a little excessive at the time, but we waited, and after those three weeks, he started to play again. For the next two weeks he seemed fine, although now I worry that he wasn't fine, but didn't want to tell me."

Five weeks after the initial concussion, Willie was taking part in an angle-tackling drill on soft ground at half speed. "Willie got hit, fell to the ground, and didn't get up," Whitey recalls, reliving every parent's worst nightmare. "I was on the other side of the field at the time. Based on the hit, I couldn't imagine that it was another concussion—he just got tapped. But when I got there I could tell something was wrong." Willie went back to the hospital, where a negative CT scan revealed it was "just" another concussion.

But after Willie returned home, things changed overnight. Willie developed amnesia. Becky couldn't believe what she saw when Willie came out of his room the next morning. "When he woke up, he didn't know the dog, and I'm not even sure he knew who Whitey and I were. As the day went on he figured out we were his parents, but I can remember him looking at me like he was trying to relearn who I was. That was so scary. He was totally dizzy, and he couldn't put one foot in front of the other. When we took him to the hospital, they said there was nothing they could do to help him." After a few weeks, his parents tried to

41

get Willie back into school. He started with half-days every other day, but struggled due to his memory loss. The school didn't think that Willie belonged in a regular classroom because he was now reading at the second-grade level. The Bauns had to convince the school that regular classes were the best thing for Willie, with the hope that he would eventually get better.

Becky often fought with the teachers. "I'd send in math work for him to do, and tell the math teacher to let him do that work instead. The teacher would call me and say, 'Well, you didn't send in work today.' I'd say, 'The work was in his pocket—he just didn't remember it was there!' Willie would wear cargo pants with four pockets. He'd have whatever he needed for each class—English, math, science, and social studies—in one of the pockets. That's how he went around school. He couldn't remember where his locker was, what to carry, or what he needed for the next class. He couldn't plan ahead."

At first Willie only realized that there was something different about him. "We'd keep telling him that he'd had a concussion, and the doctors were calling this post-concussion syndrome. I'd say, 'We'll go see the doctor, and we can ask questions if you want to.'"

After six months, Willie began getting his memory back, but no one can be sure if he will ever fully recover. Whitey worries that he's to blame for letting Willie return to the field too soon after the first concussion. "We don't know if the hits he took during those two weeks had something to do with what happened. I'll be driving down the road, and I'll start to think about it. I say to myself, 'I can't believe it. Why didn't you see? Why didn't you know? Did you get him back there too soon?' And the answer is . . . although I didn't necessarily know it at the time . . . that we did . . . I did. Living with that will be very difficult."

▼▼▼

After hearing Willie's story, I understood Dr. Chae's passion for requiring athletes to fully recover before going back out on the field. But though I understood the concept, I was a little hazy on the science. I turned to Dr. Hovda for an explanation.

"There are three scenarios that could explain why the cells die when the brain is hurt again," he told me. "First, the brain gets its fuel from blood. If you open your eyes, blood flow increases to provide fuel to the area of the brain that processes vision. After a concussion, this coupling between blood flow and metabolic demand is lost. So when you stimulate the brain, the brain will still fire and ask for fuel, but the blood flow will not increase. If this happens enough, then the cells will die from cerebral ischemia, which means that the blood flow to the area isn't enough to support the demand for energy.

"The second thing that happens is that when the brain is injured from a concussion, the neurotransmitters bind on to the receptors, they change the receptors, and they stay changed for a long period of time. One of the receptors that's changed a lot is susceptible to a compound called *glutamate*. Glutamate is a neurotransmitter in the brain that is excitatory—if you excite a cell too much it will go on to die, like a seizure. If the receptors have been changed to make them much more sensitive compared to the normal stimulation when there is another release of glutamate—which could happen from another head injury—it would overwhelm the cells, and the cells would die from what is called an excitotoxic death. This means that they fire until they die.

"The third possibility has to do with potassium being released outside the cell, causing a demand for fuel, and calcium coming inside the cell, mucking up the machinery that metabolizes fuel, called *mitochondria*. If the cell still has a high concentration of calcium, then another blow to the head will cause another flood of calcium. But this time, the calcium will overwhelm the mitochondria, and the mitochondria will die. It's similar to ingesting a toxin used in biochemical warfare, like mustard gas, that prevents the body from taking in oxygen. The cell has to make energy to survive. The brain and the body require about 116 watts of energy per hour, and if you don't make that, you start losing stuff."

The formula was relatively easy to understand. In the simplest terms, most concussions cause only temporary damage. But if an athlete continues to take shots to the head before the brain has had a chance to recover, those combined injuries cause more problems because the release of chemicals in the brain harms the interfaces between cells. That's when the athlete begins to suffer permanent damage.

Just when I thought I understood the damage caused by concussions, Dr. Chae added another process to the mix.

"While our current understanding is that a mild concussion doesn't cause brain cell death, we do believe it causes axonal degeneration. Consider the axons as 'highways' connecting the neurons. They're basically shaken by the impact. Certain types of damage trigger a cascade of events, where axons start to lose their fatty envelope. That fatty envelope is what makes the transmission of information flow properly. When you lose it, the transmission becomes much slower or gets interrupted."

Studies show concussions can change any facet of one's being that is controlled by the brain—behavior, emotion, intelligence, memory, personality, attention, mood, cognition, ability to communicate, mobility, etc. But people who are merely changed are the lucky ones. Some people don't survive the second hit.

"It's called Second Impact Syndrome, or SIS," Dr. Cantu told me. "In theory you could be at risk, but the vast majority of SIS cases occur in athletes ages twelve to eighteen. For some unknown reason, teenagers appear to be the most vulnerable."

I'd been reading about all these young athletes dying after they'd suffered two concussions in quick succession, and I was concerned. After all, I'd risked my own health for weeks after my concussions by trying to be a tough guy and continuing to wrestle. More important, I was worried that I still might be at risk in the future.

From 1980 to 1993, the National Center for Catastrophic Sports Injury Research linked seventeen deaths in football to SIS, and many more deaths have occurred since then.[14] No one is sure how and why SIS occurs, but in every case it's caused when an athlete receives a secondary head trauma before the symptoms from a first concussion have resolved. The second impacts aren't always severe; sometimes they involve a hit to the chest, side, or back that causes the head to snap back. Although it isn't clear what happens inside the brain of the athlete, what a coach, parent, or teammate sees from the outside is remarkably consistent. The athlete is usually dazed by the impact, but he remains alert for another fifteen seconds to a minute. Then he suddenly collapses to the ground, in a semiconscious state, with rapidly dilating pupils and a loss of eye movement. Then he stops breathing.

About half the athletes die from SIS, depending on the severity of the bleeding inside the brain and the medical care the athlete receives.

On September 29, 2001, high school football player Matthew Colby died fifteen hours after collapsing from a head injury he had suffered on the field.[15] He'd been complaining to friends of a headache that began after he'd received a hit on September 15, almost two weeks before. The headache persisted after a second game on September 21, and he complained again. The coaches became aware, he was held out of practice, and he received clearance from a doctor to play in the following game.

A forensic neuropathologist performing a microscopic examination of Colby's brain discovered evidence of brain trauma that had occurred up to two weeks prior to his death in the form of "neomembranes," which are spots of tissue formed after the dura—the membrane surrounding the brain—separates from the brain. In these cases, fragile blood vessels expand to fill the space, and while they are stretched, they have an increased risk of bursting, much like an overfilled balloon.

Those who survive an SIS injury may never be the same. Just over ten years ago, Brad Ames of Evansville, Indiana, returned to play football after ten days of rest following a concussion. He immediately got hit again.[16] The second brain injury severely damaged his ability to coordinate his muscles, so on most days it's difficult for him to speak and to be understood. His mind and personality remain intact. Some people who suffer this kind of brain injury lose their mental faculties to such a degree that they're unaware of having a problem. Brad is fully aware of what happened to him, but is powerless to do anything about it.

Brandon Schultz had a similar injury. His family sued the school district to help cover the estimated $12.6 million cost of Brandon's lifetime care.[17] His attorney said, "Brandon suffered a concussion during a game just one week prior to his tragic episode. He briefly lost consciousness, complained of headaches the week following the injury, and yet no school official referred him to a doctor. Had Brandon been required to see a doctor—which should always be the standard of care when an athlete suffers a concussion with ongoing symptoms—we believe his SIS brain injury would never have occurred."

Brandon's mother said, "No one instructed us that a physician should clear Brandon to play. To us it was just a headache. We had no reason to believe it was anything more than that."

Brandon continues to suffer severe physical, cognitive, and psychological problems, and will always require advanced care. He's haunted by the memory of the young man he used to be. "I still think of myself as that same guy," Brandon said. "But I'm not. And I know I'm not."

Adam Melka, a fifteen-year-old linebacker at Arrowhead High School in Wisconsin and the son of a former University of Wisconsin football player,

46

became dizzy and started vomiting on the sideline after a hit to the head. He was rushed to the hospital and underwent emergency brain surgery. His coaches and teammates were puzzled because the last hit he took wasn't an especially violent one. When Adam's father, Jim, rushed back from a hunting trip, he asked to see the game tape. Though he agreed that the final hit wasn't anything special, he noticed that Adam took an extraordinary hit earlier in the game that left him visibly shaken. "You could see him go onto his knees and bend backwards," Jim Melka said.[18] Adam survived, but has a long recovery ahead of him.

Yet many boys—and their families—and would grab at the chance to have Adam's life. Twelve-year-old Kyle Lippo, a seventh-grade football player from Round Lake, Illinois, was not as lucky. On Saturday, September 26, 2003, he told his coach during a game that he had a headache and asked to sit out the rest of the game. Five minutes later, the coach asked Kyle if he wanted to go back in. Kyle said no, because his headache was getting worse. Then he started crying, saying, "It hurts really bad!"

Kyle was rushed to a local medical center, where he was loaded onto an emergency helicopter and taken to Advocate Lutheran General Hospital. There the Boy Scout, trombone player, and student council representative died the next morning from head trauma.[19]

A few weeks later, Osten Gill, a sixteen-year-old high school sophomore from Rushford, New York, collapsed on the team bus as it was returning from a junior varsity football game. He had complained of dizziness and nausea after being hit during the game, and had vomited on the sidelines and on the bus. Osten died at a hospital several hours later.[20] Then in November of 2003, seventeen-year-old safety Edward Gomez drilled a wide receiver coming across the middle on a fourth down, forcing a dropped pass. Gomez popped up, was congratulated by his teammates, and headed to the sideline. Moments later he lost consciousness and collapsed. He died days later.[21]

Jacob Snakenberg was a freshman football player at Grandview High School in Denver. During a game, Jacob mysteriously collapsed after what appeared to be a routine tackle that did not involve contact to the head. He died two days later, and a neurosurgeon who operated on him said the cause was a recent blow to the head. In the days following his death, his friends revealed that Jacob had been suffering from headaches during the previous week, following a big hit to his head in a previous game. His father told the press he had specifically asked Jacob if his head hurt during that week, as he was concerned after watching Jacob take that blow, but Jacob had denied it.[22]

Jacob's story reminded me of something I hadn't thought about in ten years. During my sophomore year of high school, I played for a coach who had lost his own son to a head injury on the football field. I vaguely remember my former athletic trainer mentioning it every preseason. I called him to get more details. "Kurt Thyreen got a concussion in a game. He didn't tell anyone," Hersey High School trainer Hal Hilmer explained. "We later found out from his friends that his head hurt so much that week that he couldn't play his trumpet in band class. No one bothered to tell us or the coaches. He took the field for the next game, took a hit to the head that ruptured a blood vessel, and passed away."

I also read that sixteen-year-old Californian Michael Pennerman, a cousin of 1994 Heisman Trophy winner Rashaan Salaam, fell unconscious on the sideline after being tackled during a football game. He had walked off the field on his own, gone over to his coach, and told him, "It feels like somebody is pulling me to the ground." He then collapsed, and died the next day. There was suspicion that he may have suffered a concussion earlier in the game, both due to his behavior in his last minute of consciousness and because his stepfather said he was taking hits all game long.[23]

There clearly seems to be something extremely dangerous about getting hit in the head again shortly after suffering a concussion. And yet we all do it.

▼▼▼

The more I learned about the victims of SIS, the less I felt sorry for myself and the more I began to worry about all the kids still playing football. I knew that I was out of the woods; I wasn't going back to wrestling until I was symptom-free for a long, long time, and since SIS usually afflicts teenagers, I wasn't worried about dying when I did return.

But it was clear to me that these tragic injuries could be avoided if we were able to properly diagnose and treat concussions. On a personal level, I was frustrated that I didn't have the knowledge to prevent further injury to myself. It would have been nice to have avoided this whole "months of headaches and possible end of my wrestling career" thing that I was going through. But beyond any immediate thoughts of myself, I was deeply troubled by the more than 1.1 million high school football players and hundreds of thousands of middle school and elementary school kids who are experiencing concussions like mine, with far less support. Even with the unlimited medical budget the WWE seemed to have for me, it took me a long time to get the information I needed. I heard a different story about concussions from nearly every doctor I saw. Willie Baun's parents, acting on the advice of three doctors, were still unable to protect their son. Something wasn't adding up. Why did all these doctors have such drastically different information about head injuries?

Perhaps it was related to their sources of information. As a life sciences consultant to pharmaceutical and biotechnology companies for Trinity Partners, with every new project, I had to go from being a neophyte to an authority in a new area of medicine in just two to three months. I spent a lot of time at the Harvard Medical School library, reading studies that examine the current treatment methods of a specific illness and the changes in diagnosis and treatment strategies over time. It's often my responsibility to figure out how many people have a certain illness now, and how many will have it in the future.

These assignments are never easy, as the studies can often show conflicting results. Based on who performed the study, who *paid for* the study, and how the study was designed, it's my job to determine who has the most accurate information.

It dawned on me that it might be a good idea to apply my research skills to the sports concussion universe. I thought that maybe the doctors' knowledge was inconsistent because they were getting their information from different sources, some of which may have been wrong or outdated. Perhaps they were even reading studies funded by companies with a financial interest in the outcome, which can often make the conclusions of those studies . . . well, let's just say "unique." Heck, I had the time to research this—I wasn't working. It turns out that after reading just about every concussion study one could possibly get his hands on, I was proven right.

Chapter 4: Taking Care of the Kids

I would venture to say that I had between 15 and 18 concussions in my career. When my old teammates—or just guys in general—ask me about concussions, I ask them if they ever had one. They say, "No." I ask them if they ever saw stars flash before their eyes. And they say, "Yeah." I ask if they ever hit someone or got hit and had everything just fade into black. And they say, "Yeah." I tell them "That's a concussion." I've come to the realization that a lot of guys have suffered concussions, and the effects of concussions, and they don't even know it.

—Harry Carson, NFL Hall of Famer

There were times when my head hurt so bad that I felt like I was going to pass out. I was never diagnosed with a concussion; of course, I never asked the doctor to look at my head, either. It didn't mean that much to me at the time.

—Brian Daigle, former college football player

I'm afraid that these young kids don't really know what's going on. When they're a little dizzy, a little confused, or maybe something inside them says, "Hold it, I need to take a break," they don't tell us. So we say, "Okay, Joey, get back in there. Let's go!" We think, "Let me be the macho coach. Hey kid, suck it up!" The kid doesn't tell us because he doesn't know what to say. And we don't ask the right questions to find out if he has gotten his bell rung or not.

—Whitey Baun, former college football player, youth football coach

My experience over the weeks since my last concussion had taught me that few doctors, let alone athletes, understood this injury well. I knew from my prior consulting experience the answers I needed to find, and I knew that the answers that these doctors should have had at their fingertips did exist somewhere in the medical literature.

The original studies upon which modern head injury treatment is (or should be) based are buried inside medical journals, but not every doctor has time to keep up with them. But a researcher with enough time and motivation to read and analyze might find some answers. Time and motivation was about all I had.

I started to look at the concussion studies, and I soon discovered that there's a growing body of research of varying quality on high school, college, and professional football players. But I was frustrated to find that there wasn't a single study on football players who are middle school age or younger. Why wouldn't we first study the players who are least able to understand or articulate this injury? I was forced to be creative to get an idea of what was happening to the little guys.

Researching the book

An opportunity presented itself while I was driving through Cambridge, Massachusetts, one summer afternoon. I passed a field where about a hundred kids in football helmets were practicing at a summer camp, and thought it would be worth my while to park my car and watch.

After a few minutes of watching some non-contact drills, a coach blew his whistle to end the session. I recognized him—he had been a coach of mine in college. I walked over to say hello, and as we caught up with each other, I told him about the project I was working on. I asked if I could talk to a few of his younger players about concussions. He made me a deal: if I would give a talk to the whole camp about football, wrestling, working hard in school, and concussions, he'd let me talk to a few seventh- and eighth-graders one-on-one.

We had a nice group chat. The kids seemed to recognize me and were focused on who I had beaten in the WWE, and I focused on not revealing how unimpressive that list really was. When we were done, the coach started sending kids over to talk to me.

Fourteen-year-old Patrick told me that he'd never been diagnosed with a concussion, but admitted, "Once in a while I get hit hard and my head starts throbbing. Sometimes I get a little dizzy." Thirteen-year-old Keith had a similar story. He told me, "I don't think I've ever had a 'concussion.' I know I've gotten my 'bell rung' a couple of times, and I've been pretty dizzy after some hits, but that's about it. When you get a direct hit to the head, and you get up, you get a little dizzy. My teammates have had to help me off the field before, and it's taken me a while to get my bearings back, but I doubt that I had a concussion."

Fourteen-year-old Kyle had a different story. He'd been diagnosed with a concussion the previous season. "I went down low to block someone, and his knee hit me in the head. I got dizzy, my head started spinning, and I had to go to the sideline. Then I threw up. That was pretty much a concussion, they said. That's my only serious one. Sometimes after a hit, when I go back to the huddle, I'll be weaving back and forth, but by the time we get back up to the line I'll be fine. I don't consider those concussions. But ever since I got the concussion, if I run too hard or if I get hit too hard, I start feeling dizzy and tired. Then it'll go away. It comes and it goes. It happens in anything. Say I run two miles. I'm really dizzy at the end. That didn't use to happen—it's just since the concussion."

It was clear from these short conversations that these young men were suffering concussions. So why the lack of attention from the medical community? Perhaps it's because people incorrectly assume that kids are too small and too slow to get concussions. That's what Willie Baun's mother had thought. "I didn't worry about concussions at the time because the kids were all so slow, they were all so padded, and it never seemed like they picked up enough speed to bounce off of someone with much impact."

Personally, I think that no one has looked into this simply because they believe that it would be too difficult. Youth teams don't keep medical records like the upper levels of football do, and few employ medical staff. This means that there's no free data to be had. Researchers probably think that children would be poor sources of concussion histories as well. Many would doubt kids' ability to accurately say or even remember if they'd had a concussion. We certainly haven't provided much successful educational outreach to help kids understand or care about the concussions they may be getting; a recent study showed that over half the athletes at the University of Akron have no knowledge at all of the possible consequences following a head injury. If college athletes don't think that concussions are dangerous, what hope do we have for middle school students? Would they consider a concussion to be an event worth remembering?

With or without data, understanding what's happening to kids on the football field is an important question for the hundreds of thousands of youth football players and their parents. Unfortunately, we must learn our lessons from the groups who *have* been studied: college, high school, and professional football players. And here, the studies paint a disturbing picture.

Dr. J. Scott Delaney is a team doctor for the McGill University football and soccer teams, as well as for the professional football and soccer teams in Montreal. A specialist in emergency medicine and sports medicine, he was inspired to conduct multiple studies on the incidence of concussions in these sports because after a few years with the teams, he "was taken aback at how many players sat out of games due to concussions."

"Incidence" is just a fancy word for the number of concussions that happen in a given period of time. In researching early incidence studies, Dr. Delaney would have found that the largest and best-known studies claim that approximately 5 percent of football players at the high school and college levels get a concussion each season. According to my own research, just one study at that time had ever reported a number higher than 8 percent. The studies that have reported such low numbers have a common method— they ask athletic trainers how many concussions they treat each season.

Incidence of Concussions in Football According to Trainer Surveys

Study	Level	% of Players Receiving Concussion
Guskiewicz et al.[24]	High School and College	5%
Barth et al.[25]	College	8%
Guskiewicz et al.[26]	College	6%
Zemper[27]	College	4%
McCrea et al.[28]	High School	4%
Powell and Barber-Foss[29]	High School	4%

24 25 26 27 28 29

Dr. Delaney questioned that methodology. From experience, he knew that players don't always tell trainers when they've had a concussion. As he told me, "When you ask a football player if he has a headache or neck pain, he usually says, 'No.' If you ask, 'You really have no headache or neck pain?' he'll say, 'Well, just my regular headache and neck pain.'"

To get past football players' tendency to minimize their injuries at the time they occur, Dr. Delaney tried asking the players about their experiences after the season. In association with the Canadian Football League Players' Association, Dr. Delaney conducted a pilot study where he surveyed the athletes about their experiences with concussions in the CFL. To his surprise, the pilot study was a failure. Dr. Delaney discovered that players were unwilling to admit to concussions both on *and off* the field. He told me that "in the very first study, we asked players to write their names on the studies, so we'd know who'd returned them. When we got them back, almost no players had said that they'd ever had a concussion, with the exception of those guys who were very secure with their position on the team—like the star quarterback. The others were worried that it would get back to the GM that they were prone to concussions."

So Dr. Delaney went back to the drawing board. "We sent out the same study again, but this time we made it anonymous. When the players didn't have to worry about their answers being traced back to them the numbers went through the roof. They reported 10 to 40 times more concussions," he explained.

Dr. Delaney isn't the only researcher to make this discovery. The fact that the vast majority of concussions are never revealed to athletic trainers has been reported in multiple studies across numerous age groups. Post-season anonymous surveys of football players consistently reveal that about half suffer concussions each season, and many of them suffer multiple concussions.

Incidence of Concussions in Football Accoring to Player Surveys

Study	Level	Incidence	Average Per Player
Langburt et al.[30]	High School	47%	3.4
Delaney et al.[31]	College	70%	4+
Delaney et al.[32]	CFL	48%	NA
Woronzoff[33]	College	61%	NA
Gerberich et al.[34]	College	19%	NA
McCrea et al.[35]	High School	15%	NA

30 31 32 33 34 35

The wide range of findings may be easily explained by looking at the survey language. With the athletes' lack of awareness about concussions, some

56

researchers have had to try different approaches in order to get accurate data from players. Dr. Langburt and his colleagues removed the word *concussion* from their survey. They used *head injury* instead, assuming that many athletes believe that a concussion requires a loss of consciousness. They were right to consider how the injury is labeled. One survey of college football programs found that 92 percent of athletes and coaches believe that a "bell-ringer" and a "dinger" are different from a concussion. Actually, they're both just slang for a mild concussion.[36] The McCrea study, which found the fewest concussions, simply asked, "How many concussions did you have?"

When I finished reading the twelve studies, I was shocked by the wide gap between these bodies of research. When compared to a trainer-based study funded by the NCAA, Dr. Delaney's college survey would imply that only 1 out of 100 concussions are being diagnosed! He stands by his data. "We chose symptoms conservatively—these are the symptoms that you can only get from concussions. We didn't want people questioning our results."

Based on my research, my experience, and the experiences of other athletes, I have no doubt that anonymous player surveys are accurate. But I find it very strange that I'm in the minority. Dr. Delaney agrees.

"I stand on the sideline for pro football and soccer, college football and soccer, and pro boxing. When you hear some of the numbers from other studies, you scratch your head and think, 'Are they dreaming? Have they ever seen how violent this game is? Or are they just living in a lab somewhere? They can't actually believe those results.' Anybody who's been there realizes there's no way they're even scratching the surface of this issue."

There has been no similar data published at this point on the incidence of concussions in athletes younger than high school. However, if the frequency of concussions at this age is anything close, we have a lot of worry about. Dr. Chae was the first to tell me that brain development continues well into the teen years, and a brain injury at any time can permanently hinder that development.

57

"Children are a very interesting case," he said. "We think that their brains might be more flexible, and that there may be neuronal growth, but, on the other hand, they might be more susceptible to damage while they're recovering from the first injury. Because the brain is reorganizing and reformulating, any kind of injury can make that damage permanent."

Beth Adams, a neurotrauma rehabilitation specialist, treats those children who have been properly identified. I first met Beth in her Salem, Massachusetts office after Dr. Cantu recommended that I see her to help with my own recovery. As time went on, I began to ask about her experiences with younger athletes.

"I believe that there could be a lot of kids who are misdiagnosed and medicated for various behavioral or emotional problems that may actually be head-injury related. Not many studies have looked at that. My guess would be that there are kids, and you and I can probably remember who these kids were in school—the class clown, the kids who got into trouble—who also had experienced blows to the head that resulted in classic post-concussion symptoms. All of a sudden these boys were 'all over the place'—hyperactive, distracted. Many of these kids may have been hit, but the hit was never addressed as a concussion."

It's obvious to me that more attention needs to be paid to young children on the football field. But so far, we've only explored what happens to these young players in the short term. The latest and most interesting research—especially to anyone who has ever suffered a concussion— concerns what will happen to those kids when they grow up.

Chapter 5: Lost Memories

I've heard about concussions triggering Alzheimer's and some things, but nothing in real detail. To be honest, some of this stuff was presented to me, and was incorporated into my decision to retire. Some of the research is still pretty gray, and they don't know for sure, but I thought it was strong enough to make it in my interest to retire. Did it help me in my retirement? Sure, but those are all things I'd wish I'd known prior. Right now, a lot of these things are coming out after the fact, but they need to come out before the fact.

—Merril Hoge, nine-year NFL veteran

Other than being susceptible to further concussions, I don't know the long-term effects of having concussions. I feel like I'd only want to know that after I stopped playing. I wouldn't have wanted to know before, because it might have scared me a bit.

—Ray Hill, college football player

Surprisingly, the first person to tell me that there are serious, long-term consequences to concussions wasn't a doctor. Even though they were treating me for post-concussion syndrome, the doctors didn't seem to believe that telling me the really bad news was their role. Instead, I heard it from former Chicago Bear Dan Jiggetts, Harvard '76. Every Chicago sports fan knows Dan from his playing days and broadcasting career and since he and I lived within a few miles of each other while I was growing up, he had taken an interest in my career. We chatted one night at a black-tie dinner celebrating the 100th anniversary of Harvard Stadium—the nation's oldest football stadium. He asked how my wrestling career was going and I told him that I had been sidelined with post-concussion syndrome. He became very serious, telling me, "You don't want to mess with that. The players of my generation are all worried about the links they've found with Alzheimer's disease."

Despite all the doctors I had seen, I had never heard of a connection between concussions and Alzheimer's disease. Did any medical professional know? Although there wasn't an overwhelming amount of research, when we combine the studies from multiple sports, the picture becomes clearer.

Soon after Jiggetts tipped me off, I saw a possible connection between football and dementia while watching ESPN late one night. Tom Rinaldi was discussing the plight of former Baltimore Colts tight end John Mackey, at the time in his early sixties. The second tight end ever admitted to the NFL's Hall of Fame, Mackey was the first president of the newly unified NFL-AFL Players Association, and had made history as the first player to fight the NFL's restrictive free-agency and salary rules. It was his lawsuit against the NFL in 1973 that led to the free agency that football players enjoy today. Now he fights another battle—with dementia.

Mackey was diagnosed with fronto-temporal dementia (FTD) in his late fifties. Before the diagnosis he had already begun a steady cognitive decline, which included erratic behavior, memory loss, and indifference to finding a job. After watching the television program, I decided to contact Mackey's wife, Sylvia, to try to learn more about his situation. A mutual friend gave me her cell phone number, but warned me that if she didn't answer, I would probably have to try again until I got her on the phone. When Sylvia travels for work, John calls her and leaves messages. But he forgets that he's called, so he calls over and over again until he fills up her voice-mail's memory.

When I did finally reach Sylvia, she'd just returned home from an FTD conference, where she'd learned that her husband's neurological disease could be related to prior head injuries. Experts at the conference had said that among former athletes, football players and boxers are most likely to suffer FTD.

Fronto-temporal dementia is caused primarily by damage to the frontal lobe, the area of the brain behind the forehead; some doctors believe that the unique pounding that football players take to this area may play a role in their developing this disease. Though it's not known how many concussions John Mackey had suffered, as a player he was known for his toughness and durability. He never shied away from taking a hit, and only missed one game in ten seasons.

Sylvia first began to realize something was really wrong with John when he began dressing oddly and watching the Weather Channel for hours on end. He refused to read their regular mail, but answered all the sweepstakes mail. He started keeping detailed records of when he expected to receive winner checks, which would of course never arrive. The final straw for Sylvia came when she overheard him on the phone telling someone that his sister wasn't married. His sister had been married for quite a while. In fact, it was a memorable relationship because her husband was fifteen years her senior and their marriage had caused considerable drama within the family. When John hung up the phone, Sylvia confronted him. John couldn't remember his sister's husband's name—or anything else about him.

Sylvia took him for an evaluation. When they were given the diagnosis of fronto-temporal dementia, she finally understood why the man she had been married to for so many years had been fading away. Her husband had been replaced by someone who couldn't remember what happened five minutes ago, who was prone to irrational mood swings, and who now often swore at her in public.

Sylvia says that their current relationship has now become more of an attachment rather than a romance; much like a child to a mother. Sylvia is now John's caregiver. But since she has had to go back to work as a flight attendant to support them, she's away from home a lot. John attends a daycare facility that costs $1,500 a month, but he has become prone to aggression, so the facility has recommended that he be moved to a second facility—at a cost of $10,000 per month. John currently receives an annual pension of about $24,000. Sylvia claims that if playing football was determined to be the cause of his dementia, he could receive a special disability pension that starts at $110,000. "That would make all the difference in the world to me," she said.

Sylvia puts on a very strong front. However, she's worried that eventually John will be left alone with no one to care for him. Sylvia expects that John's remaining years will follow an Alzheimer's-like pattern. She's been told that he'll become incontinent, and then won't be able to walk. The last progression will be that he won't be able to eat because he will have forgotten how to swallow. There is no way for her to know when that day will come.

The evidence is mounting that even seemingly minor concussions have immediate and permanent negative consequences and may possibly set neurodegenerative processes in motion much sooner than expected. A 1999 study was among the first to quantify that damage in *active* athletes. It discovered that suffering two or more concussions is associated with long-term impairment in the speed of information processing and executive functioning (which includes abilities such as planning and organization).[37]

Although that research is both groundbreaking and sobering, it still doesn't directly explain the correlation between concussions in youths and dementia in adults. But thanks to the Center for the Study of Retired Athletes at the University of North Carolina, the connection is becoming clearer. Led by Kevin Guskiewicz, PhD, a former Steelers athletic trainer, his center investigates the full spectrum of physical and mental challenges that face retired athletes, including injuries. Dr. Guskiewicz explains, "When we began this project, we were very interested in the suspected mental decline of retired players who have had concussions. For years there's been this notion that 'clearly there has to be a link' between concussions and both Alzheimer's disease and the Parkinson's-like dementia of a Muhammad Ali. Yet there was very little substantiated research, so we began looking into it through self-reported data." Dr. Guskiewicz emphasizes that self-reported data, which is based on the memory of an individual, is not as strong as what is called "prospective data," where the researchers follow a group of people over time. However, since no long-term prospective data exists, we'd have to wait fifty years for the results of that kind of study. Right now, self-reported data is the best information we have.

Self-reported or not, the data that came out of this group's survey is astonishing. They studied more than 2,500 of the 3,700 or so retired NFL players who are alive today. Over 60 percent of former NFL players report that they suffered a concussion in their career, and 24 percent report that they suffered three or more. Compared to the self-reported incidence numbers discussed in the last chapter, those totals might seem low. Yet to truly understand these numbers, we have to look more closely. Some of the older players surveyed may not understand the modern definition of concussion. This would have led them to underestimate the number of concussions they'd had. The data indicates this was likely the case, as half of the ex-NFL players who suffered a concussion said that they'd been knocked unconscious at the time. In one of his studies, Dr. Delaney found that only 5 percent of concussed players had been knocked out.[38] If we assume that both groups were knocked unconscious at the same rate, the NFL group underreported the number of concussions they suffered by ten times.

But no matter how the concussions are counted, the trends in the data are telling. Retired players reporting three or more concussions were five times more likely to be diagnosed with mild cognitive impairment (MCI) than were retired players who reported never having had a concussion.[39] In addition, their rate of "significant memory problems" increased with each concussion.

Number of Concussions	Self-Reported Memory Problems	Spouse/Relative Reported
0	5.2%	8.0%
1-2	8.8%	11.0%
3	17.4%	15.0%

MCI is a difficult medical diagnosis to understand. In everyday living, it may be characterized by "forgetting or confusing names, telephone numbers, directions, conversations, and daily events."[40] Dr. Guskiewicz explained, "The best way to describe MCI would be as a precursor to Alzheimer's disease. Not everybody who has mild cognitive impairment converts to Alzheimer's disease, but a certain percentage does." In a separate study of a normal population, researchers discovered that a previous head injury is the second-strongest indicator of mild dementia, with mercury exposure being the first. (I find this interesting because the Mad Hatter from *Alice in Wonderland* has always been one of my favorite characters. He was so named by Lewis Carroll because mercury was once used in hat manufacturing, causing many "hatters" to develop psychosis from mercury poisoning.)[41] Extrapolating a connection between trauma and later life problems from survey data can be difficult. There can be other causes, like steroid use or pain issues, that can cloud the picture. The only true way to know what happened to the brain is to physically look at it, and luckily, that opportunity was just becoming available.

Chapter 6: Two Autopsies

We ought to be talking about some of the things that are happening to us now. I'm sure they're not isolated events. That's one of the reasons all those guys showed up at the health screening put on by the NFL Players Association. We want to know what the hell is going on.

—Pete Cronan, nine-year NFL veteran

There are so many professional football players who are breathing, and look fine, but they have so many internal injuries. You have to read the obituaries to get the real story.

—Whitey Baun, former college football player, youth football coach

I can't imagine what it would be like to have depression that's caused by getting concussions. I don't think I want to know. Right now, I'm having fun playing. I'm going to keep doing what I'm doing. But should I be thinking like this? I'm not too sure.

Steve, high school football player

The image of NFL Hall of Famer Mike Webster playing center for the Pittsburgh Steelers is permanently etched in the memory of any serious football fan. Although I was only twelve when he retired from football, I clearly remember him as the player who never wore sleeves under his uniform, even in sub-freezing temperatures. His pale, oversized biceps hunched over the football always stood out on television; they were the calling card of a man whom many considered to be the toughest player in all of football.

65

Mike Webster played in the NFL for seventeen years, fifteen of those for the Pittsburgh Steelers. He started in 150 consecutive games. With four Super Bowl rings, seven All-Pro seasons, and nine Pro-Bowl selections, his success on the field is virtually unmatched. Yet Mike Webster didn't find the same success off the field. After his premature death, he became a focus of the media once again.

When he passed away in September 2002, at the age of fifty, the Associated Press reported, "The Steelers initially said that Webster died of a heart attack but later declined to comment. Webster was diagnosed with brain damage in 1999, an injury caused by all the years of taking shots to the head. Webster's doctors said several concussions damaged his frontal lobe, causing cognitive dysfunction. The progressively worsening injury caused him to behave erratically, and Webster briefly was homeless, sleeping in bus stations several times when he could not find somewhere to stay."[42]

Most newspaper accounts didn't capture just how difficult life had become for Mike Webster after football but sportswriter Greg Garber did.[43] According to Garber, as Webster's mental capacity waned, he was involved in a series of failed businesses that left him broke and homeless. At times he took a laundry list of drugs: Prozac for depression, Paxil for anxiety, Ritalin or Dexedrine to keep calm, Klonopin to prevent seizures, and Eldepryl, a drug indicated for patients who suffer from severe Parkinson's disease.

By 1997, he told a doctor that his daily headaches were "blowing the top of his head off." He would ask his children to use a Taser gun to stun him into unconsciousness so he could sleep. His arrest for forging Ritalin prescriptions had a morose back-story. His doctor had given him a pad of signed, blank prescriptions because Webster moved a lot and often lost his pills—a result of his homelessness and memory impairment. His income usually came from autograph signings, and he sent most of his money to his wife and four children. He was offered assistance from many former teammates and for a short time was supported by Pittsburgh Steelers' owner Dan Rooney, but Webster was too

66

proud to accept their charity. Instead, he tried to come up with new business plans that would put him back on his feet. Sadly, he no longer had the ability to see any of those plans through.

Before his death, people who knew of Mike Webster's deteriorating mental health were left to speculate if it was related to his football career. After his death, that speculation was put to rest.

▼▼▼

Bennet Omalu is a neuropathologist with the Allegheny County medical examiner's office in Pittsburgh, Pennsylvania. He met Mike Webster the day after Mike died. "I was watching ESPN the morning after he died," he says. "Everyone was battering him: talking about how he died poor, how he didn't manage his resources well, etc. It struck me, because I knew that long-term play in contact sports can have adverse effects.

"I came to work and found Mike Webster's embalmed body on the autopsy table. I asked why he was in our office, and I was told that his physician had written 'chronic concussive brain injury' on the death certificate, which implies that an element of trauma contributed to his death. I began by removing his brain; I am a board-certified neuropathologist as well as a forensic pathologist and epidemiologist. I subjected his brain to very extensive analysis. I confirmed that he had structural damage to his brain consistent with chronic traumatic encephalopathy (CTE), which is often described in boxers. This was an important finding, so we published it."

When Dr. Omalu's paper was published in the prestigious medical journal *Neurosurgery*, it sent shockwaves through the medical community.[44] Whereas chronic traumatic encephalopathy is well established in boxing, Dr. Omalu's diagnosis was the first case of CTE ever found in a former professional football player. CTE is also known as *dementia pugilistica*, or "punch drunk" syndrome.

67

A 1969 study found that approximately 20 percent of boxers eventually develop clinical symptoms of CTE, and many believe that it's the cause of Muhammad Ali's very public neurological decline.[45]

The symptoms of CTE include cognitive impairment, Parkinsonism, a loss of coordination and balance, and behavioral changes. The cognitive symptoms can easily be confused for Alzheimer's disease.

"CTE is very similar to Alzheimer's," Dr. Omalu said. "When you have shearing forces [stress on the connections between neurons], there is disruption of what we call the skeleton of the nerve fiber, which are proteins. The nerve cell makes an attempt to reconstitute itself. Over the years, the nerve cell loses its ability to hold these proteins together. Now these proteins start becoming redistributed in the brain abnormally. Certain proteins will accumulate and take on abnormal shapes and forms in brain cells, and these brain cells begin to die. That is what I see in the brain."

Study after study reveals this pattern—traumatic brain injury causes tau proteins to break away, creating "neurofibrillary tangles."[46][47] NFTs have been found in the normal head-injury population, and specifically, in the boxing population.[48]

I asked Dr. Omalu how he knew Mike Webster had had CTE and not a standard case of Alzheimer's disease.

He answered confidently, "This was not Alzheimer's disease because the topography of CTE is distinct." After doing my research, I knew that by 'distinct topography', he meant that the distribution of NFTs within the brain is different. In Alzheimer's disease, they appear predominantly in the deep layers of the brain. In CTE, they're concentrated in the superficial layers—near the surface of the brain. To a neuropathologist performing an autopsy, they are clearly distinct diseases.

▼▼▼

Chance brought Dr. Omalu into this growing area of research, and inspired by his findings, he proposed new studies and sought the cooperation of NFL doctors. "The NFL never responded to our letters," he said.

Instead, the NFL attacked the research. The medical leadership of the NFL wrote a published letter to the editor of *Neurosurgery* stating that the conclusion of CTE was "based on a complete misunderstanding of the relevant medical literature on chronic traumatic encephalopathy of boxers (*dementia pugilistica*)."[49] They concluded the letter saying, "We, therefore, urge the authors to retract their paper or sufficiently revise it and its title after more detailed investigation of this case."

However, there were holes in their criticism. The NFL doctors wrote: "Omalu et al. go on to state that 'there was no known history of brain trauma outside professional football.' In fact, there was no known history of brain trauma *inside* professional football either." I hope they meant to say "brain injury" and not "brain trauma," but perhaps they were trying to convince us that playing in the NFL does not involve getting hit in the head.

I was shocked that the NFL doctors had made such a bold attack. From the research I had read, the Mike Webster paper seemed like the logical progression of decades of research. Dr. Omalu read my mind. "That's another problem we had with the NFL. It's not like this paper is coming out of the deep blue sea," he said. "There are antecedents. There are hundreds, if not thousands, of papers out there pointing to this trend! It's established that people in contact sports like ice hockey, soccer, boxing, rugby, and football manifest long-term neuropsychiatric decomposition. This was just the very first time that it had been discovered in an NFL player."

But that wasn't the end of the story for Dr. Omalu. Nearly three years later, he showed up at work and found another former Pittsburgh Steelers offensive lineman on his table. In June 2005, Terry Long, age forty-five, was found unconscious at his home. He died at the hospital hours later. Tests revealed that Terry Long had committed suicide by drinking antifreeze.[50]

Examination of his brain revealed that, like Mike Webster, Terry Long had also suffered from CTE. Dr. Cyril Wecht, the Allegheny County coroner and a co-author on the Long paper, noted that CTE is "a general term that we would use to denote changes in the brain of a degenerative nature. These changes can be from one intensely traumatic injury, or they can be from repetitive and cumulative injuries, which is what we believe happened here."[51]

Toward the end of his life, Long was known for making poor decisions, indicating his brain may not have been functioning as well as it once had. Three months before his death, he was indicted by a federal grand jury on charges of fraudulently obtaining loans for a chicken-processing plant. Prosecutors alleged that in 2003 he had burned down the plant for the insurance money. He had filed for Chapter 11 bankruptcy protection just days before his death, estimating that he was more than $1 million in debt.[52]

When the Allegheny County medical examiner's office publicly announced that CTE was a contributing factor in Long's death, it was national news and led to an interesting debate.

Dr. Omalu was quoted saying, "Terry Long committed suicide due to the chronic traumatic encephalopathy due to his long-term play." Dr. Joseph Maroon, the Steelers neurosurgeon, responded, "I think the conclusions drawn here are preposterous and a misinterpretation of facts. I think it's fallacious reasoning, and I don't think it's plausible at all. To go back and say that he was depressed from playing in the NFL, and that that led to his death fourteen years later, I think is purely speculative."[53] Dr. Maroon was right that Dr. Omalu had gone too far into speculation. It is difficult to connect a disease to an act as complex as suicide. But the underlying finding, that this former player had a degenerative disease linked to trauma, was significant.

When I began this journey I shared Dr. Omalu's optimism that the NFL would aggressively seek the answers to the many questions about concussions plaguing this sport. But based on the NFL's actions over the last decade, I'm no longer so optimistic.

Chapter 7: What Is the NFL Doing?

One year Paul Tagliabue, NFL Commissioner, was interviewed on concussions by reporters at the Super Bowl, and he says something like, "Worrying about concussions is a function of pack-journalism." We expect a player in his forties to come out of the game with aches and pains that maybe prevent him from picking up his child. But not to be able to identify that child is an entirely different matter.[54]

—Leigh Steinberg, NFL agent

Some football trainers send people who have been unconscious back into the game. What is it going to take to get these guys on board?[55]

—Dr. James Kelly, neurologist

I think the NFL will always look for a way to deny, deny, and deny. They want no part of [the Mike Webster case] because there are some players who could join together and bring a class-action suit against the NFL.

—Harry Carson, NFL Hall of Famer

I first learned about the NFL's concussion experts while I was watching television one day in November 2003. It was five months after my last wrestling match, and I had just started paying attention to the media's coverage of concussions. A friend told me that the HBO show *Inside the NFL* was going to air a feature on the research of the Center for the Study of Retired Athletes (CSRA), specifically on the link it has found between multiple concussions on the football field and an increased risk of depression.

72

Inside the NFL introduced the Center's findings, and then showed the NFL's reaction. The NFL spokesperson was Dr. Elliott Pellman, the New York Jets team doctor who also serves as chairman of the NFL Subcommittee on Mild Traumatic Brain Injury. I was eager to hear his thoughts on these provocative, but not unexpected, findings. To this day, I'm still shocked by his official response to the research: "When I look at that study, I don't believe it," Pellman said.[56]

I did a double-take. "I don't believe it" was not the reaction I'd expected from a man of science. Pellman was strangely defensive and dismissive. I figured that he could disagree with the study's findings in two ways: he could either find fault with the methodology (how the CSRA had conducted the study) or the conclusions (what the CSRA had inferred from the data). Instead, he took a rare third path—personal experience and anecdotal evidence.

"I don't believe those numbers. I have not seen that depression, that melancholy, that was described in that study."

I saw the show months before I read any research on the short-and long-term associations between depression and concussions, so I didn't immediately realize how unlikely it was for Dr. Pellman to be so unfamiliar with depression in concussed football players. I thought to myself, Pellman must know that just because he hasn't seen depression himself doesn't mean that it doesn't exist. (I've never seen a germ, but I still wash my hands.) Besides, what are the odds that an NFL team doctor has the time to treat a large group of retired athletes, which was the subject of this research?

I became more disillusioned with the NFL's top concussion expert when he went on to offer an alternative explanation for why ex-NFL football players would be suffering from depression at such a high rate: "You take any professional, and give them a window of opportunity of which 4, 5, 6, 7, 8 years is the pinnacle of their career, of which they've done what they've loved, what

73

has consumed them, and now push them into an entirely different profession . . . what type of effect would that have on you?"

Pellman constructed a story line that makes sense, but if that were true, why isn't the same thing being found in every other sport? Pellman continued to confuse me. He said, "If we take a look at the tools we have now, there is no one else who is finding that element."

Pellman was trying to isolate the study as an aberration, yet this study was supported by decades of research linking depression and traumatic brain injury. You can play along at home by searching for the term "depression" with either "concussion," "traumatic brain injury," or "head injury" at the National Library of Medicine's medical journal search engine at http://www.ncbi.nlm.nih.gov/PubMed. [57] [58] [59]

In fact, Pellman's claim was so dubious that even *Inside the NFL,* which has a working relationship with the NFL and probably doesn't want to rock that boat, noted, "But *Inside the NFL* did find several studies, published in prestigious journals and dating as far back as 1994, that do indeed suggest a connection."

All in all, I found the show very disturbing.

▼▼▼

The NFL's subcommittee on mild traumatic brain injury was formed in 1994 by then-Commissioner Paul Tagliabue. Dr. Elliott Pellman was chosen to chair the committee because of his experience treating former Jets receiver Al Toon, a prominent player who retired with post-concussion syndrome. Pellman described how he came to his position. "From the beginning of his professional career, Mr. Toon began to incur what we now recognize as concussions. . . . Unrecognized by everyone, including myself, these concussions began to worsen in the later years of his career. . . . On the basis of my experience with Mr. Toon, I was invited to the Commissioner's office to offer my limited insight

74

into this problem. The Commissioner and I realized that we had many more questions than answers. . . . I was asked to mount an effort to answer these questions."[60]

The committee includes a neurosurgeon, a neurologist, a neuropsychologist, a biomechanical engineer, and an epidemiologist, but curiously is headed by Pellman, who is trained as an "internist and rheumatologist."[61]

Two years after it formed the committee, the NFL began a five-year study on concussions in the NFL. They studied a league that lacked uniform concussion treatment guidelines or standards, which has led to some curious, controversial, and even comical sideline concussion management in the NFL.

In October 2004, Brett Favre suffered a concussion in a game against the New York Giants. Favre was slammed to the ground by defensive lineman William Joseph. Packers coach Mike Sherman said Favre was a "little cloudy" after the hit, and the medical staff asked that he be taken out of the game.[62] Backup Doug Pedersen went in for the next two plays. On the sideline, Coach Sherman then asked Favre if he felt okay.

Favre, as most competitive athletes would, said yes. Sherman, without consulting with the team doctor or trainer, put Favre back in, where he immediately threw a 28-yard touchdown pass. Sherman said, "The doctors later told me that they didn't want to put him back in the game. The doctors hadn't exactly cleared him. So I was in error putting him back in the game." Giants quarterback Kurt Warner spoke with Favre as he came off the field and reported that Favre didn't remember the touchdown.

Kurt Warner was a victim of the same lack of communication just a year earlier. While playing for the St. Louis Rams, Warner suffered a concussion in the first half of a game against the New York Giants. The team doctor cleared him at halftime to return to play. In the second half, Warner was having trouble deciphering the plays. Clearly, he hadn't recovered. When the doctor was asked by the press why Warner had been allowed to continue to play in the second half even though he still appeared to be suffering from the effects of the concussion, the doctor said, "That's a coaching decision, not a medical decision."[63] If you notice, that hierarchy is the polar opposite of what Green Bay Packers Coach Mike Sherman had said about the Brett Favre incident. Apparently whether a doctor or coach has the final say over medical decisions varies by team.

Sometimes a player is told that he didn't have a concussion even though he believes that he did. After a game against the Cleveland Browns, Cincinnati Bengals wide receiver Chad Johnson told the press that he had suffered a mild concussion and didn't remember much after being tackled on a reception, including a 46-yard touchdown catch he'd made in the first quarter.[64] Yet Head Coach Marvin Lewis told the press that if Johnson had actually suffered a concussion of any sort, he wouldn't have been allowed to continue playing.

"I can say 100 percent, unequivocally, that our medical staff wouldn't have allowed it," said Lewis. "[Wide receivers coach] Hue Jackson did say at a point that for a while after the touchdown catch, Chad wasn't feeling quite right, so they took him out for a few plays. But he cleared up, went back into the game, and was fine. It's fun and cool to be injured like the other guys once in a while."[65] So Johnson got tackled, didn't feel well, and the trainers thought enough of it to pull him from the game. But the coach says he didn't have a concussion. Who would you believe? The player or the coach?

Some coaches even have trouble understanding the definition of a concussion. After one game, the press asked Pittsburgh Steelers Head Coach Bill Cowher whether Duce Staley had suffered a concussion. He answered, "No, he was just a little groggy."[66] He was asked, "Did Ben Roethlisberger get knocked woozy?" He answered, "Yes . . . I think on the one point after his scramble . . . [but] there is no concussion." According the NFL's concussion definition, Cowher was 0 for 2 on those diagnoses.

Sometimes players convince officials to let them stay in after they've obviously suffered a concussion. In 2005, Dallas Cowboys offensive lineman

Rob Petitti was kneed in the side of the head in a game. He got up woozy and was unsteady on his feet. According to one journalist, the official noticed the injury, but Petitti convinced him to let him stay in, and the Dallas sideline did nothing. Before the next play, Cowboys quarterback Drew Bledsoe called timeout. Petitti could barely stand. When the timeout was over, Petitti stayed in the game.[67]

Sometimes the public relations department and the coaches end up on different pages. In 2004 San Diego Chargers center Nick Hardwick sustained a concussion in the first quarter of a game against the Raiders. The team announced that Hardwick would not return for the rest of the game. In the third quarter, he was back in the lineup. "I was out of it for a little while," said Hardwick, whose head began to clear in the middle of the second quarter. "I didn't know what was going on. I didn't know any plays. I didn't know what was what."[68]

The San Diego Chargers sideline was also the setting of one of the better-documented cases of confusing concussion treatment. In 2004 Drew Brees sustained a concussion during a Chargers-Jets game after taking a helmet-to-helmet hit from Jon McGraw. One play later, after a LaDainian Tomlinson touchdown, Brees went to the sideline, where the trainers asked him some standard concussion questions. "A couple of them I thought I answered OK, and the others maybe not," Brees said.[69] The trainers cleared him to go back in.

Offensive coordinator Cam Cameron asked Brees how he was feeling. "I guess I told him 60 percent," Brees said. "I just arbitrarily threw out a number. They saw me stumbling around on the sideline trying to pick up a ball to get loose again before I went back out."[70] Drew did go back out. In the huddle, Tomlinson noticed that Brees wasn't himself. Brees threw a touchdown pass and returned to the sideline. Coach Cameron told head coach Marty Schottenheimer about his conversation with Brees. The head coach had yet to be informed about the concussion. Without consulting team physicians, Schottenheimer immediately decided that Brees was done for the day.

Backup quarterback Doug Flutie remembered, "Drew didn't want to give up his spot. Not only did he have me as a backup, but the team had drafted Philip Rivers in the off-season. So when Brees got hit, and we all knew he was a little off, I picked up a ball and started warming up. But Brees went back in there and played really well, even throwing a great touchdown pass. So I put the ball down and stopped warming up. Then out of nowhere the offensive coordinator came over and said, 'You're going in.' I said, 'Are you serious?' I guess the doctors had been trying to evaluate Brees every time he came to the sideline during those 11 or so plays, but he just kept telling them he was fine."

I guess those doctors didn't have the authority to hold Drew out for a series to fully evaluate his condition.

That decision was covered in the San Diego sports pages that week; some sportswriters supported Schottenheimer for being concerned about Brees's well-being, while others admonished him for playing doctor. But the fact is that Brees was allowed to continue for eleven or twelve more plays while still symptomatic from an obvious concussion.

Two of the best-known sports concussion treatment guidelines, written by the American Academy of Neurology and Dr. Robert Cantu, recommend that any player with a concussion be monitored for at least fifteen minutes after a mild concussion, because symptoms can sometimes get worse or may not appear for a few minutes. The guidelines were created to protect a player from the consequences of secondary impacts, and because a concussed player is less able to protect himself from injury on the field. Even Elliott Pellman has published a paper discussing how some NFL players' symptoms are worse the day after the injury than the day of the injury, suggesting that "the mTBI sets off intracranial processes that result in worsening cognitive functioning over the first twenty-four to forty-eight hours after the injury."[71] Brees is the poster boy for fifteen minutes of rest, as Schottenheimer told reporters after the game, "I think it was something as he continued to play, it got worse."[72]

When Brees's teammate LaDainian Tomlinson was informed that the team expected Brees to play the next week, he said, "I don't think he should. We're talking about someone's life here . . . For the safety of him, he shouldn't be out there. This could really affect him in the long run. In the short term, it isn't important for him to be playing with a concussion."[73] Tomlinson got it.

Others don't. These examples pale in comparison to the sideline care that the NFL's concussion guru, Dr. Elliott Pellman, gave to Wayne Chrebet, the latest NFL player to retire prematurely from multiple concussions. Understanding NFL concussion care can be difficult because doctors are rarely allowed to explain their sideline decisions to the media. Dr. Elliott Pellman is not one of those doctors. His explanations to the New York media revealed a great deal about his unique opinions on concussions.

The Curious Case of Wayne Chrebet

On November 2, 2003, New York Jets wide receiver Wayne Chrebet suffered a concussion in a game against the New York Giants. By all accounts, he lost consciousness for about a minute.[74] Photographs show that Chrebet was still lying face down on the turf when three members of the Jets medical staff reached him.

A number of return-to-play guidelines for concussions exist so that medical personnel will know when it's safe for a player to return to the field. Each guideline varies slightly, but they all consistently say that if an athlete is knocked out for any length of time, he shouldn't return to the game. If Pellman had been following the Cantu guidelines, he would have advised holding Wayne Chrebet out for at least two weeks. If Pellman were using the American

Academy of Neurology system, he would have rushed Chrebet to the hospital for overnight observation and kept him out of action for at least a week.

But Dr. Pellman cleared Chrebet to go right back into the game. It would be the last game Chrebet played that season.

All concussion guidelines leave room for clinical judgment, meaning that a doctor always has the right to overrule the guidelines. However, when the New York media forced Pellman to justify his decision to return Chrebet to action, he didn't use clinical judgment as his defense. Instead, Pellman applied some rather bizarre logic.

Three days after the game, Pellman was asked whether Chrebet was suffering post-concussion syndrome. He answered, "I don't know if Wayne is post-concussed or not. The fact that I don't know is why I'm a little nervous."[75] It isn't easy to say whether Wayne was suffering from post-concussion syndrome, as there is no true clinical definition. But Wayne was certainly suffering from post-concussion symptoms, as "Chrebet complained [to Pellman] of fatigue and some headache-like pain Monday night and early Wednesday" (the two had no contact Tuesday).[76]

Ten days after the game, Chrebet was placed on injured reserve (IR) for the season. The New York media began asking Pellman more pointed questions. It was obvious to everyone that when Chrebet returned to play in the Giants game, he had either not recovered from his concussion, or he had been exposed to secondary trauma, making the injury much worse. Or both.

Dr. Pellman defended his actions by saying, "The decision about Wayne returning to play was based on scientific evaluation and medical evaluation. That evaluation and that decision made no difference as to what's happening today."[77] He added, "Let's say I didn't allow him to return to play, and he played the following weekend. The same thing could have happened. I can only go by what we find scientifically."[78]

I'm not sure if the medical evidence supports those statements. Most, if not all, brain trauma experts agree that there is a period of vulnerability after a concussion occurs, where further trauma can cause greater injury or even death (see chapter 3). Had he rested for a week, Chrebet would have had seven days to flush out the potassium and calcium that had collected in the wrong places in his brain while restoring normal cerebral blood flow.[79]

To add insult to secondary injury, Pellman told the press, "This will not be something that I will be concerned about for months, but it's been more than just a few days. There was no concern on any of our parts that Wayne will have any long-term problems."[80]

Perhaps the strangest exchange happened only moments before Chrebet went back into the game. According to Pellman, he'd told Chrebet, "This is very important. You can't lie to me. There's going to be some controversy about going back to play. This is very important for you, and this is very important for your career. Are you okay?" Chrebet reportedly answered, "I'm fine."[81]

Logic tells us that a man with a malfunctioning brain and without medical training would be a terrible judge of whether or not he should go back into the game. Logic tells us that a brain-damaged player with a large personal and financial incentive to lie to get back in the game is not the best person to ask. But perhaps Pellman simply isn't aware of that logic, nor of the concussion guidelines that urge doctors never to ask players if they are "okay."

When Chrebet was placed on injured reserve for the remainder of the season, a reporter asked Pellman if Chrebet would be at greater risk for future concussions and post-concussion problems. Pellman answered, "Is Wayne more susceptible now to these injuries? I do not know. But one of the things I believe is to try and prevent that susceptibility [by giving] the person a chance to recover." [82]By this I guess Pellman means that NFL players should have a chance to recover when the game is officially over, but not during the game.

Somehow Pellman was pulling off an amazing balancing act. A week earlier Pellman had said that he didn't second-guess sending Chrebet back into the game, implying that Chrebet wasn't at further risk.[83] Then a week later, he said that rest lowers the risk of further injury. He seemed to be creating some alternative medical universe where Chrebet wasn't at risk for further injury immediately after the concussion, but was suddenly at risk ten days later. Again, let me say that this same doctor published a paper suggesting "that the mTBI sets off intracranial processes that result in worsening cognitive functioning over the first twenty-four to forty-eight hours after the injury."[84] But I guess this just didn't hold true for Wayne Chrebet.

Now I understand why Pellman said that he'd told Chrebet on the sideline, "There's going to be some controversy about going back to play." To me, it sounds like Pellman was sending a lamb to the slaughter, and, to cover himself, pawned off the responsibility for his actions onto the lamb.

Chrebet's story does not have a happy ending. The injury he received in the Giants game was his fifth recorded concussion since his freshman year of college—but may have been his sixth or seventh.[43] More than a month after the injury, Wayne said, "It just feels horrible, feels like people say you fell into a black hole. You wait to come out again. It's a crazy thing. Every morning you wake up feeling hung over, like you had the worst night of your life."[85]

In the off-season, the Jets renegotiated Chrebet's contract to include a concussion clause.[86] Normally, if Chrebet were to end up on injured reserve, he'd be paid his full base salary of $1.5 million. The Jets added an unprecedented clause in his contract stating that if he ended up on IR from a concussion, he would earn only $500,000. In essence, the Jets gave Chrebet— the kind of guy who would get knocked unconscious and beg to go back in— increased financial incentive to hide any concussions from the team the next season.

Chrebet's 2004 season ended with another concussion; he received this one during the last game of the regular season. He sat out the Jets playoff game. His career finally came to an end when he suffered a concussion against the San Diego Chargers on November 6, 2005. His teammates were reportedly shaken by the sight of Chrebet as he lay unconscious on the field, his legs frozen in the air, and again in the locker room as trainer David Price had to help him undress. Chrebet was placed on the IR.[87] He was still suffering from symptoms daily when he officially retired on June 2, 2006, saying, "You wake up every morning like you have a hangover. I don't know why that is. I've been told it goes away eventually. I look forward to that day. You deal with a lot of inner demons and mixed emotions when you go through something like this. I go through a lot of days where I struggle. I'm not the same as I was years ago, let's put it that way. I wouldn't say you get used to it. You learn to expect it."[88]

From these examples and others, Dr. Elliott Pellman and the NFL team doctors seem radically out of step with the research and recommendations of the rest of medical community. Being a team doctor is a prestigious position, so the explanation could legitimately be that the NFL doctors are more qualified than their counterparts. But since many teams no longer choose their team doctors, there may be no correlation between being a team doctor and being a good doctor. A recent *New York Times* article exposed the current trend of doctors paying teams for the "right" to treat players because the promotional advantage is so lucrative.[89]

With doctors "paying to play," the reason for their laissez-faire treatment of concussions may be much simpler. Dr. Delaney explains, "At the pro level, if you practiced the most conservative guidelines, you probably wouldn't be a pro doc very long. And that's the sad truth." Many doctors believe that paying teams creates a direct conflict of interest, as the doctors might be tempted to protect the team's interests rather than the players' in order to maintain their position.[90]

But Pellman's achievement of such a prestigious position might be the most interesting tale. As I've explained, some were surprised when the NFL appointed Pellman, who is not a neurologist, to head up its concussion committee. Pellman is no stranger to such controversy; he briefly became a household name in March 2005 for a string of missteps.

Pellman had been hired by Major League Baseball (MLB) as a medical advisor, and he defended its steroid policy before Congress in 2005. After giving a very pro-MLB opening statement, Pellman was hammered by several members of Congress on his lack of knowledge about MLB's steroid policies. It turns out that Pellman didn't know that players were allowed to leave the room for an hour in the middle of a drug test, and that they could be fined rather than suspended for positive tests.[91]

Representative Tom Lantos, a Democrat from California, called Pellman "pathetically unpersuasive," and said that he sounded like a tobacco industry official. Lantos also pointed out that Pellman's testimony undermined the contributions of the rest of the medical panel.[92] Representative Henry Waxman, another Democrat from California, said, "Major League Baseball told us Dr. Pellman was their foremost expert, but he was unable to answer even basic questions about the league's steroid policy at the hearing."[93]

This is the same Elliott Pellman who'd said in 2002 (before he was hired by MLB), "The players and the team owners have sold their souls to the devil with steroids, and I know, because I've been treating professional athletes since 1986."[94] That is quite an about-face.

Days after the hearing, the *New York Times* broke the story that Pellman had falsified his résumé.[95] Among four inaccuracies, Pellman claimed to have a medical degree from the State University of New York at Stony Brook. The truth is that Pellman graduated from the Universidad Autonoma de Guadalajara, in Mexico, and received a certificate of completion from SUNY Stony Brook.

He was later awarded an MD degree by the New York State Department of Education.

Mexican medical schools have lower admissions standards than U.S. medical schools do. According to the *New York Times,* Dr. Pellman said that he had enrolled there in 1975 because of poor grades as a biology major at New York University. Dan Brock, director of Harvard Medical School's Division of Medical Ethics, said, "If I told you I graduated from medical school in the United States, and I went to Guadalajara, then I think I would have deliberately misled you, so I would say that was unethical." [96]

If the NFL is wrong about its treatment of concussions, this could cause a serious problem for youth football. Many experts realize that NFL concussion management guidelines are followed at the lowest levels of the game.

Dr. Heechin Chae said, "Trainers or physicians at the college or high school level need some kind of example to follow. So if the NFL has standards, they're going to follow that standard too."

Others believe that the concern lies less with the youth trainers who follow the lead of the NFL, and more with the young players who try to emulate their NFL role models. After watching Brett Favre suffer a concussion, and then go back into the game to throw a touchdown, one Wisconsin high school football player remarked, "I kind of wonder how they can do it yet we can't do it, but it was amazing how he went right back in and threw a touchdown."[97]

The NFL's unique perspective on concussions goes beyond treatment and interpretation of other groups' research. The NFL got into the concussion research business itself in 1996, and its five-year study has been released in an eleven-article (thus far) series in the medical journal *Neurosurgery,* with Pellman listed frequently as the primary author. The papers have caused a controversy in the medical community. As one prominent researcher (who asked not to be named due to a business affiliation with the NFL) told me, "Where it's challenging for someone like me is how the NFL is extrapolating their research to the entire population, and how they say they don't have a head injury problem, because they clearly do. The fact is those papers are becoming everyone's gospel, and that's dangerous."

The most controversial paper is Part 4, regarding players who sustained more than one concussion. Pellman says that their research did not find a higher risk of repeated concussions in players with previous concussions, and that there was no "7- to 10-day window of increased susceptibility to sustaining another concussion."[98]

Neurosurgery is a "peer-reviewed" journal, meaning that every article is sent to prominent doctors for their comments before it's published, and then the study and the comments are published together. Dr. Julian Bailes explains, "Editorial comments provide the reader, most of the time a physician, another point of view or context from other experts in the same field." Dr. Cantu was one of the article's reviewers, and noted: "At first glance, the NFL experience with single and repeat concussion (no difference) and management (more than 50 percent of players return to the same game, including more than 25 percent of those with loss of consciousness) seems to be at odds with virtually all published guidelines and consensus statements on managing concussion."

Another doctor wrote, "Unfortunately, the present article in this series of studies on professional football players has several flaws with respect to the study design, data collection, and data analyses. . . . The article sends a message that it is acceptable to return players while still symptomatic, which contradicts literature published over the past twenty years suggesting that athletes be returned to play only after they are asymptomatic, and in some cases for seven days." He goes on to point out, rightly, that the studies the NFL tries to discredit have collected more data more often, using more sophisticated tests, including computerized neuropsychological screenings. The NFL data was based solely on clinical analysis, verbal questions, and included some pencil-and-paper tests neuropsychological tests, which are either less sensitive and/or more subjective than the methods the NFL group chooses to bash.

Part 6, which deals with neuropsychological testing and concluded, "There is no evidence in this study of widespread permanent or cumulative effects of single or multiple mTBI's in professional football players," was also blasted by the peer reviewers.[99] The first reviewer called the conclusions "premature."

The second said the results should be interpreted with "caution," especially considering that 78 percent of concussed players chose not to take the neuropsychological tests. That means four out of five players refused to be tested. Why would an athlete refuse the test? My guess is that it's for the same reason that people pulled over on suspicion of driving drunk refuse a breathalyzer test—because they don't want anyone to have proof that they were compromised.

The third reviewer called the methodological choices "perplexing." The fifth reviewer pointed out the same flaws the others had, while expressing exasperation that Pellman drew the conclusions he did considering that the NFL study only looked at short-term symptoms, and by virtue of the study design, that it didn't follow players who had retired from the cumulative effects of concussion. (You won't find cancer in a study population if you take out the people who have it!)

Even the fourth reviewer, Dr. Joseph Maroon, the Steelers neurosurgeon wrote, "It is specifically recommended that the statement that there are no widespread permanent or cumulative effects of single or multiple mTBIs in professional football players be softened somewhat."

Perhaps the most concerning statement was made in Part 5:

This 6-year study indicates that no NFL player experienced the second-impact syndrome or cumulative chronic encephalopathy from repeat concussions. While the study did not follow players who left the NFL, the experience of the authors is that no NFL player has experienced these injuries. This finding may lead to future research aimed at challenging two of the expressed rationales for developing management guidelines to prevent the second-impact syndrome and cumulative chronic brain injury from repeat concussions. [100]

These statements were also hammered by the reviewers. One put the odds of finding a case of SIS, a rare event, in the NFL was one every 375 plus years. And the claim that not finding CTE—a disease that can only be diagnosed after death—in an active living player is evidence of anything is absurd. And yet the NFL docs proposed to use this data to *kill* concussion management guidelines. We're back to asking Wayne Chrebet how he feels—once he regains consciousness, of course.

This strong backlash from their peers makes me wonder why the NFL doctors were trying so hard to make the case that multiple concussions are no worse than a single concussion, and that there are no negative long-term consequences from concussions. I can't come up with an answer. Maybe, as NFL Hall of Famer Harry Carson told me, they're worried about lawsuits from players.

But let's say that the NFL doctors are correct. Let's say that, because the NFL players are older, they're not exposed to the risks younger players are. If that were true, then we would have to find another way to spread the word about the risks of concussion to younger players, because the NFL may not be incentivized to play that role. The *Christian Science Monitor* reported, "In its TV ads, the National Football League emphasizes the hard hits, the quarterback sacks, and the razor-edged intensity of the professional game. But when it comes to youth sports, the NFL is calling for a tamer approach, one that de-emphasizes violence and competition and emphasizes safety, fun, and teamwork."[101] Scott Lancaster, the director of NFL Youth Development, says that it has a three-pronged plan to "take out all the negatives and emphasize the positives."[102] The NFL has put over four million children through its numerous youth programs, which include Junior Player Development, High School Player Development, Pass, Punt, and Kick, USA Football, and NFL Canada.

Scott Lancaster gave a seminar at a conference on marketing to children in 2005 that was called "Making Your Brand Kid-Cool and Mom Acceptable." According to Leigh de Armas, a journalist who attended the conference, Lancaster said that children are important to the NFL because getting the attention of a kid means better odds of creating an adult football fan with some discretionary income.[103]

But Lancaster knows that the NFL can't get to kids without going through moms. "It's important to create a product that moms will embrace," he reportedly said. "One of the most radical things we did with our football clinics is we made soccer moms the coaches of tackle football. A lot of times you'll hear a kid say he can't play football because his parents don't approve, or they don't want him to get hurt. By bringing the mother in to coach, we were not only empowering the mothers, we were appealing to the fact that when children reach the ages of between 12 and 14, mothers will want to spend more time with their kids. This is the age when a lot of kids start slipping away to do their own thing. So by involving the mom, we were not only getting parent participation, it's great exposure for the brand."[104]

By itself, the NFL's marketing message to children isn't that bad. Many companies use similar tactics. But something changes when you combine a marketing program aimed at children and parents that is meant to "take out all the negatives and emphasize the positives" with a top doctor's radical statements such as, "If there's normal testing and a player feels good, what's the contraindication to letting him play? There really is none."[105]Based on its past behavior, I think we can be confident that the NFL is not going to sound any alarms about concussions in children. As Dr. Art Day, director of the Neurological Sports Injury Center at Brigham and Women's Hospital in Boston, says, "You're asking the fox if there's a particular problem with hanging around the henhouse. Pellman works for the NFL. Until there's definitive evidence otherwise, he's going to take that tack that managing concussions isn't a problem. Will Mercedes tell you they're not the best car?" [106]

Part 2: 2006 – 2013

Chapter 8: Taking the Fight to the Front Page

Head Games was first published in October 2006. I could never have anticipated where it would take me, or how it would affect the sports concussion controversy.

To be honest, I struggled at first to get people to read *Head Games*. For some reason people didn't embrace a professional wrestler lecturing on neuroscience. There was also a "dissemination of information" problem. Most of the sports leagues, from professional down to youth leagues, had been dismissive of and threatened by the concussion issue, and they didn't want to draw any attention to it.

The only strategy to raise awareness I could afford was through the free media, but there were problems there as well. The youth concussion angle was a tough story for the media at the time. They were covering an invisible injury that most stakeholders, including parents, coaches, and even medical professionals, weren't worried about. The NFL aspect of the story was more interesting, but there I struggled to get reporters, some of whom I knew personally, to write about it. Many sportswriters would tell me privately that they agreed with everything I wrote, but if they wrote about it they would be blackballed by their team or the league—losing access to interviews with the players and coaches, thereby destroying their career.

Everything began to change about a month after publication. On November 20, 2006, former Philadelphia Eagle Andre Waters, now a forty-four-year-old college football coach, shot himself in the head. That was the day that inspired me to go from being an observer to an activist.

I was back working at Trinity Partners, and I read about Andre's suicide on the Web. The article mentioned that "he was known as one of the NFL's hardest hitters and often was fined for some of his tackles."[107] He was nicknamed "Dirty Waters" because he wasn't afraid to lead with his helmet or hit low. That phrase brought back memories for me, as I could vaguely remember watching Andre Waters play against my Chicago Bears as a ten-year-old in the late 1980s. His Eagles teams, led by stalwart defenders like Reggie White and Jerome Brown, were marked in my memory because they were tough as nails.

I inferred from his style of play that Andre may have suffered some concussions, and I wondered if he might have been suffering from CTE when he killed himself. When he played, concussions were rarely recorded, but I decided to Google his name and the word *concussion* to see if I could find something. The results of my initial online search were a shock. In 1994, Waters claimed, "I think I lost count at fifteen .... In most cases, nobody knew it but me. I just wouldn't say anything."[108]

At this point in time, I was so naïve that I assumed other people knew about the Mike Webster and Terry Long CTE diagnoses, and so I expected to read in the paper the next day that the medical examiner planned to study his brain to see if Andre had CTE. I watched the news closely for the next three days but didn't see anything, so I decided to cold-call the medical examiner (ME) to ask if he planned to test for CTE.

I told the ME about the research on concussions, CTE, and depression, and asked if he was going to look for CTE. He told me that he would not be, as he didn't believe there was a connection between concussions and depression. I asked if I could send him a number of publications supporting the theory, and he claimed he would take a look. I immediately emailed him the studies, and waited patiently by the phone for over a week. In the meantime, Andre Waters was buried, and I assumed I missed my chance. After ten days I called again. The ME said that after briefly reviewing the papers he still didn't believe that

CTE had anything to do with the cause of death, so he wouldn't perform any studies. His job was to simply find the cause of death, and in this case it was obvious—a bullet through the brain.

But instead of slamming the door in my face, he left it open a crack. He told me that, per state regulations for a death not of natural causes, he had retained five small sections of Andre's brain. He told me that if I could get his family's permission, and find someone else to perform the tests, he would release the tissue.

That was an unwelcome suggestion. When I decided to call the ME, I simply wanted him to do the tests. I never thought that I would have to get involved in this macabre situation, and I certainly never thought I would have to call a deceased person's family within weeks of the funeral to ask for permission to study their relative's brain tissue.

The person I would have to call, Andre's next of kin, was his eighty-five-year-old grieving mother. I was scared to make the call. I had a vision that when I asked for Andre's brain, she would have a heart attack on the other end of the phone and I would be blamed. One thing I've learned through this work is that people accept burying a parent—that is the natural way. But burying your own child—even an adult child—is a parent's worst nightmare.

But I also knew that a positive finding of CTE in Andre Waters might be a game-changer. The NFL could argue that Webster and Long were isolated cases as long as they remained isolated. But if there were more cases of CTE identified, the link between the game and the disease would become impossible to dismiss. Andre Waters was also well liked as a player and a human being. He would give the media a reason to cover the issue. He could be a face of the disease. Before I called Andre's mother, I needed to secure the other half of the equation—the lab tests. That decision was easy; I only knew one neuropathologist, Dr. Bennet Omalu. He agreed to study it if I could get permission.

Now I couldn't back out. I started writing down reasons to press forward to boost my confidence:

One: It can help a lot of people.

Two: It might help the family understand what happened.

Three: It's just a little phone call. Even if it makes them sad or angry, they'll get over it.

Four: Don't be a coward.

I started building a strategy for the call. My primary goal was simply to keep Andre's mother on the phone long enough to explain why I was calling. That meant I had to explain who I was, the underlying science, the importance of a finding, and as much information as I could cram in *before* I asked for his brain. At this point in time, three and a half years after my last concussion, I was still post-concussed and still had constant headaches. I didn't trust my ability to think on my feet, so I wrote out a speech.

It began, "My name is Chris Nowinski and I'm a medical researcher focused on concussions in sports. I am very sorry for the loss of your son, and I'm very sorry to be calling under these circumstances [pause], but I work with some doctors that are studying the long-term effects of concussions in football. Have you heard about concussions being connected to things like depression?" If she said yes at that point, I figured I would have a shot. If she said no, it would be an uphill battle. I was ready to mention that I played football too, and, to bolster my credibility, that I'd written a book about it. A single mistake in execution would result in the phone being hung up, especially if they learned *what* I really wanted before they knew *why* I wanted it.

When I was ready, I reached out and grasped the phone receiver, punching in the numbers slowly and anticipating the sound of an old woman's voice. Instead I heard the voice of a much younger woman. Caught off-guard, I stumbled through the opening of my monologue. First came my condolences; then I went into who I was and why I was interested in concussions in football. Finally, I told her that I thought Andre could still help a lot of people. Then I asked, "Who am I speaking with please?"

She said, "Hold on a minute." Silence. I heard her talking to someone else. She got back on and said, "I'm Andre's sister. Let me have you talk to another one of Andre's sisters." My head dropped. I'd have to say everything all over again! The new sister got on the line and I gave the rehearsed speech a second time, this time more slowly and clearly. It ended with, "So I think if we examined his brain, we may have a better understanding of why this happened and be able to prevent this from happening in other people." She listened patiently, and told me she'd have to discuss it with the family and would call me back. I hung up, discouraged. The family was respectful and open-minded, but I didn't expect to hear back.

Twenty minutes later my phone rang. There was another voice on the end of the line. The family had given Andre's niece Kwana Pittman the task of figuring out if I was a crackpot. Kwana was about my age and currently enrolled in some graduate-level biology courses in preparation for a potential career change. She was also skilled in using the Internet for research, and had Googled me. Thank goodness for Wikipedia. It was a strange role reversal—I wanted to talk about Andre, but now I had to talk about me.

Kwana was moved by the fact that I was actually suffering from too many concussions myself. Kwana later told a reporter, "I said, 'You know what, the only reason I'm doing this is because you were a victim. I feel like when people have been through things that are similar or the same as another person, they can relate and their heart is in it more. Because they can feel what this other person is going through.'"[109] She saw value in the research and said she'd try to convince the family to participate. A couple days later she called back and said that the family would move forward with the donation.

Within a week the brain was on its way to Bennet Omalu. The tests would take a few weeks. I took that time to learn more about Andre.

Friends and family described Andre Waters as kind, giving, and a jokester with a great sense of humor. He was a great American success story, born in humble circumstances in Belle Glade, Florida, a town of about 15,000 on the southeastern shore of Lake Okeechobee where half the population is African American and one-third live below the poverty line. Belle Glade is no Florida beachfront paradise; it is also known as "Muck City" due to the damp dirt in which locals grow sugarcane. Those sugarcane fields were where his mother worked, and Andre would often pitch in as he got older.

As a great athlete, football was Andre's ticket out, and he started playing football as a sophomore in high school, playing well enough to earn a scholarship to Cheyney State College outside Philadelphia, and eventually earn a spot in the NFL. As a strong safety for the Philadelphia Eagles from 1984 to 1993 and the Arizona Cardinals in 1994 and 1995, Andre was a star. He led the Eagles in tackles four times and was an All-Pro in 1991. But he never forgot where he came from, buying his mother a house and a car as soon as he was able to, keeping his Christianity a central part of his life. His agent said he donated a higher percentage of his salary to charity than any other player he represented.[110]

Andre's first recorded concussion happened in high school. Andre told a reporter, "My junior year at Pahokee (High School), we had a game against Glades Central, and I hit their tight end early in the first quarter and got knocked woozy. To this day I don't know how I finished the half. I just played on instinct."[111] He continued to get more concussions in the NFL. "I hit Paul Palmer, a running back, helmet to helmet and I had a hard time getting up because my equilibrium was off," Waters said. "I don't think the coaches even realized it; they figure I always get up slow, anyway."[112] Waters' personal policy was to never take a play off. "I'd sniff some smelling salts, then go back in there."[113] After suffering a concussion in an NFL game on a Sunday, he had a seizure on the flight home. He was back practicing on Tuesday.

But after football went away, Andre slowly began visibly changing, and not for the better. He wasn't the same happy-go-lucky guy. He was occasionally depressed. Those in the media and many around Andre usually chalked it up to Andre missing the glitz and glamour of the NFL and the million-dollar paycheck. After all, who wouldn't miss that?

But Andre's life was still moving in a positive direction, but he soon began having problems with his memory. He took a job as the defensive coordinator at Fort Valley State University in Georgia, a Division II school. Even they noticed something was wrong. His head coach Deondri Clark told me the staff used to tease him that, "He's had one concussion too many," never believing that might be the actual problem.[114]

His problems with short-term memory were eventually joined by paranoia. His mother, Willie Ola remembered, "One time he told me I moved his keys. He kept saying, 'Momma, you had to have moved my keys.' He found them in his pants pocket in the closet, but he still accused me of moving them."[115] Another time he got lost driving from his mother's house—the one he bought her—back to his home in Tampa, a trip he had made many times, and had to call a friend to guide him back.

The symptoms became increasingly bizarre and worrisome. A friend confided to Andre's mother that he dropped by Andre's one day and found him crying, pleading over and over, "I need help, somebody help me." But no one ever knew exactly what was wrong or how to help him.

Andre began having suicidal thoughts. It began as talking about it, and then progressed to attempting it. Twice Andre was discovered in the garage with the engine running, attempting to kill himself through carbon monoxide poisoning. Eventually Andre chose a method that no one could stop.

Around 1:00 a.m. on an otherwise uneventful Tuesday morning in Tampa, Florida, former Philadelphia Eagle safety Andre Waters, sitting alone in his home, put a gun in his mouth and shot a bullet through his brain. He died instantly. He left no note.

▼ ▼ ▼

While the tests were being performed, I continued to think about the implications of a positive finding. A third case of CTE would be a big deal. One case is an anomaly, two is a coincidence, but three is a trend. This was important, and people would need to hear about it. Most people never knew about Webster and Long's CTE diagnosis. It wasn't mentioned much outside of local newspapers and a single Associated Press report. If Waters had CTE, the world needed to know.

At this point I had no idea how to spread information like this. I had written a few articles for SI.com, and for a moment thought that perhaps I could write the story. Then it dawned on me that if I wrote it, I would not be seen as a neutral observer. I could be easily dismissed by the NFL and the public as a guy trying to draw attention to his book.

Then I decided to call a reporter named Alan Schwarz, a baseball writer I'd met in the summer of 2005. When I was furiously writing *Head Games,* I realized I had no idea how to get a book published, and that it was pointless to continue until I figured that part out. The only person I knew who had ever published a book was Ken Leiker, who had edited the WWE book *Unscripted* and interviewed me for it. I called Ken, whom I hadn't spoken with in over three years, and told him about the project. Ken told me to call Alan.

Alan Schwarz had just published an engaging book on statistics in baseball, *The Numbers Game: Baseball's Lifelong Fascination with Statistics.* Alan was a graduate of the University of Pennsylvania and a follower of Ivy League football. For the past fifteen years he had been a baseball writer for *Baseball America, ESPN The Magazine,* and occasionally the *New York Times.*

Schwarz & Nowinski

Alan remembers our first conversation well, later telling an interviewer, "[Chris] calls me up and says, "I'm hoping you can help me figure out how to get this thing published or see if you like it."

Alan invited me to send the manuscript. He remembers, "I saw the manuscript—I still remember my reaction—it wasn't the main narrative, it was the footnotes that blew me away. I mean this guy had really done his work. It wasn't just some vague rant by a wrestler; it was a scholarly work done by a Harvard grad who happened to wrestle. And I was like, 'This is really good.' I didn't quite understand everything going on. I had, like everybody else, thought that a concussion was a brain bruise. I didn't know."

Alan was helpful beyond my wildest expectations. He invited me to New York and we met for coffee before I headed over to a meeting he set up with Time Warner Books. I still remember him walking in, and I never could have anticipated what was to come out of that first meeting. Alan is 6' 3", skinny and a bit gangly, with dark hair and penetrating eyes that always keep you guessing what's going on behind them, which I assume can be very helpful in reporting. He prepped me for what I could expect from Time Warner. Although it was a positive meeting, Time Warner and eventually other publishers thought the book wasn't commercial enough, so over a year later *Head Games* was bought by a small publisher.

I didn't speak with Alan again until December 2006, when I called about Waters.

"Hi, Alan, I'm not sure if you remember me, but this is Chris Nowinski, the guy who wrote the—"

"Yes, Chris, of course I remember you," Alan all but interrupted. "How am I going to forget the Harvard football-playing wrestler who wrote a really well footnoted book about concussions?"

I explained, "I have something that I think is very important, and I'm not sure what to do with it. And you're the only one who ever took me seriously. So I'm wondering if you could give me some advice on what to do here."

I told Alan what was happening, and he said, "Would you mind if I called the *New York Times*? I think they'd be interested." At the time Alan was a freelancer writing a Sunday biweekly column "Keeping Score" with another reporter for the Times where he applied statistical analysis to ongoing sports news. Alan called back a few minutes later and said, "Can you come to New York? They want to meet you." I couldn't believe it!

In retrospect, the *New York Times* was the perfect outlet to take on this issue. They weren't worried about losing access to players. They were used to taking on important and controversial issues. And, as we'd later find out, they had the budget and commitment to put a reporter on this issue full time.

In addition to finding the right paper, I had found the perfect reporter for the issue. While a football reporter seemed like the obvious choice to cover the story, for them it could be career suicide to ruffle the feathers of the NFL. Alan was primarily a baseball writer. He didn't care about burning all his bridges in football because football wasn't his beat, or his passion. On top of that, he had a unique background for a sportswriter. He had majored in mathematics at Penn, having planned to be a high school math teacher. He would eventually break stories on misinterpreted data by the NFL, but he also had the logical mind of a mathematician; things were either right or wrong, truth or distortions. He wanted to find the truth.

▼ ▼ ▼

The tests came back from the lab early. Dr. Omalu emailed me on January, 4, 2007, to tell me that Andre had tested positive for CTE. We called the Waters family to tell them the news. They did not seem surprised. We made the decision that the world needed to know, so on January 18, Alan Schwarz broke the story on the front page of the *New York Times*: "Expert Ties Ex-Player's Suicide to Brain Damage." One of the greatest rewards was the reaction of the Waters family. "Chasing brains," as it's been called, carries huge risk, and among the largest is the risk of breaching the trust or taking advantage of a grieving family. Alan asked that question. "We always had the question of why—why did my uncle do this?" said Kwana Pittman, Andre's niece. "Chris told me to trust him with all these tests on the brain, so that we could find out more and help other people. And he kept his word."

▼ ▼ ▼

I was overwhelmed with emails of support after the Waters story was published. I had finally found a way to get the word out. Not everyone was convinced, however. On the day the story broke, William Rhoden, a columnist for the *New York Times*, reached out to Gene Upshaw, the executive director of the NFL Players Association and a Hall of Fame offensive tackle for the Oakland Raiders. Rhoden wrote, "Upshaw sounded annoyed by the buzz created by the article. 'I think everyone is getting a little riled up because this guy's out there trying to sell this damn book.' Upshaw was referring to Chris Nowinski, author of *Head Games: Football's Concussion Crisis*." [116]

That quote came as quite a shock! I was young and naïve at the time, but I figured that the person theoretically in charge of protecting the interests of NFL players would be appreciative. It quickly dawned on me that while I was

101

helping the players, I was also exposing that Gene Upshaw should have been doing more. He was downright defensive, saying, "But it's not like we've been just sitting on our hands. That's what's being implied here, that no one is looking at this, that no one's studying this, that no one cares about this. If that was true, I'm irresponsible and I haven't been doing my job, and neither has the NFL."

Upshaw wasn't the only person who wanted to ignore the Waters findings. I realized that for momentum to be sustained Andre couldn't remain the only face of the issue, because Andre couldn't speak for himself. I needed Ted Johnson to come forward.

Ted Johnson was one of the toughest middle linebackers ever to play for the New England Patriots. Born in California, Ted was a second-round pick out of the University of Colorado. He had 757 tackles over ten seasons for the Patriots, including three Super Bowl victories. Ted abruptly retired right before the 2005 season due to post-concussion syndrome, although he didn't realize it his disorder had a name. Ted's head hurt when he hit people, and he said he knew he was done when "I couldn't imagine sticking my head in there again." Ted was one of the best at using his head as the point of attack; one of his nicknames was Cement-Head Ted. He was famous for a helmet-to-helmet collision with Jamie Nails, the Miami Dolphins 320-pound guard, in 2003 that cracked Nails's helmet *in half.*

Ted and I were introduced by a mutual friend in early 2006, as Ted was struggling with cognitive problems, lethargy, and had become addicted to Adderall, a stimulant, to feel "normal," as he put it. I went to Ted's home in Wayland, Massachusetts, to learn more about his problems and interview him for *Head Games.* I told him about my experience with concussions and post-concussion syndrome (PCS), and he asked me to repeat it. I said, "Repeat what?"

"Post-concussion something."

"Post-concussion syndrome?"

"Yeah, that. What's that?"

Although he had retired due to PCS, Ted had never heard of the term! I explained what it was, and that it was frequently caused by a concussion on top of a concussion that you haven't recovered from. He leaned in and asked me, "Can you keep a secret?"

He recounted a story from 2002 where he suffered a concussion in a preseason game. It was near the Patriots sideline and everyone saw him lose his balance getting up after a tackle, so they physically pulled him off the field and held him out for the game. When Ted arrived at the first contact practice four days later, he assumed there would be a red jersey in his locker. Players get a red jersey when they are not cleared for full contact practice, and Ted had yet to see a doctor to be cleared from his concussion. Ted remembers, "There is no red jersey in my locker. I was like, 'That's weird.' So I went to my trainer—who was in his first year, I might add, so this guy doesn't want to make enemies with (Head Coach Bill) Belichick—and I said to Jim, "There's no red jersey in my locker...did you guys clear me to practice?" "Oh, absolutely not—no, no, no— you should be in red," he stammered. Ted was given his red jersey and headed out to practice.

Ted got a surprise visitor on the field a short while later. "After individual period, the assistant trainer comes up to me and hands me my blue jersey. So I'm like, 'What the f**k is this?' He said, 'I was told to bring this to you.' I was infuriated, man. I was infuriated because I assumed Belichick had him go get the blue jersey. But I'm stubborn, and prideful, and I put the thing on. Well, the next period is nine on seven, and the first play was an iso [a play where Ted is blocked by a fullback with a three-yard running start] to me. I'm not sure that

103

was designed, but I wouldn't doubt if it was. So, of course, the first collision I don't black out, but that warm feeling comes over me, everything *slows down.*" Ted had another concussion, and only a few days since his first.

Ted was never the same. He sat out a few games and then returned, struggling with his memory throughout the season and increasingly suffering what he called "mini-concussions." He had frequent vision impairment on the field, and often had to have his teammates take the signals from the sideline. In 2004 the problems continued. Ted told me, "We won the Super Bowl, but the whole offseason was weird; I wasn't myself. I was unengaged, didn't want to hang out with my kids or work out—all I wanted to do was watch TV." By that time, he had become addicted to Adderall, daily taking two to three times the prescribed dose and either finding multiple doctors or running out and going through withdrawal.

I asked Ted if I could put that story in *Head Games: Football's Concussion Crisis.* I knew that it would blow the roof off this issue. Ted refused. He didn't want to tarnish the reputation of the Patriots. Instead, Ted offered to write the introduction to the book and simply go public with his personal struggles, but not tell that specific story about being hit in practice.

I accepted his terms and kept his secret, and was excited about what he wrote, which included, "It's an old line, but I wish I had known then what I know now. I wish I met Christopher Nowinski years ago, when the information he has shared with me— and is about to share with you—could have made a major difference in my life."

Unfortunately, members of Ted's family did not agree that he should take his struggles public. They were concerned about Ted being labeled "damaged goods" and struggling to find employment in the future. Admitting to a drug addiction combined with memory problems and lethargy is not exactly stellar résumé material. But I wanted Ted to tell his story, because *somebody* that people cared about needed to tell the truth. Perhaps I was being selfish. Just because I was willing to share my weaknesses with the world didn't mean it was the right move for everyone. Over time I've learned to respect and appreciate those willing to step forward with their struggles, like Hall of Fame former New York Giants linebacker Harry Carson, and I don't think less of people who aren't ready. Their circumstances are different. I don't know if I would have been so honest if I had children or a mortgage.

Under pressure from his family, Ted pulled his introduction to *Head Games* one week before it went to print. I was crushed, but Ted and I remained friends and continued to share tips on trying to overcome PCS. When the Waters story went public, I felt a new urgency to find someone to speak out. The day the *New York Times* article ran, I called Ted and invited him out to dinner. I grabbed my copy of Schwarz's article and took a taxi to his apartment at the Ritz Carlton in downtown Boston where he had been living since separating from his wife.

While Ted grabbed his jacket I put the Waters article on his kitchen table and said, "Hey, you should read this article when you get back." I hoped it would inspire him to tell his story. Initially I thought I wouldn't bring it up during dinner and let him read the article and think it was his idea to go public, but over dinner at his favorite South End restaurant, Stella, I found I could not hold back.

Ted had the same reaction that I did to Alan's story and decided then and there at the restaurant to step forward and tell his story. Ted later told me that while he read the full article he thought, "When a guy just takes a gun to his head … and none of the family knows why? I said I have to tell my story—you know why? Because if I don't, it'll happen again and nothing will change. Nothing would change. I told my story for one reason and one reason only. It was to help the guys that have retired from the game, that are still in their beds going 'what's wrong with me?' Their marriages are falling apart, and they can't find work … and they don't have a name for it. Now when you don't really have a name for what you're fighting, you don't really stand a chance."

I urged Ted to let Alan Schwarz write his story in the *New York Times,* but Ted felt that he owed Jackie MacMullen from the *Boston Globe*, so he told both of them and the story ran in both the *New York Times* and the *Globe* the Friday before the Super Bowl. The issue finally had a name that could speak for himself, who could say how terrible is it to live with PCS and possibly CTE. "I don't like the new Ted. Oh God, man. I don't want anyone to see the new Ted. On bad days that's why I stay in bed. I used to have patience, I used to listen. I was a good listener, you know? I don't like it at all."

▼ ▼ ▼

After the Super Bowl the issue continued to gain momentum. Alan Schwarz was hired by the *New York Times* as a full-time reporter and was told to keep writing about concussions. Due to pressure created by Alan and by some important investigative work by Peter Keating at ESPN on additional problems with the NFL and some *Neurosurgery* articles, Dr. Elliot Pellman resigned as the chair of the NFL's MTBI Committee on February 28, 2007.

Though Pellman's resignation was initially perceived as a positive step for player safety, in reality he still sat on the committee and was the liaison between the committee and the NFL, so the NFL's stance on CTE remained the same. Pellman's replacements seemed more out of step with the science than he was. New co-chair Dr. Ira Casson told reporter Ken Murray that he wants to answer the ominous question "of whether or not a career in the NFL results in any kind of chronic brain injury. We don't plan to change anything in the committee. We are planning to continue the work that [Pellman] started. If we can do half the job he did, we'll be doing well."[117]

It was about this time that my respect for Dr. Cantu grew as he became more outspoken on the problems with the NFL's research. The concussion expert world is very small, and rarely are credible doctors willing to be openly critical

106

of one another. But Alan Schwarz needed a credible expert to say what we all knew—that the NFL committee was dangerously wrong in their views. Bob was the right person for the job. When he started speaking out against the NFL's statements, research, and policies, reporters couldn't find anyone who could discredit him—he was an expert, and had a track record of being reasonable and fair—so his criticism was immensely powerful both in the media and behind the scenes. I will always admire him for sticking out his neck when he was talking about the NFL committee to Alan Schwarz: "I find it very worrisome. They say one thing in one place and in other places other things. They're going against a ton of peer-reviewed, very well scrutinized, multiple academic research centers. And their science is very suspect."[118]

Because print media had broken through, television finally started to take an interest in the concussion story. At the time I believed they had hung back further than print media because of the lucrative multibillion-dollar contracts to broadcast games, along with fees for NFL highlights, made crossing the NFL financially dangerous. HBO's *Real Sports with Bryant Gumbel* was the first to reach out to me. They asked if there were former athletes other than Ted who wanted to tell their story. There were. I had just received an email from the ex-wife of Gene Atkins, a former safety for the New Orleans Saints and Miami Dolphins. She said Gene, who was forty-two at the time, had played at the same time as Andre Waters and the same position, and was dealing with everything she read about Andre. She called it a "five-year downward spiral," and she wanted to know if we could help him while he was still alive.

Gene had struggled since retiring. He was arrested multiple times. He was arrested in May 2004 for domestic violence. According to the police report his wife reported Gene had shoved her against a wall, bit her, choked her, and hit her with a remote control.[119] Gene was charged with attempted second-degree murder in 1998 for allegedly hiring three men to firebomb the home of a former business partner. He was acquitted.

Due to the sincerity of the email I received from his ex-wife, I didn't think Gene was the man his rap sheet said he was. On a phone call with his current wife, she told me that Gene had attempted suicide multiple times, but survived through his family's intervention each time. That was the trigger that made me feel obligated to help. I'd taken the Waters story public so that people could recognize symptoms and intervene prior to suicide. Ted Johnson had done the same, and so I found an anonymous donor to fly Gene and his current wife to Boston to see Dr. Cantu, and the family allowed it to be filmed by HBO.

Dr. Cantu gave Gene a neurological examination. A standard part of the exam is to repeat six digits forward. Dr. Cantu asked Gene to repeat back, "9-7-8-4-3-2." Gene could only remember "9-7-8," which was extremely abnormal. But it was the next question that has haunted me, as well as viewers of the piece ever since. Dr. Cantu asked Gene to say the months of the year in order. Gene started, "January, February... April."

Dr. Cantu stepped in and asked Gene to say them in order, saying to Gene, "Like: January, February, March, April...."

Gene raced through what he just heard, "January February March April," and then paused, eventually saying softly, "June..."

"What comes before June?" Dr. Cantu interrupted.

Gene paused. "July?"

I was sitting next to his wife during that conversation. I couldn't look at her, only imagining what was going through her mind at that moment. Thinking about my own future, I imagined the strength it would take to stick by someone with early onset CTE. Gene and his wife separated not long after the visit.

In the same episode, Dr. Casson was interviewed by Bernie Goldberg and downplayed a connection between brain trauma and later-life impairment.

Goldberg: Is there any evidence as far as you are concerned, that links multiple head injuries with among pro football players with depression?

Casson: No.

Goldberg: Dementia?

Casson: No

Goldberg: Early onset of Alzheimer's?

Casson: No

Goldberg: Is there any evidence, as of today, that links multiple head injuries with any long-term problem like that?

Casson: In NFL players? No.

Retired players have referred to him as "Dr. No" ever since.

Chapter 9: SLI and the BU CSTE Are Born

There is absolutely no evidence to suggest a connection between the NFL and dementia.

—Greg Aiello, NFL spokesman, April, 2007[120]

It was clear the NFL was going to dig their heels into the ground and was bracing for a long fight. I believed that turning the NFL was the key to changing worldwide sports, so I needed to fight back.

I'd learned a few lessons at this point. The first was that neuropathology was working as a way to raise awareness of CTE and the consequences of brain trauma. The media was finally covering the topic, and the stories they told resonated with people. But I also realized that for the brain donation concept to continue successfully, it needed more infrastructure and oversight. It wasn't going to last if it was a guy chasing brains in his spare time and sending them to a doctor who I later found out was working on the cases in his garage, publicly claiming to speak to the ghosts of those he studied. [121] [122]

To set up a system to ensure this work continued would require funding, staff, and facilities, and the one place I could think of that existed to meet all those needs was a university medical school. Figuring out the right partner would take time, so until the program could find the right home, it needed to become a legitimate organization. A not-for-profit seemed like the most logical structure; families needed to trust that the donated brains were not going to an organization focused on profit.

The first person I called was Dr. Cantu. My vision was to continue the work by creating a 501(c)(3) focused on raising awareness and funding for the research, and then eventually partner with a top-tier medical school to conduct

110

the research. He told me he liked the idea and would participate, and asked for a proposal. I then called Dr. Omalu, who agreed to be a member of the team. Eventually a few others joined. I named it the Sports Legacy Institute, known as SLI for short. "Sports" was the first word because that was our focus. The word "legacy" was chosen for two reasons. One was to inform the brain donors and their families that their gift would have a far-reaching, permanent, and positive impact on sports. The second reason was to emphasize the fact that sports concussions leave a permanent legacy in their brain. We have to continually ask, "What is the legacy that youth sports leaves on our children's futures?" I incorporated SLI in Boston on June 14, 2007.

The evidence continued to accumulate. In March, 2007 I received a tip from a doctor that there was another brain out there that should be studied. Justin Strzelczyk was an offensive lineman for the Pittsburgh Steelers who began exhibiting bizarre behavior shortly after his retirement. His mother, Mary, told me Justin's abnormal behavior started slowly. He wouldn't do the dishes. He wouldn't do the laundry and his house became a sea of clothes. He began buying new shirts instead of washing old ones. He became short-tempered, and his daughter started avoiding him.

Mary knew something was wrong with his head. They went to an IMAX show together, and the movie opened with a kaleidoscope-like display of colors and lines. Mary asked Justin, "Is that visual like the thoughts racing through your head?" She remembered, "First he got *really* mad. Then he started to cry." Toward the end, he began complaining of hearing voices from people he called "the evil ones."[123]

Justin had some sort of breakdown on September 30, 2004. While driving in the morning he caused a minor accident, and rather than stop he left the scene.

The police found him, but he refused to pull over, giving them the finger and throwing beer bottles at them. Eventually he led police on a 40-mile high-speed chase throughout upstate New York. He drove the last 15 miles on three tires and a rim, as his tire had been punctured by spikes police put in the road.[124] He crossed the highway median for the final three miles and was going nearly 90 miles an hour when his pickup truck collided with a tractor trailer, killing him instantly. Sections of his brain were kept by the coroner per state regulations, and I received permission from his mother to send the tissue to Dr. Omalu.

Justin was found to have CTE, and Alan Schwarz wrote about it on June 19, 2007, the same day the NFL held their first "concussion summit" outside Chicago with outside guests including Dr. Cantu. Roger Goodell hosted a press conference afterward and announced a number of concussion measures, including:[125]

1. A "whistleblower" system to provide a way for players who feel pressured to return too soon to report it to the NFL (a.k.a. the Ted Johnson Rule)

2. The dictum that medical concerns should override competitive concerns *(because apparently it had to be said)*

3. Mandatory neuropsychological baseline testing for players

4. Player education on concussions will become more of a focus

5. Equipment rules regarding player safety will be more strictly enforced

Despite these measures, the NFL was still not fully owning the problem. When Alan Schwarz asked Goodell about Strzelczyk's CTE, Goodell focused on the lack of documented concussions in football, telling him, "There's no record of a concussion. He may have had the concussion swimming."

Alan Schwarz asked, "He could have had a concussion swimming?

Dumbfounded, Goodell answered, "My brother had a concussion swimming. He hit his head on the side of the pool. Come on, Alan, it does happen. A concussion can happen in a variety of different activities."

At this point four out of four deceased former NFL players had been diagnosed with CTE.

Alan Schwarz asked, "Four out of four. Are you suggesting that all four men sustained their damage in fields other than football?"

An interviewer later asked Alan Schwarz what he was thinking when Roger Goodell told him that. He answered, "Do you really want to know? I'm scared out of my mind. I'm standing there talking to the commissioner of the National Football League basically dumping at his feet a problem that I knew in my bones was going to be immense for him. And in a way, I was becoming the math teacher that I had always planned on being. All I wanted to do was get him to understand the probabilities at work here. That it wasn't just me being in a pain in the ass, it was the fact that when you're four out of four for a million-to-one shot, something's up."

In August the NFL distributed a concussion education pamphlet. It noted signs and symptoms and encouraged players to report their symptoms. It also downplayed long-term effects, with the Q & A section saying:

Q: If I have had more than one concussion, am I at risk for another injury?

A: Current research with professional athletes has not shown that having more than one or two concussions leads to permanent problems if each injury is managed properly. It is important to understand that there is no magic number for how many concussions is too many. Research is currently under way to determine if there are any long-term effects of concussion in NFL athletes.

113

Research is under way to determine *"if"* there are any long-term effects? Well played, NFL.

▼ ▼ ▼

On June 25, eleven days after the formation of SLI, my friend and former colleague at WWE, Chris Benoit, was found dead, along with the rest of his family. Eventually it became clear that he had murdered his wife, Nancy, then his seven-year-old son, and then committed suicide. The media immediately connected the events to his known use of steroids, but I had a different theory. I didn't know Chris well, but we had some interesting interactions. I was wrestling in Cincinnati in the WWE developmental program at the Heartland Wrestling Alliance in late spring or summer 2002 when Chris was returning from neck fusion surgery. He spent a few weeks training with us, and knew a wrestler named Race Steele, whom he used as his training partner. Race and I were friends, so Race invited me to a few of these private sessions—just the three of us. At the time I'd only been training for about eighteen months and was still working on making the basics look convincing. One weakness I had was that I threw a bad forearm to the head. It looked weak. Chris threw one of the best in the business—it looked like it killed guys, but you could barely feel it. I asked him to teach me.

First, Chris threw some forearms to my head and to Race's head so I could watch and feel the move. Then he bent at the waist and said, "Now you hit me."

I was stunned. I said, "You just had surgery, why don't I hit Race?"

He said, "No, no, hit me. Let's go. Lay it in."

I threw a couple of weak forearms, scared to death I was going to injure him or cause him pain. He stood up straight, looked me in the eye, and repeated his request, "Come on, hit me."

He bent over again. I wound up and—*WHACK!*—I tattooed him in the side of the head. I took a step back and said, "I'm so sorry!"

He looked at me, smiled, and bent over, saying, "Good, now do it again."

We spent more time on it, and a few other things that afternoon. When a big star takes you under his wing and teaches you a few things, you are forever grateful. Chris always treated me well over the next five years.

My alternate theory as to what contributed to those tragic events of 2007 was based on a conversation I had with Chris about a year prior in the locker room of the arena in Manchester, New Hampshire. At this point I was still working as a spokesperson for various WWE community service programs, including *Smackdown Your Vote*, and I would occasionally attend shows near Boston to catch up with the guys.

I ran into Chris in the locker room in Manchester. Few guys were interested in my concussions or the book I had been working on for a few years at that point. In fact, I don't remember anyone asking for a lot of detail about what I had found; that is, except for Chris Benoit. He was sitting to my left on a bench in the locker room before the show. He never gave me a hard time for retiring and asked me for an update on *Head Games*. I remember him asking me how many concussions I'd had, trying to understand how many it took to end my career. I told him, "I've had at least six."

I turned the question back at him. "How many have you had?"

"More than I can count," he answered. Benoit was known to be extraordinarily tough, and preferred if you wrestled "stiff"—meaning erring on the side of hitting someone painfully with a punch rather than missing them. Yet he rarely missed time for injury, so it was very likely that if anyone had concussions and wrestled through them, it was him. At the end of our conversation he asked if he could give me his phone number, and if I could give him a call. I'd never had his home number, and considered it an honor. I was also nervous about calling him, so I waited a couple weeks. When I did call, he didn't have anything specific to say—he actually seemed confused as to why I'd called him. It was an awkward and short conversation.

When I heard about the murders I immediately thought of that locker room conversation and realized that the questions he asked and giving me his number might have been a cry for help. Ted Johnson and I had talked about trying to prevent tragedies by creating awareness, but this was one I missed. I was certain that Benoit had suffered from CTE.

I called Chris's father a few days later with my theory and to ask for permission, and he agreed. Chris Benoit's brain was the first that I acquired outside of professional football. Dr. Omalu found that he indeed had advanced CTE when he committed those heinous acts. Whatever role steroids may have played in the situation, I believe he would never have become a murderer without the brain disease.

▼ ▼ ▼

Taking the Benoit case public was also the beginning of the end for some of the original members of the SLI team, and nearly the end of SLI. I'd added some other members to the team on Dr. Omalu's advice who had endeared themselves to Dr. Omalu, but I quickly found they did not conduct their affairs in a way I would ever be comfortable with. Although Dr. Omalu and I worked well together, the balance we'd had fell apart. After a bizarre series of events I was forced to exert my control over SLI so that this important work could continue the right way. It was an ugly split, and I had doubts that SLI would survive. It was a struggle for me, as I'd never had conflicts with people I had worked with. The work had become such an uphill battle—both behind the scenes and in the public sphere—that I started having doubts about anyone really caring about what we were trying to do; I was worried they were just humoring a post-concussed kid. Then I had one of those moments that usually only appears in movies.

I'd been a Smashing Pumpkins fan since I first heard the song "Today" from *Siamese Dream* in 1993 during my sophomore year of high school. They were my favorite band, and I was crushed when they broke up in 2000. Billy Corgan, the frontman, songwriter, composer—for all intents and purposes, the band—happened to be a big wrestling fan, and we met in 2005 at Wrestlemania, and again in 2007. When the band regrouped for the *Zeitgeist* tour in 2007, Billy offered me tickets to the show at the Orpheum Theater in Boston, and invited me backstage before the show.

I was basically at a low point professionally. It was almost worse than retiring, because this idea I had to start an organization that would save lives and provide meaning to my injury was falling apart before my eyes. I remember walking up the back stairs before the show to the tiny dressing room. Billy greeted me and we stepped outside. I remember clearly that he had his back against the wall standing on one leg, with the other knee bent and his foot flush with the wall behind him, a scarf around his throat to keep his vocal cords warm, and a guitar around his neck. While he strummed along on the guitar, he started telling me how proud he was of me. He'd been following the entire story through the media, from Waters to Strzelczyk to Benoit, and thought it was so cool the way I was fighting the big corporations.

I told him how much trouble I'd been having with some members of the original team. Billy mentioned how familiar it sounded, like the split he'd had with the original members of his band. He advised me to cut ties and press on, because the cause was just. He said it was, "God's work." And he thought I was the right guy to lead it. Whether or not that was true, it was one of the coolest

117

moments of my life. And it turned out to be great advice. And the show rocked that night.

SLI pushed along, with me operating as executive director and Dr. Cantu as medical director, but we continued our search for the right university partner. I was introduced to Dr. Bob Stern, a neuropsychologist and now a professor of Neurology and Neurosurgery at Boston University School of Medicine, who at that time focused solely on Alzheimer's disease. I shared my vision for SLI partnering with a medical school and doing work that would change the world. Dr. Stern was a believer, and he recommended that instead of partnering with concussion experts or traumatic brain injury experts, that we look for neurodegenerative disease experts. The model for CTE research was not concussion, but Alzheimer's disease and fronto-temporal dementia and amyotrophic lateral sclerosis (ALS), also known as Lou Gehrig's disease. He also thought that Boston University might be the right place to do it. They had one of only thirty Alzheimer's Disease Research Centers that are funded by the federal government through the National Institute on Aging, which is part of the National Institutes of Health. They also had a world-class neuropathologist named Dr. Ann McKee.

Dr. McKee is one of the most interesting people I know. When I first visited her office at the Bedford VA Medical Center, I was shocked by what I found. It wasn't the brains in freezers or the morgue drawers that said "Feet this end." It was the football memorabilia. Dr. McKee was born in Appleton, Wisconsin, and was a Packers fan to the core. Her brothers played in college, and she kept a Brett Favre bobblehead next to her brain slides.

By 2007, Dr. McKee was an established expert in Alzheimer's disease, Parkinson's disease, amyotrophic lateral sclerosis, and aging. She already led the brain banks for the Boston University Alzheimer's Disease Center, the Veterans Administration National ALS Brain Bank, the Centenarian Study, which studied people who lived to one hundred years of age, and the Framingham Heart Study, the largest controlled population study in history. I asked her if she could add a CTE brain bank to her lab. Dr. McKee was already interested in CTE as she'd identified it in two ex-boxers she studied as part of her VA responsibilities.

On top of her expertise in disease, Dr. McKee was also an expert in the protein that broke down in CTE: *tau.* She'd been fascinated by it her entire career and tested every brain in her lab for tau, which was not a standard practice elsewhere. As an added bonus, her lab had a unique ability to process the brains in such a way to create visually stunning pictures of the brain. Whereas most labs had to chop up the brain in order to show a handful of magnified cells, she could cut, process, and photograph an entire brain slice, which allowed a layperson to see the disease in its entirety, rather than a cell at a time. Dr. McKee was also an artist, so she approached displaying the disease with an artist's eye, and was able to create images and collages that were stunning. At this point in time many scientists still argued that CTE was just another form of Alzheimer's disease, which many people get, and not a unique disease caused by trauma, so Dr. McKee's experience, reputation, and technical skills would be key to changing hearts and minds.

Ann McKee

Dr. Stern met with the dean and rallied departments to financially support this fledgling endeavor, and in 2008 the Center for the Study of Traumatic Encephalopathy at Boston University School of Medicine (BU CSTE) was launched with a commitment of nearly $150,000 from the university. It was technically a partnership between SLI and BU, with Dr. Cantu, Dr. McKee, Dr. Stern, and myself serving as co-directors. Soon the VA joined the partnership, and provided the lab space and much of Dr. McKee's staff. I considered it quite an accomplishment to find two researchers who were already set in their careers to shift gears and focus on CTE.

In September of 2008 we announced, through Alan Schwarz and the *New York Times*, our first definitive case of CTE as the BU CSTE. Former NFL player John Grimsley, an All-Pro middle linebacker for the Houston Oilers and Miami Dolphins, died at the age of forty-five of a self-inflicted gunshot wound. According to his wife, Virginia, his short-term memory had begun failing him to the point that he would take a list every time he left the house for errands because he would frequently forget where he was headed. Eventually he started calling home because he'd forget again, and Virginia would gently remind him he had a list in his pocket telling him what do to. He had also begun to develop a short fuse, although he had not yet become violent.

The medical examiner initially thought the self-inflicted gunshot wound was a classic suicide, but eventually ruled that the death was an accident and that the most likely scenario was that John had forgotten he had a bullet in the chamber while cleaning his gun.

While he was alive John and Virginia had watched the HBO *Real Sports* episode on CTE the year prior. At the time, Virginia said they both suspected John's advancing problems were caused by CTE. When I called their house the day after his death, the phone was answered by Virginia's friend. She told Virginia, "There is a Chris Nowinski from Boston University on the phone for you."

120

"Tell him I know what he wants and he can have it," she said, referring to John's brain. It was direct evidence that the media campaign was working.

In the same *New York Times* article we announced that sixteen athletes were pledging to donate their brains upon death to the BU CSTE. I had already grown tired of calling up widows who had just lost their husband or children who had just lost their father. If athletes signed up in advance, it would make my life easier, and it would also help scientifically as we could set up a longitudinal registry and interview participants annually before we eventually acquired their brain. Currently we had to rely on the recollection of concussion history and symptoms from their families, which had weaknesses. That longitudinal study is now called LEGEND, and has over 500 participants and a couple years of data.

The key to getting people to donate their brain to you is, of course, trust. The first sixteen athletes were not random. They were almost entirely good friends I had known for years, had watched the concussion issue gain momentum, and trusted me not to mess with their brain or their legacy after they passed. Publicly, we said Ted Johnson was the first to sign up because it was great for public relations. In reality he was second. He wouldn't agree to it until I got Isaiah Kacyvenski to do it. Isaiah was an eight-year NFL veteran who happened to be my former roommate at Harvard, where on the football field we were self-dubbed as the Polish Connection (his idea, but my Dad made the T-shirts). I knew if I couldn't get Isaiah, I couldn't get anyone. After the usual, "Dude, you want my brain?" he recognized the importance of the project and jumped in, and other people were then willing to follow.

Isaiah is an interesting story. He's the all-time leading tackler in Harvard football history and overcame a tough enough upbringing that Oprah had him on her show that highlighted people overcoming difficult childhoods. He was the hardest working guy in the NFL for eight seasons, starting 22 games but was best known as a special teamer and fearless wedge-buster.

While he was generally supportive of my concussion advocacy, he also was concerned that the original *Head Games* would cause a backlash in his direction. Therefore, he demanded I not include his name in the book, and I was not allowed to mention his name or our friendship to anyone in the NFL. He also refused to read the book because he believed he had to be fearless to do his job. His contract was up after the 2006 season, and his wife, now ex-wife, called me and asked me to postpone the book until after Isaiah signed with a new team, just in case there was backlash. I refused ... It is ironic that the book did end up hurting Isaiah financially more than anyone else, but not for the reasons we thought.

Isaiah had six successful seasons with the Seattle Seahawks. In 2006, in the middle of his seventh season, he was cut for a weekend to make room for an injury replacement, with the expectation he would be re-signed the next Monday when the injury replacement was no longer needed. His reputation was so strong that he had no fewer than eight teams call his agent that weekend, and because he didn't respect how the Seahawks handled the situation, he signed with the St. Louis Rams rather than re-signing with the Seahawks.

The Rams played Seattle a few weeks later, and Isaiah got a concussion on a kickoff. "It was the one hit in my life that I never saw coming," he said. He popped up and began making his way to the wrong sideline, forgetting he was no longer with Seattle, "which was embarrassing." When he headed back to the correct sideline, he recalls, "I remember looking up at the scoreboard and seeing half of it disappear." He was attended to and given a concussion evaluation by the medical staff. In his post-concussed state Isaiah passed the sideline concussion questions, which in 2006 weren't standard and included questions like asking him to name the months of the year backwards—"Which I can always do, whether I'm concussed or not," he told me.

"I remember the one thing that scared me was them holding up a smelling salt and putting it right under my nose, and I took a huge whiff, which is crazy...nothing. And they said 'Did you take a whiff?' I'm like yeah I just took the biggest whiff I could. They snap two of them, put two of them under there, took two more huge whiffs...nothing. They were like 'Wow, we've never seen that before.'"

"What followed should never have happened," Isaiah remembers. "Twenty minutes go by, some of the vision's back. It wasn't perfect and I remember the doctors coming back to me and saying, 'You ready to go back in the game?' And I said yes. And I think if you ever put it in a player's hands, the player is always going to say yes."

Isaiah finished the game. He felt terrible but continued to practice and play, and in the next game against the Carolina Panthers, "my whole goal of that game was to not have anybody touch my head; I didn't want anybody touching me." Isaiah survived that game, but wasn't so lucky the next week versus the San Francisco 49ers. He was knocked unconscious making a tackle on a kickoff. "I remember coming to with like the whole side of my body and my face all the way down to my arms and my legs like just absolutely numb. They carted me off the field."

Isaiah Kacyvenski

Due to the severity of the symptoms Isaiah had to miss three games, and he only returned for the last two games, and not because he was healthy, but because "I was going to be a free agent again, so I wanted to make sure teams knew I could be ready to play." It was November of that fall that Andre Waters committed suicide. I told Isaiah that we were studying his brain that December, and that the results would go public as soon as we knew them. He asked me if I could delay releasing the findings until he signed his new deal. Isaiah recalls, "I remember saying 'If you've waited [this long], you could just wait a little longer.'"

Isaiah was concerned because he was the only guy in the NFL to have two concussions on his injury report in 2006. He was certainly not the only player to have two concussions; players are fully aware that having two concussions in a season can get them labeled a "concussion case" and they won't get signed anywhere again, so they hide second concussions even more than first concussions. Isaiah was knocked unconscious by his second concussion and couldn't hide it. He had a suspicion that he might have acquired that label, and years later he said to me, "I don't know if you realized how impactful it was going to be. I was just hedging my risk. This had potential to really blow up in my face."

I refused my best friend's plea to delay the Waters findings. I knew it was ethically the right thing to do—I'd never forgive myself if, as we delayed for Isaiah's contract, another former athlete with CTE took his life because he didn't understand what was wrong with him and didn't get help. Part of me thought Isaiah was just being paranoid, and another part thought that I was doing him a favor if I killed his career. He remembers me having the gumption to say, "Isaiah, if you end your career tomorrow it will be a good thing. You're going to thank me in twenty years."

Isaiah's intuition was correct, and he was labeled a concussion case. He remembers, "So after the article appeared in the *New York Times*, I went from six, seven, eight teams interested in me [when he was cut during the season] to a big fat zero teams being interested in me [after the season]. I had an old coach that was in the Pittsburgh Steelers system and they had been looking at me and he said when it came down to it, after this article broke they had talked to their doctors and I had been tagged as a concussion guy moving forward. I really was in limbo for the whole off-season, and the team that did give me a shot was the Oakland Raiders, but instead of the $500,000 plus signing bonus I should have received, they offered me $30,000."

So, in conclusion, my crusade cost my best friend around half a million dollars, and now I have to pay for dinner when we go out for the rest of eternity.

Chapter 10: Getting on the Inside

I think that there are many questions that still are out there as to whether there is a kind of traumatic encephalopathy associated with football. I think we don't know. I think that there is not enough scientific evidence to say that there is.

—Dr. Ira Casson, Co-Chair of the NFL MTBI Committee, January 28, 2009[126]

Now that I had a solid base underneath me with SLI and the BU CSTE, I was ready to go back on offense. We started the year with the bold move of announcing two more cases of CTE, and I chose to do it with a press conference at the Super Bowl. With our limited funding, if we could only afford to raise awareness through free media, we'd have to go to where the media is, and that was Tampa, Florida, at the end of January 2009. There were thousands of members of the media at the Super Bowl, and for our press conference we were able to entice only about twenty to cross the street to the Marriott Hotel to hear what we had to say about the most important issue in sports.

The first was Tom McHale, the defensive player of the year in the Ivy League in 1987; as a lineman for Cornell he terrorized teams. He went on to play nine years in the NFL for the Tampa Bay Buccaneers, Philadelphia Eagles, and Miami Dolphins. After retiring Tom owned and operated three successful restaurants in Tampa and raised three boys with his wife, Lisa. He started abusing painkillers for musculoskeletal pain from football injuries in 2005. That caused lethargy, so he began to use cocaine to feel better. Lisa found out and sent him to rehab. He would get clean and then fall right back into his old habits, and over the next three years he continued to abuse drugs while failing rehab three times. He eventually died on a friend's couch from what was deemed an accidental overdose.

126

I called Lisa to ask for Tom's brain, and luckily she allowed it, but she told me that Tom would be our control brain, "Because Tom was never diagnosed with a concussion." Sadly, Lisa was wrong; Tom had moderate CTE, and it likely contributed to his addiction and the cognitive issues he was trying to combat with the drugs. That made six of six retired NFL players over the age of twenty-four who had CTE.

In addition, we released the findings of CTE in the brain of an eighteen-year-old named Eric Pelly. At the time we couldn't release his name for legal reasons, so we told the world that an anonymous eighteen-year-old was a football and rugby player, and that he'd had multiple diagnosed concussions. In fact, he died at his kitchen table a week after the last concussion, and to this day no one is certain why.

Isaiah Kacyvenski joined me at the Super Bowl in Tampa, which was very helpful. I was persona non grata to the NFL, but Isaiah had access to every event, including the Commissioner's Ball, with an unnamed "plus one." I entered the affair nervously, as I didn't know if I'd be thrown out if I was recognized. It's a heck of a party if you ever get a chance to go; within ten feet of the door Isaiah and I were already chatting with Drew Brees about the concussion issue, and I was gaining allies quickly. Our real goal that evening was to meet with Kevin Mawae, the president of the NFL Players Association, because I felt that the NFLPA needed to be a bigger voice in the public battle.

The NFLPA had to make a move, because it was difficult to convince the world that the NFL was playing fast and loose with the truth if the organization with the job of protecting players wasn't saying the same thing. At the time they were accepting the research conclusions of the NFL with little dispute, partially because they weren't able to commit the same resources as we had. Their medical director, Thom Mayer, MD, was only part-time, and he had no concussion advisors of his own to turn to and no structure with which to compete. My goal was to convince Kevin Mawae to start a concussion committee to combat the NFL's.

As Isaiah and I weaved through the crowd looking for Mawae we were blocked by a large group moving en masse. It was Commissioner Goodell and his entourage. Isaiah jumped in front of him and stuck out his hand, "Commissioner, I'm Isaiah Kacyvenski and—"

The Commissioner cut him off and smiled, "Sure, Isaiah, how are you?"

Isaiah ignored the question and said, "I'd like you to meet my former roommate at Harvard"—Goodell locked hands with me before looking at my face— "Chris Nowinski. Chris has been very active on the concussion front and…"

I felt Goodell's grip tighten. Roger Goodell either has an impressively strong handshake or he was giving me a special hello. Or both. Goodell's smile dimmed, but he remained polite and professional. "Of course I know Chris. Thank you for all you are doing and if you think there is anything more we can do, never hesitate to call my office."

I said something inconsequential and the meeting was over. It was wild. We pressed on in our search and randomly ran into Sean Morey, an eight-year NFL veteran special teams ace. I hadn't seen Sean since I played against him in college, and I first got to know him when he hosted me on my recruiting trip to Brown in 1996. Sean retired as the all-time leading wide receiver in the history of the Ivy League.

We told Sean of our goal of meeting with Kevin Mawae. Sean knew it wouldn't be easy to get to Kevin that night, and since Mawae had personally appointed him to serve on a joint Player Health & Safety Committee, he insisted we update him before making any introductions. He was interested in the concussion issue; he had struggled with them himself over the years, and had idolized his former teammate, Ted Johnson. He also respected Isaiah's football acumen, so he knew if Isaiah was involved that it was serious.

Sean had a bigger passion for the issue than we realized. As one of the longest-playing NFL veterans, he now felt strongly it was his duty to learn more and give back by educating his fellow players. Getting Sean fired up about concussions was like catching lightning in a bottle. Although his second Super Bowl appearance was just days away, he refused to leave that night until he heard everything.

We never met with Kevin Mawae, but that didn't matter because we had spoken to the right guy. I would see Sean again in May in New York City, and by that time he'd done his homework. He had torn apart the Congressional Research Study, studied all the pertinent articles he could get his hands on, and read *Head Games* so many times that the pages of his copy were falling out. By that time, he was fully committed to the cause and had been trying to get the wheels churning at the NFLPA. He had presented the current CTE research to Kevin Mawae and other Executive Committee members at the NFL Combine, where the NFLPA had held its inaugural Player Safety Summit.

Morey was in New York that May to attend a major meeting at NFL headquarters. Dr. McKee had finally been invited by the NFL MTBI Committee to NFL headquarters on Park Avenue, and Sean was attending on behalf of the NFLPA. When Dr. McKee accepted the invitation, she requested that I be allowed to join her. Dr. McKee didn't want to get sucked into the politics of the game that was being played, and she thought that my presence would assure a collegial and productive discussion, as there would be another witness to whatever was about to happen. Dr. Casson called her back and denied her request to bring me, saying it was a "doctors only meeting." Her reply was, "No Chris, no meeting," and shortly thereafter I received a gracious invitation.

I wish I could share the details of the meeting, but we all agreed to try to build trust and not divulge this specific meeting through the press. I will simply say that it was odd that at Dr. Casson's "doctors only" meeting that there were two defense attorneys in attendance who worked for the NFL. It was difficult not to think they had invited us there to present the latest science only so they could prepare a defense for future lawsuits. After all, the doctors shouldn't have needed us to explain to them what they already should have known.

Later that June, Sean would pitch the NFLPA's new executive director DeMaurice Smith to form their own concussion committee, and in October, Smith created the NFLPA Mackey-White TBI Committee, co-chaired by Sean Morey and Dr. Thom Mayer. The players were now willing to share in the responsibility to get this issue right; after all, their brains, livelihood, and quality of life were on the line.

▼ ▼ ▼

That same month the Zackery Lystedt Law passed in Washington State. Zackery was a young man whose life changed one Friday night in October 2006. Zack suffered a concussion in the first half of his high school football game. While making a tackle his head struck the ground, and he stayed down for a minute clutching his helmet while his head throbbed. Four plays later he was put back in. At some point his brain started bleeding, and at the end of the game he collapsed and was airlifted to a trauma unit where he underwent emergency surgery. Three months later, when he awoke from his coma, he faced a new reality. It would be three years before he could stand again, and during that time he chose to become a powerful spokesperson for concussion legislation.

It was a brilliant plan. Zack and his team of experts thought, "Why wait for people to come along voluntarily? This is about protecting children, so why not consider this an extension of existing child abuse laws?" The law as crafted focused on three things:

1. Athletes, parents and coaches must be educated about the dangers of concussions each year.

2. If a young athlete is suspected of having a concussion, he/she must be removed from a game or practice and not be permitted to return to play. When in doubt, sit them out.

3. A licensed health care professional must clear the young athlete to return to play in the subsequent days or weeks.

It was such a simple model that a version of the Lystedt Law has now been passed in over forty states. It took a lot of hard work by a lot of people to get these laws passed through each legislature one by one—I know because SLI led the charge in Massachusetts and became the sixth state to do it. A lot of folks deserve thanks and acknowledgment, but I think we cover them all by saying: Thank you, Zack!

Chapter 11: Time for a Showdown

In October 2009 the issue finally rose to a boil. First, *60 Minutes* did a feature on our work when we broke the news that former Minnesota Viking Wally Hilgenberg, a four-time Super Bowl champion, was suffering from CTE when he died of Lou Gehrig's disease. Then Malcolm Gladwell wrote an article for *The New Yorker* comparing the NFL to dogfighting, focusing on CTE. We released the finding that NFL Hall of Famer Lou Creekmur, who died of dementia at eighty-two, had CTE. Lou's case was especially important because Lou played prior to the steroid era, meaning that steroid use, which was still cited by the doubters, was not the cause of his CTE. Lou also made it eleven for eleven retired NFL players over age twenty-four with the disease.

But the finding that put the issue over the top was, ironically, a study commissioned by the NFL. They had hired the University of Michigan to survey the health of former NFL players from a number of different angles. Over a thousand players answered the survey out of a randomized list of 1,625, and while most findings were expected, one stood out:

Have you been diagnosed with dementia, Alzheimer's disease, or other memory-related disease?		
	US Population	**NFL**
Age 30-49	0.1%	1.9%
Age 50 and above	1.2%	6.1%

The study revealed that NFL players age fifty and above were five times more likely to have been diagnosed with "dementia, Alzheimer's disease, or other

132

memory-related disease," and players age 30 to 49 were nineteen times more likely! The report was leaked by an NFL insider to Alan Schwarz because the person was concerned that otherwise the study may never see the light of day.

The NFL was nearly out of defenses, as this was their own study that they approved and funded. Yet they tried to distance themselves from it. Dr. Casson again led the charge: "What I take from this report is there's a need for further studies to see whether or not this finding is going to pan out, if it's really there or not. I can see that the respondents believe they have been diagnosed. But the next step is to determine whether that is so." [127]

NFL spokesman Greg Aiello was also out of logical defenses. Aiello said, "There are thousands of retired players who do not have memory problems"; and "Memory disorders affect many people who never played football or other sports." [128] Those statements are scientifically silly. There are thousands of smokers who never developed lung cancer, but that doesn't mean that smoking is considered to be safe. It's all about the numbers and the relative risk, and now the numbers existed.

That was enough to interest Congress to hold a hearing by the House Judiciary Committee. I was invited to testify, along with Dr. Cantu, Dr. McKee, and SLI board member Dr. Eleanor Perfetto. Chairman John Conyers, a Democrat of Michigan, pressed Commissioner Goodell to say whether or not there was a connection between brain trauma and later-life mental impairment. He refused to give a yes or no answer, saying the doctors could better answer the question. The hearing ended without the NFL admitting a problem, and nothing was resolved. Later, Linda Sánchez, Democrat of California, told Alan Schwarz that the committee requested Dr. Casson be there to defend his statements, "but obviously he was a no-show." [129]

The next few months were a time of soul searching. What would it take to put us over the top? We all felt as if we were on the cusp of something big. The

NFL continued to tweak their policies and rules, and we played the waiting game.

I made strategic moves to keep the issue moving forward, keeping the NFL on the defensive. The Collective Bargaining Agreement between the NFL and the NFLPA was about to expire in a year, and the NFL and NFLPA were both already fighting for the moral high ground. The fans knew there would be a lockout and the 2011 season was in jeopardy, and the NFL and NFLPA were both trying to portray the other group as greedy and immoral.

We reached out to the NFLPA to discuss collaboration on our research. The NFLPA decided it was going to encourage players to sign up to donate their brains, and for families to donate if a loved one passes away. It would ensure that the pace of research would quicken. They would be the first major sports organization to give our research the stamp of approval, and we had a press release drafted and ready to go on Monday, December 21.

As we were putting the finishing touches on the agreement, Congress moved again. They weren't satisfied with the last hearing and on December 17 called for a second hearing, to be held on January 4, 2010, in Detroit. Again I was invited and looked forward to another opportunity to participate, especially with Dr. Casson now confirmed to be there.

I thought the NFLPA collaboration would help in the Congressional hearing, because it would make the NFL look as if they didn't want to know the truth. But that press release never got any attention, because somehow the NFL scooped us. I got a phone call on Sunday morning, December 20. I remember it well because it was at about ten o'clock and I was snowed in inside my apartment. It was from Howard Fendrich, a reporter from the Associated Press, asking my reaction to the NFL donating $1 million to the BU CSTE.

"What?" I asked.

I told him I had no idea what he was talking about and would have to get back to him. I called my colleagues and the BU communications department. I knew that in October Dr. Cantu had been invited to meet with Roger Goodell one-on-one to talk about what the NFL should be doing, and one of the things we asked for was the same thing we asked from the NFLPA—that the NFL encourage players to be involved in research. We didn't ask for money, because the NFL had a poor track record for funding research that people trusted and we knew it could compromise our reputation.

Our response to reporters was, "We haven't discussed funding with the NFL. Any financial support from the NFL would need to be free of any real or perceived conflict of interest." The headlines and leads told another story, with the AP reporting, "The NFL is partnering with Boston University brain researchers who have been critical of the league's stance on concussions, it was revealed Sunday."[130] Yet this was a one-way partnership, as we hadn't been consulted on whether we wanted to join. In addition, the NFLPA partnership we did negotiate was buried, and no one remembered it.

What happened next was even more unexpected. Later that day Alan Schwarz called the NFL to discuss the million dollar donation, and he got the quote that changed *everything*. Greg Aiello, NFL spokesperson, said:

"It's quite obvious from the medical research that's been done that concussions can lead to long-term problems."

What? Come again? Alan pointed out that his statement was the first time anyone from the NFL had "publicly acknowledged any long-term effects of concussions, and that it contradicted past statements made by the league, its doctors and literature currently given to players." Aiello responded, "We all share the same interest. That's as much as I'm going to say."

We won!

We were all stunned. Congratulations were made all around. So many people worked so hard to make this happen, and it was a victory for everyone. The families who had lost loved ones to CTE, what we call at SLI our "Legacy

135

Donor" families, were overjoyed. I received a bottle of champagne in the mail from Virginia Grimsley, the widow of John Grimsley, and the card said simply, "Congratulations!"

Things changed very quickly. By the next football season, there was a poster hanging in the locker room of every NFL team informing players about concussions. It included the quote: "According to CDC, 'traumatic brain injury can cause a wide range of short- or long-term changes affecting thinking, sensation, language, or emotions. These changes may lead to problems with memory and communication, personality changes, as well as depression and the early onset of dementia. Concussions and conditions resulting from repeated brain injury can change your life and your family's life forever.'"

But there was little time to celebrate. Although we had won the awareness battle in the United States, the problem was beginning to go global.

Chapter 12: Taking the Fight Global

My first real exposure to the global concussion crisis came in 2011, when I was named an Eisenhower Fellow. The Eisenhower Fellowships program was established in 1953 as an international leader exchange program to honor President Eisenhower's devotion to world peace. For my Fellowship I traveled to six countries in Europe to spread concussion awareness and build research collaborations. I was amazed at how much concussion awareness varied by country. In Switzerland, Dr. Beat Villiger introduced me to the "Respect the Head" campaign he had helped create in Swiss youth ice hockey, which included compulsive concussion education.

In Germany, professional team doctors told me they were not aware of any concussion experts in the country to whom they could refer patients to with post-concussion problems. In fact, I was told things were so bad there that if an athlete developed PCS but had a negative MRI (which is almost always the case) they were labeled as having *psychiatric* problems. This label meant it wasn't an injury caused by the sport, and therefore insurance would not cover the athletes' treatment.

The country with the most public concussion discussion was Ireland. Two rugby players, Bernard Jackson and John Fogarty, had recently retired because of concussions and had gone public, like Ted Johnson in the United States. Fogarty was still suffering from memory loss, headaches, and emotional changes after retiring, and Jackson acknowledged that the more than 20 concussions he suffered in his last three seasons had left damage.

While in Dublin I met with the International Rugby Board (IRB), the international governing body of the sport. In 2011, there was not a lot of reliable data on the scope of the concussion crisis in rugby. CTE had yet to be found (or

137

looked for) in a former rugby player, although the sport had a concussion rate similar to American football. Historically, rugby had a conservative approach to concussion. If a player was diagnosed with a concussion and did not have access to a trained medical professional, they were to rest for a minimum of 14 days and could not return to match play for at least 21 days.

One major difference between rugby and the sports I was involved with, like American football and ice hockey, was that rugby does not allow for free substitution of players. Rugby union, the most popular type of rugby worldwide, only allows 7 substitutions during games that field 15 per side. In addition, there are no stoppages of play built into the game. The game is rarely stopped, and usually only for the most severe injuries. With only one referee for a game involving 30 people even severe injuries can be missed, so injured players are routinely examined on the field by medical personnel while the game continues to rage around them.

With limited substitutions and no stoppages, it is impossible to properly assess a suspected concussion without losing one of the 7 substitutions. A player cannot be assessed properly on the field while the game continues. The solution, proposed by the Irish sports medicine physicians I met with, was to get the IRB to allow for a "Brain-bin."

In 1991, during the height of the AIDS crisis, the IRB had created a substitution exemption commonly known as the "Blood-bin," which allowed for a player to be substituted for up to 15 minutes while they are have a cut closed or a wound bandaged. It was a progressive move that limited the risk of other players contracting blood-borne diseases.

Now, twenty years later, the IRB was again in an awkward situation. Having a Blood-bin, but not a Brain-bin, did not make sense. Temporary substitutions were allowed to prevent the exceedingly rare chance of disease transmission but denied to allow for near certain chance of additional brain damage from continuing to play after suffering a concussion?

When I raised that point with the IRB, I was told that the decision makers believed that a Brain-bin would be abused by teams – they would cheat to have a strategic advantage. Rugby had been burned by a small number of high profile incidents where coaches had forced players to use oral blood capsules to allow for a late game substitution. Those coaches were severely punished when the ruse was discovered.

As an outsider, I was confused. The IRB had already shown the model – yes, there might be rare cheaters, but if they are severely punished, cheating will remain rare. But the IRB wasn't moved. They made a poor choice - rather than expend the effort to police cheating on a "Brain-bin," they will likely have to spend exponentially more time and resources fighting future lawsuits from players who claim they were injured by not having a Brain-bin.

In 2012, the IRB had a change of heart and introduced a trial of what they called the Pitch-Side Concussion Assessment (PSCA), which allowed a player to be temporarily substituted for a concussion assessment. While the PSCA was an important step, the critical flaw was that they only allowed the player to be removed for a maximum of five minutes, which is far too short for an accurate assessment. Compared to the Blood-bin, it is bad medical policy. Fifteen minutes for blood, but only five minutes for a complicated clinical assessment of the brain?

Dr. Barry O'Driscoll, a former elite rugby player for Ireland, had represented the IRB at recent international concussion meetings and had served as a medical advisor for fifteen years. He fought the five minute limit and, after his objections went unheeded, chose to resign rather than support such a flawed program. He explained, "Concussions in rugby has a long history, and for many, many years… if you had a suspected concussion, you were out for three weeks. Two years ago, they came to a conclusion that with minor traumatic injury, over seven days with no symptoms at all, you can be declared fit. Last year, rugby decided a player with a suspected concussion would come off for five minutes,

139

and then go back if he passed the most perfunctory of tests.... Well, it's almost a joke to me, really."

Dr. O'Driscoll continued, "Everybody else is getting much more careful about concussions. We are putting concussed players back on the field after five minutes. I objected to this, strongly and in writing, and to the chairman of the international board, but they stuck to doing it, and I was out. They said to me, 'You can't compare rugby with NFL.' But the forces are exactly the same! My point was, it's not that you can't, but you *must* compare it. The only research done that I've been able to find shows that the incidence of concussion in rugby football is slightly higher than that in American football. And yet, they say, 'You can't compare the two.' That's sticking your head in the sand."

The issue came to a boiling point in March, 2013. I was in Edinburgh, Scotland to film the documentary that accompanies this book and was back at the hotel after attending the Scotland-Wales Six Nations tournament game. We were watching Ireland play France on television, and we saw Dr. O'Driscoll's nephew Brian, perhaps the greatest rugby player in the history of Ireland, suffer a concussion on the field.

We only noticed it because there was a stoppage in play because another Ireland player had been knocked unconscious. Of course, the game did not actually stop because the player was unconscious – it continued for at least fifteen seconds, and the French team was using his limp body as a pick, forcing the Irish players to run over top of him. When the game finally did pause, it became apparent Brian O'Driscoll had also suffered a concussion, as two members of the team staff were standing under each arm and holding him up. He could not even stand on his own. Eventually, along with the unconscious player, O'Driscoll was escorted off the pitch, still showing obvious and serious signs of a concussion. I assumed Brian was done for the day - if that occurred in the US, there was no way we would see him back on the field

Yet somehow, just a few minutes later, O'Driscoll ran back onto the field to the roar of the crowd. I was confused, as the Six Nations had refused to adopt the PSCA, so there was no way he could have been evaluated for a concussion and return. The mystery was solved when on a close-up I noticed that he was now wearing a giant bandage taped around his head. They had sent him back under the rules of the Blood-bin! I did not even notice he was bleeding when he left the field. Brian finished the game.

Brian's uncle, Dr. O'Driscoll, saw this as more evidence that rugby was not on top of the concussion issue. Dr. O'Driscoll later found out that during Brian's time in the Blood-bin, the team medical staff attempted a superficial concussion test. He said, "They told me when they asked Brian the score, he gave the right score because he looked over the doctor's shoulder at the scoreboard, the massive scoreboard that was up there."

Dr. Barry O'Driscoll

When Brian O'Driscoll returned to the game, doctors and advocates watching knew it put him at personal risk for problems like sudden death from Second-Impact Syndrome. However, when those same experts publicly called out the team in the press for improper medical care, they were not just thinking about Brian's safety. They recognized that the culture of the game is set on television by the pros, so if pro rugby players are allowed to return after a clear concussion, coaches and parents would model concussion care for children the same way, and children would be put at risk.

141

Fourteen year old Ben Robinson showed the world this nightmare scenario was real. Ben played rugby union for his school in Carrickfergus, Northern Ireland. He loved the game and was so excited to play in a big game on January 29, 2011 that the night before the game he watched the rugby film *Invictus* before falling asleep in his rugby kit, dressed ready for the big match the next day.

Ben was on the small side and during the game was involved in a lot of big hits. A hit early in the second half knocked him down, and he stayed on the ground for 90 seconds. He needed to be helped to his feet, but he was not removed nor assessed for concussion.

Within four minutes he took another major blow to the head. Holding his head, he walked to his coach. Ben's mother Karen remembers, "There were stoppages, and I knew they were for Benjamin. I saw the coach doing the fingers test, moving them from left to right." The coach was performing a test which is no longer considered a standard part of a concussion assessment as it is not a useful indicator of concussion. Almost everyone passes, whether or not they have a concussion.

Ben passed and was sent back in. The game stopped at least three other times because Ben was unable to get up after a hit or was showing other obvious signs of concussion. Yet he remained in the game. Video footage shows Ben talking to his teammate, who later told the coroner that Ben told him, "I can't remember the score." At one point Ben even turned to his mother and said, "I don't feel right." When Ben's mother expressed her concern directly to the referee, feeling that Ben should be removed, the referee told her to calm down. Soon after, the game was stopped because Ben was down again, and this time he didn't get back up.

Ben died from his brain injury. Ben's parents claim they were told by the Ulster branch of the Irish Rugby Football Union that it was probably a freak accident, the result of one bad tackle and a single blow to the head. The coroner decided to investigate the case and found that Ben's brain study revealed he actually had three separate, distinct brain injuries. The final cause of death was Second-Impact Syndrome, which means it could have been prevented had Ben been removed from play. The coach and the referee failed Ben. They were either unaware of the guideline that Ben should have been removed, or they were not properly trained on how to respond to an athlete displaying obvious concussion symptoms. Ben was the first proven case of SIS in rugby in the United Kingdom.[131]

▼ ▼ ▼

The PSCA came under fire in July, 2013, when the British and Irish Lions, an all-star team, traveled to Australia to take on the Australian International team, the Wallabies. During the game, Wallabies' player George Smith took a massive blow to the head and was knocked senseless on the ground. Medics immediately came onto the field to attend to him. When they finally got George Smith to his feet, he was unable to walk under his own power to the sidelines – he had one man under each arm. Smith himself said after the game, "It obviously affected me. You saw me snake dancing off the field." There was no way Smith should have been back on the field, as he was showing clear signs of a concussion. Yet the PSCA was given, and as Smith told reporters, "I passed the [concussion] tests that were required within those five minutes and I got out there."[132] If George Smith could return after such an obvious concussion, the system was not working.

I am hopeful the five minute limit to the PSCA is quickly eliminated. It is impossible to rule out a concussion in only five minutes. Many concussion symptoms are delayed, and the longer a doctor has, the more accurate his assessment will be.

More importantly, if I was a player, I would ask: What right does the IRB have to rush my personal doctor? If it is my brain and my health, I would have a real problem with a bureaucrat telling my doctor that he better hurry it up and make a rushed decision. It is not right to sacrifice an athlete's health for the sake of tradition. No sports league should force a doctor to rush a diagnosis, especially if the only downside is the remote possibility of cheating. As a culture, we need to stop worshiping the traditions of sports ahead of the welfare of the players.

Chapter 13: CTE in Rugby

One of the problems holding back concussion awareness more globally has been the lack of confirmed CTE cases in sports like rugby and soccer. Proof of CTE has been the key catalyst to creating concussion policy change. Second-Impact Syndrome (SIS) has always been tolerated by the sports community, and it was never enough to create major change. It could always be dismissed as a rare event. So in the absence of concern about CTE in specific sports, there tends to be little dialog on the concussion issue. The fastest way to create safer sports globally is to find CTE in more sports.

Luckily, other experts around the world have developed an interest in CTE and have begun seeking out brains for study. Dr. Willie Stewart of Glasgow (Scotland) Southern General hospital was the first, and an ideal, doctor to take on this task. A fit neuropathologist with a close cropped buzz cut, Dr. Stewart is a former rugby player and still a devoted rugby fan. He wants the game of rugby to have a bright future, and it is his belief that addressing the concussion and CTE issue appropriately is essential for rugby to endure. His philosophy is simple; "Just as we discourage people from playing on with a damaged knee, so we should strongly discourage people playing on with a damaged brain."[133]

Dr. Willie Stewart

Dr. Stewart leads the Glasgow Traumatic Brain Injury Archive, famous for its unique contributions to understanding the human pathology of brain injury dating back over several decades. After years of quietly making his interest in potential CTE cases known to other researchers and coroners, he received a phone call from a colleague who had just received the body of former rugby player who died with dementia at a relatively young age. The family was willing to have his brain examined for research purposes, not knowing what the possible diagnosis or link to his rugby playing days might be.

After performing dozens of tests on the brain over a period of weeks, the local laboratory's suspicions were aroused that this was unusual pathology, with the abnormal *tau* protein in a distinct pattern, raising the possibility of CTE and so Dr. Stewart was called to consult on the case. After lengthy review and the addition of yet more tests, the diagnosis was confirmed. Dr. Stewart was saddened by the results, and telling me, "My worst fears of CTE in a game I loved were confirmed. Although it was blindingly obvious cases would appear once we started looking, deep down I had hoped to be proved wrong."

Thus this case became the first diagnosis of CTE in someone whose exposure to head injury had come solely through rugby (our team at Boston University had identified CTE in athletes who played rugby, but rugby was not their primary cause of exposure to brain trauma). At the time of this writing, the case is working its way through the legal system as part of a coroner's inquest, so there are no further details, but that didn't stop the news from sending shockwaves through the sport.

The news broke in August, 2013, and the story quickly went global. Following in the footsteps of the NFL, the members of the international medical leadership of the rugby world minimized the connection to the sport. Dr. Simon Kemp, medical director of the Rugby Football Union in England, told the *Daily Mail,* "We understand that there is no proven causal relationship between head injuries sustained while playing rugby union and the reported cases of CTE and early onset dementia."[134]

I was surprised by this reaction, as it appeared rugby leadership had not learned from the mistakes of the NFL. In 2007, in the early days of modern CTE research, the NFL made similar statements, but beginning in 2009, in the face of additional evidence as well as public pressure, the NFL softened their position. Despite the about-face, the NFL was sued by more than 4,500 former players and their families for, in part, being dishonest and misleading about the dangers associated with brain trauma from concussions. In August, 2013, the NFL and the plaintiffs announced that they had agreed in principal to a $765 million settlement to compensate players who suffered from neurological diseases that could be attributed to brain trauma.

Part of the problem, and the reason there is a debate, is that we have imperfect information. Both sides of the debate have to base their decisions on limited knowledge, partially because CTE research was neglected for so long. In examining the limited information, there are some things that we know for certain. Potentially the most important data is that no one has ever been diagnosed with CTE without being exposed to extraordinary brain trauma. Through the end of 2013, not a single researcher around the world has claimed to find CTE in someone that never had single or multiple brain injuries.

An additional important piece of evidence is that there is no other variable that links the diagnosed CTE population. That population now includes not just athletes and military veterans but also victims of abuse, an epileptic, a circus clown, and three developmentally disabled persons who deliberately, repetitively banged their heads against surfaces. No one has put forth a reasonable hypothesis for another causative factor. At this point, it cannot be drugs, alcohol, or lifestyle, and it is increasingly unlikely we'll stumble across a magic genetic connection or environmental hazard.

Therefore, the current data implies causation, but does not prove it to the highest standards of medical evidence. Therefore, to say there is "no proven causal relationship between head injuries sustained while playing rugby union and the reported cases of CTE," as Dr. Kemp did, is technically accurate. However, I do not think it is responsible, unless one adds the caveat that, "while not proven, all evidence points to a causative relationship."

Casting doubt upon "proven" causal relationships is an old tactic that was expertly deployed by the cigarette industry in defending against the connection with lung cancer and heart disease. For CTE, "demonstrating cause and effect" to the highest level of medical evidence is likely impossible. To reach the highest standards, we would have to take a group of identical twin babies and divide one sibling from each set into two groups. One group would get hit in the head over their lifetime, and the other group would not. If we controlled for every other variable, we'd have a perfect study. Any study short of that will always allow a critic to cast doubt that the connection is not yet proven.

To be fair, I can't be sure Dr. Kemp didn't add any caveats to his statement, and the reporter chose not to print it. After a decade in the field, and having met nearly all the critics in person, we aren't as far apart scientifically as it appears in the media. Nearly every critic who is demonized in the press is a person who has dedicated his or her career to sports safety and honestly believes he or she is handling the information appropriately. Our disagreements are usually on the strength of the evidence, the urgency of the issue, and how we talk to the public about the information we have.

Part of the reason Dr. Kemp may have felt confident in making his statement is that he was not basing it on his own research. He was quoting the *Consensus Statement on Concussion in Sport* from the 4th International Conference on Concussion in Sport held in Zurich, Switzerland in November, 2012. Since 2001, many of the world's experts have gotten together to issue consensus statements on sports concussion policy – in Vienna in 2001, Prague in 2005, Zurich in 2008, and Zurich again in 2012.

These meetings, and the publications that always follow, have been critically important in achieving major policy breakthroughs. The policy to no longer return athletes to play the same day of a concussion, a standard today, was first recommended in 2008 by these experts, and they were the first major group to say it. Actually, that is not entirely true – the Statement only recommended youth players not return the same day, but wrote, "Occasionally in adult athletes, there may be return to play on the same day as the injury." North American sports quickly ignored that recommendation, partially due to public pressure, as there was little evidence adult brains are so different from youth brains.

The Zurich statements have made similar odd statements when it comes to other issues that cover professional athletes. Along with drawing the somewhat arbitrary line between return to play of adults and children, they have made curious statements about the long-term consequences of brain trauma. In the 2012 statement, CTE was given all of one paragraph in a twelve page document, despite the explosion of research and data in the field! The entire statement read, "Clinicians need to be mindful of the potential for long-term problems in the management of all athletes. However, it was agreed that chronic traumatic encephalopathy (CTE) represents a distinct tauopathy with an unknown incidence in athletic populations. It was further agreed that a cause and effect relationship has not as yet been demonstrated between CTE and concussions or exposure to contact sports. At present, the interpretation of causation in the modern CTE case studies should proceed cautiously. It was also recognised that it is important to address the fears of parents/athletes from media pressure related to the possibility of CTE."

As you can see, CTE was played down, and their statement 'that a cause and effect relationship has not as yet been demonstrated between CTE and concussions' is being parroted worldwide by professional organizations. To provide some background on the meeting, the organizations that host and fund the meeting are Fédération Internationale de Football Association (FIFA), the International Olympic Commission (IOC), the International Rugby Board (IRB), and the International Ice Hockey Federation (IIHF). It is actually held at FIFA headquarters. Those groups have significant influence in which experts are invited and asked to sign on to the Statement. There are no player associations or advocacy groups formally involved.

Given their history and structure, I can't help but question what was behind the Zurich group's perspective on CTE. If the US based National Football League & National Hockey League held a conference in 2012 that claimed, not only is there no cause and effect, but also told doctors it was important to address the fear of CTE caused by media "pressure," I think Americans would recognize the massive conflict of interest.

So far, the conflict of interest inherent in that "consensus" statement on CTE has been questioned more often privately than publicly. It was also not a true "consensus" statement, as the CTE language was vigorously opposed by Dr. Robert Cantu, one of a handful of doctors that was an author of all four statements, and he was not alone.

The IRB has also expressed annoyance at the CTE issue. The IRB medical director, Dr. Martin Raftery, wrote an editorial on behalf of the IRB for the British Journal of Sports Medicine, which was published October 4, 2013.[135] In the opening paragraph, he wrote, "The public debate regarding the link between CTE and head injuries in sport is emotive as well as distracting. The media focus has been positive in that it has raised public awareness of concussion but the same media focus could have negative consequences by

- Reducing sports participation and undermining the health benefits of exercise
- Forcing sports to adopt hastily developed and evidence deficient risk management strategies"

150

It's always amazing to me when a medical leader disparages the lack of evidence on CTE in one sentence and then makes statements with zero evidence, like CTE hysteria could be "Reducing sports participation and undermining the health benefits of exercise". Just so everyone is on the same page, no cause and effect relationship between CTE awareness and declining sports participation has been demonstrated.

To address the concerns raised, I predict that, rather than turning athletes into couch potatoes, awareness about concussions will push more athletes into lower risk sports. Our message is that sports and exercise have many benefits, but we have yet to discover a single health benefit associated with brain trauma.

Regarding the complaint that sports are being "forced" to adopt "hastily developed" strategies, that claim speaks less to media pressure and more to the neglect of sports to appropriately address the risk of CTE. Sports have been on the clock since Dr. Harrison Martland's 1928 "Punch Drunk" article and have had 85 years to conduct CTE research and make any of the changes sports are scrambling to make now. In 1928, Martland quoted a 1927 paper that said, "It is no longer possible to say that 'concussion is an essentially transient state which does not comprise any evidence of structural cerebral injury.' Not only is there actual cerebral injury in cases of concussion but in a few instances complete resolution does not occur, and there is a strong likelihood that secondary degenerative changes develop." [136] We have made shockingly little progress since then, despite Martland's call to action: "It is the duty of our profession to establish the existence or non-existence of punch drunk by preparing accurate statistical data as to its incidence, careful neurologic examinations of fighters thought to be punch drunk, and careful histologic examinations of the brains of those who have died."

Rugby leadership has already begun distancing itself from its comments for most of 2013. When Dr. Stewart went public with his CTE case, the IRB began toning down their comments, and in mid-November, Dr. Raftery issued a new statement on the importance of concussion care and said, "CTE is a form of dementia, and there are studies about boxers and American football players who have suffered repetitive head injuries, so we recognise that there might be a potential link."[137]

It was rewarding to see the IRB finally move toward a more nuanced statement. They were already making an effort to change the culture of concussions in sports by holding conferences, developing education programs, and continually reviewing the rules. They have even named a new advisory committee that includes Dr. Cantu and Dr. Stewart as two of its four members. However, culture change truly begins with being honest with the players about the risk. Give them informed consent, and let them play a role in changing the game. If players are not told about the risk of long-term consequences from brain trauma, why would they change their behavior?

The IRB's timing was good, as another rugby CTE case was about to be unveiled by our research team, and this one had a name. The family of Barry "Tizza" Taylor, a former professional rugby player and coach in Australia, had donated his brain for research after watching him suffer through dementia. It began in 1993 at age 57 with memory problems and erratic behavior, interlaced with outbursts of anger, and progressed over 20 years. Taylor began playing rugby at age 10; He played for 23 years, playing 235 games for the Manly Club.

The man responsible for getting Tizza's brain examined was a former player of his, Peter FitzSimons. After retiring from professional rugby, FitzSimons became a columnist, a best-selling author, and television reporter. Fascinated with and concerned about our CTE research, Australia's Channel Seven *Sunday Night* sent him to Boston to interview our team, resulting in a well-produced feature.

FitzSimon's also interviewed a former Australian Rules football player who is playing a Ted Johnson-like role in Australia by coming forward with his symptoms while still alive. Greg Williams, a very successful pro, now suffers from severe memory problems at 49. During the televised interview, with his wife beside him, Williams admitted he didn't remember where he went on his honeymoon, and couldn't remember the middle names of his children. The Australian Football League Players Association has taken notice of the global concussion conversation and by 2013 had already advocated successfully for major changes to the game and a strong educational campaign.

Taken aback by what he found, FitzSimons decided that rather than be a casual observer, he would get involved. Like me with my many concussions, FitzSimons figures he might have a stake in the result of this work. When he heard about Coach Taylor's passing, he was the one that reached out to the family and facilitated the donation, and he was the one that found the doctors at the University of Sydney, where he is a trustee, to retrieve the brain. It was no small feat, and the world owes him a lot for his effort, as I suspect that Tizza Taylor will have a profound impact on the rugby world.

Barry "Tizza" Taylor

Chapter 14: The Most Popular Sport in the World

A sport with considerable brain trauma that has remained under the radar on the concussion discussion is association football, or as we call it in the United States, soccer. (In this section, I will refer to it as football out of respect to my international friends, but in the rest of the book it is soccer). Football is the most popular sport around the world. The *Fédération Internationale de Football Association* (FIFA), the sport's governing body, estimates that over 265 million people play the sport.[138] The concussion issue has been on FIFA's radar for a long time, as evidenced by their involvement in, and now hosting of, the Zurich consensus meeting.

Football is an interesting lens through which to see the concussion problem, because it is a true global sport. Rugby, while global, was exported by the countries of the United Kingdom and thrives in former colonies like South Africa, New Zealand, and Australia, making English the primary language of rugby. Culture change in rugby will be easier than in football, which has ten times as many players and dozens of languages.

This year the Zurich consensus meeting began with a two day session that was open to medical professionals and educators. Anyone in the field was able to sign up online. The most interesting aspect was who attended. If my memory serves me correctly, of about 100 people that chose to attend, the conference announced that nearly all attendees were from either the United States, Western Europe, Canada, Australia, and South Africa. There were only two doctors from all of Asia (Japan), few from Eastern Europe, perhaps one or two from Central and South America, and South Africa was the only country represented in Africa.

154

Concussions do occur in those countries, but for a long list of possible reasons, they are not yet a major part of the emerging world dialogue. I expect that education, wealth, and the sports culture are the likely reasons why the concussion discussion is currently limited to a few regions.

Education plays an obvious role. No one sought medical attention for concussions anywhere just a few short years ago. Now that families are educated in North America, it is standard to see a doctor after a concussion; it is law in some states for youth sports athletes. Because of the jump in volume of patients in the United States seeking concussion care, our Sports Legacy Institute recently launched a directory of dedicated concussion clinics at www.ConcussionClinics.org, and we quickly found that over 500 have popped up in the United States in the past few years.

Wealth also plays a role. Concussion is a first world problem. When resources are limited, and doctors are limited, even if people were educated it would be unlikely that they could afford to seek out medical care for a concussion. With a shortage of doctors, it is far less likely that doctors would specialize in concussion.

The sports culture also plays a role. Contact sports involving repetitive brain trauma are not universally popular. Some cultures have a lower tolerance for youth brain trauma. As a former sociology major, I would love to see this formally investigated, but I can supply only one anecdote. On my Eisenhower Fellowship, I spent a week in Brussels as part of a special European Union visitors program. The other members of my small group included a staffer at the Gates Foundation, a Rosenthal Fellow, and a Turkish professor of economics.

When I told the economist about the work I do, and how it was a struggle to get people to open their minds to a connection between repetitive brain trauma and brain damage, she was surprised. She told me that in Turkey, they have two words - *dayak aptali* and *dayak salagi* – that both mean, loosely translated, "a child who has been beaten in the head so much that they have become an idiot."

The term stems from a push against child abuse by parents, but I can't think of a similar word in the English language that connects IQ and brain trauma, or at least not one that is utilized in the US. I would be curious to see how Turkey would react to children playing American football.

Another reason for the limited worldwide interest in concussion consensus meetings might have has to do with the popularity of sports within those countries. Why individual sports are popular in some places and not in others is beyond the scope of this discussion, but it is interesting to note that the Zurich participant-base was primarily composed of countries where their top three most popular sports included either American football, rugby, or ice hockey.

Outside of the United States, concussion does not yet appear to be a major concern in professional football. The best example of the confusion about modern concussion care occurred in the English Premier League on November 3rd, 2013. Tottenham's goalkeeper Hugo Lloris took a knee to the head from Everton striker Romelu Lukaku. He was clearly knocked unconscious, albeit briefly. The Tottemham medical staff eventually got him to his feet and looked like they were going to simply walk him to the sideline – he was done for the day. Lloris walked slowly and looked to be talking to the medics, perhaps trying to convince them that he was good to play, which concussed athletes often do as they feel the pressure of the game and are trying to make a decision with a malfunctioning brain.

After what seemed to be minutes, Lloris reached the sideline. If he stepped over the line to be formally assessed, he wouldn't be allowed to return. He appeared to realize it, and stopped. At the same time, the manager Andre Villas-Boas came over and spoke to the medics. A few seconds later, Lloris turned heel and ran back to the goal to play. He was left in the game.

After a summer of high profile concussion stories, the London media was now becoming educated on concussions and questioned the coach after the game. Villas-Boas, apparently unaware of appropriate concussion care, told the BBC

"He doesn't remember [the collision] so he lost consciousness. It was a big knock, but he looked composed and ready to continue. Hugo seemed assertive and determined to continue and showed great character and personality. We decided to keep him on based on that. The call always belongs to me."[139]

The fact that the coach has the final word on medical decisions, rather than the doctor, is unacceptable. What's worse, the fact that he thought a concussed Lloris showed "great character and personality" by continuing is unacceptable – it is the kind of language that a teenager remembers when they or their teammate is in the same situation and contributes to preventable brain damage spreading like a virus throughout football.

Luckily, both the media and FIFA attempted to use the case as a teaching moment.[140] FIFA's chief medical officer Jiri Dvorak was unequivocal, saying, "The player should have been substituted. It's a 99% probability that losing consciousness in such an event will result in concussion. We have a slogan: if there is any doubt, keep the player out." Dr. Dvorak rebuffed the coach's statement that Hugo's assertiveness provided evidence he was ready to play, saying, "When he has been knocked unconscious, the player himself may not see the reality."

Dr. Dvorak hinted at the policy problem in the Premier League when he said, "I do not know the details, but I know that the Premier League doctors are extremely good, and I can imagine that the doctor may have recommended he be replaced." Again, Villas-Boas was so unaware of current concussion care that he admitted to the media, "The medical department was giving me signs that the player couldn't carry on because he couldn't remember where he was....It was my call to delay the substitution, you have to make a decision in situations like this. From my knowledge of football he seemed OK to continue." I cannot imagine an American coach making the same statements today and not losing his job.

Football is clearly in need of concussion awareness, as some studies have shown that it has a similar concussion rate to American football. One study of university football players found that over 60% admitted having concussion symptoms during the previous season, but only one of five realized that having those symptoms after an impact was a concussion.[141] Players can take thousands of headers a season. Football must be creating cases of CTE, but it is not discussed.

The fact that there is virtually no CTE discussion in football is surprising, especially considering there is already a proven case in the academic literature and another in the English court system. Geddes and colleagues published a confirmed case of CTE in a 23 year-old amateur football player in 1999. He was said to be a prolific header and also to have suffered one severe brain injury. Perhaps because he was not named, and there is no personal story, it has remained out of sight. [142]

Jeff Astle was a member of England's 1970 World Cup team and beloved player for West Bromwich Albion, playing 361 games and scoring 174 goals.[143] He was a prolific header, and when he died at 59 with dementia in 2002, the coroner ruled "death by industrial disease," concluding, on the review of a neuropathologist, that his dementia was brought on by repetitive heading of the soccer ball. The governing body in England, The Football Association, continues to claim, "There remain conflicting opinions on the possible effects of frequent heading of a football over time."[144]

I am hopeful that the story of Patrick Grange changes that. Patrick was an elite soccer player in the United States (I will revert back to soccer since Patrick was an American). One of the greatest players ever in the state of New Mexico, he played college soccer for the University of Illinois-Chicago as well as the University of New Mexico, where he led the team to the Sweet Sixteen in 2004. After a few years of semi-pro soccer, he officially retired but still played for fun – until one day he noticed his calf was not working.

In 2010, at the age of 28, Patrick was diagnosed with Amyotrophic Lateral Sclerosis, or ALS. ALS is a rapidly progressive, invariably fatal neurological disease that attacks the nerve cells responsible for controlling voluntary muscles. It strikes about 5,000 Americans a year. Most sufferers eventually die of respiratory failure within five years of diagnosis because they can no longer perform the function of breathing. When Patrick was told of his diagnosis by the doctors, his family told us he cried and said, "I don't want to be a burden to my family." He died only 17 months later, at the age of 29. He was the youngest person ever diagnosed with ALS in New Mexico.

A few short years ago, no one would have connected Patrick's death to brain trauma or CTE. But Dr. Ann McKee had changed that in 2010. The first former athlete to learn of the connection was the American football player Kevin Turner. Kevin Turner was a hard-hitting fullback for the Philadelphia Eagles and New England Patriots after playing for the Alabama Crimson Tide. He retired after the 1999 season and struggled with drug abuse and gambling problems, eventually losing his money and getting divorced. He once told me that he nearly called me in 2008 as he was learning about CTE because he wondered if that could have contributed to him going from a meticulous, focused, and vice-free player to his current out-of-control state. But he never called.

Two years later he finally got up the courage to call, but now he had a bigger problem. "Have you ever heard of a connection between Lou Gehrig's disease and brain trauma? I was just diagnosed with it," Kevin asked. I told him, "Actually we are about to publish that Dr. McKee did find a connection."

Athletes in some contact sports have been suffering ALS at a higher rate than the normal population, but the cause had been unclear. Dr. McKee was curious as to why, and asked me to get the brain of Wally Hilgenberg who died in 2008 at the age of sixty-four of ALS after winning four Super Bowls for the Minnesota Vikings. When she looked at his brain, she was shocked to find he didn't have any normal pattern of disease that she had seen in other ALS patients. Instead, he simply had advanced CTE, the CTE had spread to and was severe in parts of the brain that linked to his ALS symptoms. ALS is a poorly understood disease, and while 5 to 10 percent of cases are believed to have genetic causes, the other 90 to 95 percent have an unknown trigger. ALS is one of a group of diseases that affect motor neurons, and includes all types of what is termed Motor Neuron Disease (MND). ALS is a name for clinical symptoms, and not the name for a specific type of pathology. There are likely dozens of pathologies that cause different motor neuron diseases that are all called ALS.

Dr. McKee then studied Eric Scoggins, a American football player for the University of Southern California and briefly for the San Francisco 49ers, who died at forty-nine of ALS. She found the same thing. Next, she studied a professional boxer who died of ALS. She concluded that the cause of his ALS appeared to be related to CTE as well, and she published a paper explaining the link.

Dr. David Dodick, Professor of Neurology at the Mayo School of Medicine in Rochester, Minnesota, explains the connection between CTE and ALS more clearly; "How can repeated trauma to the head give rise to a disorder like ALS, for example, which is a spinal cord disorder? This abnormal protein that accumulates can spread from neuron to neuron, from the upper parts of the brain, be distributed throughout the central nervous system, including the spinal cord, leading to ALS."

Dr. David Dodick

Dr. McKee essentially discovered a new disease, which she named CTE-MND, and her findings may account for the increased risk of ALS symptoms in people with a history of brain trauma. In 2012, the connection that Dr. McKee found pathologically was finally supported epidemiologically. First, a well-controlled study from Italy found that patients reporting three or more traumatic injuries in their lifetime, or even the previous ten years, were more than three times more likely to develop ALS.[145] Later that year, a study was published finding that NFL players who played at least five seasons between 1959 and 1988 had a four times greater risk of dying from both Alzheimer's disease and ALS.[146] (The authors attributed the Alzheimer's spike to misdiagnosed CTE).

Patrick Grange's family was aware of Dr. McKee's discovery, and I was able to work with them to obtain Patrick's brain for study. Patrick was diagnosed with Stage II CTE by Dr. McKee, the second of four pathological stages. In fact, he had the most advanced case of CTE that we had seen in someone in his twenties – more advanced than any American football player, even more advanced than Derek Boogaard, the enforcer for the New York Rangers of the National Hockey League, who had participated in 174 fights in professional hockey and an unknown number prior.

How could a soccer player have such advanced disease? We don't know, but it might have something to do with all the headers he took over the years. His mother Michelle remembers, "We had a net in the backyard, and at three (years old), Pat was throwing that ball up and hitting it into the net, at three. And I'm saying all day. On the five year old team, to him, that was really fun. He thought doing headers was hot shot."

He was known for his aggressive heading throughout his career. His brother Ryan remembers, "Pat used to score a lot of goals with his head. I can't say that I've had any severe concussions. Maybe minor ones, but I've avoided trying to put myself in that position, really. I didn't score any goals in college. And that maybe is the difference between getting a concussion and not. Pat scored a lot of goals, and you have to put your head on the line."

Pat's high school coach, Lucien Starzynski, remembers Pat suffering a lot of brain trauma. When Lucien was interviewed for the *Head Games* documentary, he even taught Pat's father Mike about Pat's concussion history.

LUCIEN: Do you know how many concussions Pat had?

MIKE: He had one.

LUCIEN: He had one at Gallup. Do you remember when he fell in the turf that one year?

MIKE: No.

LUCIEN: And he hit the ground, and I remember when he fell and didn't brace himself with his arms.

MIKE: Really? Didn't know that at all.

LUCIEN: Yeah, concussed. But I didn't know back then.

MIKE: Nobody did.

LUCIEN: And knowing what I know now, I put Pat in on a concussion that day.

Coach Starzynski believes Pat's techniques may have caused additional brain trauma just playing the game. "He had that combination of incredible technique, and... this sort of reckless quality to him, where he sort of plays without fear. He always said, 'If you hit the ground hard, and you get fouled, the referee is more likely to call the foul.' So when he would fall sometimes, he wouldn't break his fall with his arm."

Pat never blamed soccer, and loved the game until the end. His mother Michelle remembers, "You know (with ALS) everything goes. Pat couldn't talk. We had a board with all the alphabet letters and we had yes and no. We knew it was coming, we knew it was gonna be that day or the next day, and the TV was not on, and I said to our nurse, 'This is probably the first time you've been here when soccer hasn't been on,' and he said, 'Yeah, it is. That's really strange.' And

I said, 'God, maybe Pat wants it on,' so we held up the board, we said, 'Pat, do you want soccer on?' And he looked at the board, and he looked at yes, so we flipped the TV on, and soccer was on when Pat passed."

Patrick Grange

The vast majority of concussions in soccer occur from heading the ball or the act of attempting to head the ball, in which a player's head collides with another head, an elbow, a shoulder, or the ground. Cindy Parlow Cone knows that all too well. Cindy was the youngest soccer player to ever win an Olympic gold medal and a World Championship, at the age of seventeen. Her first diagnosed concussion was in 2001 while playing for the Women's United Soccer Association. She remembers, "My poor parents were watching the film at home, and I was going up for a header, and one of my own teammates hits me in the temple. You just see my limp body fall to the ground."

Cindy's memory of that event is still fuzzy. "I don't remember getting hit. I remember watching the ball come to my head and I was trying to time it correctly and then the next thing I remember is everyone standing over me seeing if I was okay. No one knew that I was knocked out because I wasn't knocked out for very long."

In 2001 people didn't take concussions as seriously, so Cindy continued to play. "I actually continued to play until half time and then there was only three or four minutes left to the half and I remember I couldn't feel my fingertips. I knew something was wrong so immediately I went to the trainer and was like, 'something's wrong with me.'"

Cindy's second diagnosed concussion happened in 2003 in the World Cup consolation game. Cindy recalls, "I ended up getting hit in the jaw and get spun around and land. Abby Wambach falls on top of me. She actually wakes me up, and then I continue to play. Julie Foudy, who was one of our captains, asked me what run I'm making on the corner kick. She's like, 'Hey, Cindy, can you make the slot run?'

"In a high-pitch noise I go, 'Yeahhh.' 'Cindy you okay? And I go, 'Yeahhh.' She's like, 'Can you make it to half?' I just answer—and this is all from her because obviously I don't remember any of this—'Sure, what half is it?' She runs to the sidelines tells them to sub me out, and I'm subbed out after that and I had a lot of symptoms post that. I still don't remember the entire day, leading up to the game, the night after the game, none of it. I just remember waking up in my hotel room, looking at my parents with this very worried look on their face."

Cindy was never the same after those concussions. "After that every time we'd do heading in practice or if we had a really hard header in the game I would see stars. Some people consider that concussion. If you count all those we're talking triple digits,"

To this day Cindy still struggles with those concussions. She confided, "I'm going to worry my family now. My parents don't need to know all this, but right now I have frequent headaches, and a lot of jaw pain and neck pain. I'll be driving down the road and forget where I am, and people say, 'Well, oh, that's normal, everyone does that every once and a while.' But when you do it all the time, it's a problem. I always keep my GPS on, even when I'm just driving around Chapel Hill with roads that I know by heart just because every once in a while I'll freak out and not know where I am."

Cindy Parlow-Cone

What happened to Cindy is happening to girls around the world. Personally, I think soccer is a beautiful sport. Without heading, soccer is very safe for the brain relative to other sports. The head medical officer for FIFA appears to be willing to lead soccer to a safer place. I think that begins by having a global discussion about at what age to introduce headers and how, once it is introduced, we can set limits for amateur players.

And that leads to a larger discussion – knowing what we know now, what should we do?

Part 3: Solving the Concussion Crisis

Chapter 15: Updating the Science

When I look at sports now, I see a blank slate. We created all of these sports without incorporating our current knowledge of the consequences of brain trauma. The rules of all sports are frequently changed. In the case of professional sports, they are sometimes changed in the middle of season. Therefore, I expect significant changes to sports to make them safer. The hard question is: how far do we go? Our challenge is this: how do we reform sports to a point where we can be confident that children will only walk away from sports with the positive lessons sports teach and not with permanent brain damage or disease. Sports are important and have many redeeming qualities. However, there are zero redeeming qualities to brain trauma and brain disease.

There is no clear answer, so we have to make decisions based on the best information we have today. Therefore, before we get to changes that I propose, we should review our current knowledge. Thanks to all the pioneering research performed by our team and many other groups, it has become clear that the concussion crisis extends far beyond football and into all sports, both genders, and all ages. The finding of CTE in so many former athletes is a clear wake-up call that it is time to update science, sports, and policy. This section begins with a word of warning. Some like to call the brain "the last frontier," and the truth is that we don't really understand the brain well. Every change we make will have unseen, unknown, unpredictable, and sometimes immeasurable consequences.

166

Policies that we think are safe now we could find out in the future are not. To put brain trauma in perspective, when I speak to groups of parents and coaches, I always ask, "How many of you have been hit in the head hard *one time* in the last year?"

Consistently I get one or two hands raised. Then I ask, "Has anyone been hit in the head hard over three times in the last year?" Usually no one raises their hand. I then contrast that by showing them published data revealing that their children take hundreds or even thousands of blows to the head a year in the name of sport. Outside of sports and abuse, getting hit in the head on a regular basis is not a normal part of life. Therefore, it is very unlikely that the human brain evolved to handle this trauma well.

Most adults do not voluntarily engage in activities with significant brain trauma. When they do, we usually have to pay them a lot of money, like in professional sports. Only kids will do it for free.

Sometimes I wonder if we should step away from adult-designed sports for children and see what they came up with themselves. I can imagine that in this kid-controlled game, the first child who took 1,000 blows to the head might raise their hand and say, "Hey guys, how about we play something else?" When this is all taken into consideration, my gut tells me that hitting children in the head on a regular basis, for any reason, is probably a bad idea. Next we will review the latest research on what can go wrong.

Post-Concussion Syndrome

Post-concussion syndrome is a devastating disorder. I believe that I no longer deal with PCS, but I had a very rough time overcoming it. My last concussion was in June 2003, but PCS was a daily issue for me for five years, through June 2008. My sleepwalking, officially known as REM behavior disorder, was one of the worst parts. I had to be sedated every night so that when the dream behavior would occur, I didn't have the power to get up or do something violent to myself or others.

However, the medication was so powerful that it interrupted normal sleep patterns, meaning no matter how much I slept, I felt tired. I needed to get off it, but I was scared to death of what might happen the first time I acted out without the medication. It was nerve-wracking, but after three and a half years, I was finally able to wean off the medication, and I haven't needed it since.

For me, the headaches were the last lingering symptom. It took nearly five years for a headache to not be a daily or near daily occurrence. Unfortunately I'm still not, and never will be, 100 percent. I get bad headaches whenever I "over-exercise," as I call it. That means any time I go over 85 percent exertion, meaning any sprinting, heavy weight-lifting, or challenging myself at sports or in the gym. Sometimes I overexert in pickup basketball because it's a close game or a tough opponent. More frequently it is in an exercise class I take at the gym. Although the class has fat guys and women twenty years older than I am, I'm usually the only person stepping out to lower my heart rate or quitting early because I've gone over my limit and have developed a headache. It's depressing, to say the least.

Unfortunately there have been few major scientific breakthroughs with post-concussion syndrome since 2006. It still appears clear from empirical evidence that athletes are more likely to suffer PCS if they return too soon or suffer "too many" concussions.

NHL star Sidney Crosby of the Pittsburgh Penguins may be the most high-profile recent example of how a mishandled concussion can put a career at risk. In the Winter Classic on January 1, 2011, Crosby took a shot to the head from the Washington Capitals' David Steckel. He got up slowly and awkwardly but returned to the game. He was not diagnosed with a concussion, although it is unclear if he reported symptoms or even was evaluated for concussion.

168

On January 5, only four days later, Crosby played against Tampa Bay and took another shot to the head. The next day it was announced by the team that he had a concussion and was expected to miss at least a week. On January 28, he was cleared for light workouts, but symptoms returned. He didn't play a game again until November 21, almost ten months later, but still scored two goals in his comeback. On December 7, the team announced he'd miss two more games as a precaution after taking a big hit, but it was clear that hit brought back symptoms and he missed over a month. Eventually he returned and finished the 2012 season.

I like to use Crosby's example because it illustrates not only the complexity of PCS, but also how helpless we are to "fix it" at this point in time. The best player in the NHL couldn't play for nearly all of 2011, which cost the Penguins and the NHL a lot of money, but the failure to recover quickly was not for lack of trying. Crosby saw just about every specialist out there, as well as laypeople with unproven theories. PCS remains without a simple and effective diagnostic tool, and is difficult to treat.

PCS is in fact more and more treated like a diagnosis of exclusion, meaning that doctors work hard to try to rule out other disorders. Non-PCS disorders could be contributing to PCS, so I always instruct PCS victims to fight back and never give up. There might be a therapy out there that allows you to make your life more livable. Causes of symptoms worth exploring:

1. A neck injury that occurred at the same time of the brain injury.
2. Hormonal disorders. The pituitary gland sits just underneath the brain, and trauma can damage the tissue.
3. Sleep disorders. Sleep apnea, especially for big guys, can cause cognitive problems and fatigue.
4. Depression. Injury or losing one's identity and support structure can cause depression, which can cause a range of symptoms, including cognitive problems.

169

5. Migraine. Although I am concerned when a preexisting or new migraine condition is cited as the cause of PCS headaches, migraine can complicate PCS.

6. Vestibular problems. Sometimes trauma can cause balance issues that are centered in the brain, but also in the inner ear. Therapy can improve symptoms.

7. Exercise. Lack of exercise can cause depression. However, exercise while recovering from a brain injury can cause serious problems. Some researchers are exploring mild exercise to help PCS victims recover and feel better.

In no way do I encourage anyone to pursue any specific PCS treatment. I am not a doctor. However, it may be worth exploring these possibilities with your doctor.

If everything else is ruled out, then you might just have to wait out the symptoms. Many of us have done it, and can testify that there is a light at the end of the tunnel. You'll reach the end of the tunnel, too.

There is no question PCS is a real problem and in some cases cannot be solved during an athlete's short career window. Many famous athletes have retired due to PCS since I wrote the first edition of Head Games, and one I have gotten to know well is former NHL star Keith Primeau. Keith retired in late 2006 due to ongoing symptoms after a fifteen-year career with the Detroit Red Wings, Hartford Whalers, Carolina Hurricanes, and Philadelphia Flyers. Keith never recovered from his fourth diagnosed concussion, but he knows he had many more. He said, "I know that over the course of my career that there were many more times that I was concussed, and not only concussed, but played through concussion-like symptoms. But I really only began documenting it in 1997."[147]

Keith Primeau

Keith fought valiantly through his symptoms. "For the better part of a year I tried to put myself in a position to return to play, I continued to work out, as I said, the entire time. Even in the spring of 2006, after the October '05 concussion, I started practicing with the team, heading into the playoffs. But it became a distraction. I stopped practicing with the team only to go back to my own workouts again."

Keith continued fighting and training through symptoms all summer, and when camp started again in August, he was still hoping that he'd wake up one day and feel fine. After speaking with his athletic trainer about his symptoms, the athletic trainer said, "Keith, we applaud your courage and we thank you for your efforts, but I'll never give you permission to play again." At that point Keith felt his career was over.

Six years after his last concussion, Keith still suffers through symptoms, and he is clearly frustrated. "Right now I'm in a good place, but over the course of the last two years, I have been able to say that I'm in a good place only to regress back to not a very good state," he said. "Most constant symptoms for me are headaches and head pressure. There's times where I get extremely fatigued, irritable, light-headed ... sometimes difficulty with vision."

The bigger fear that people like Keith and I live with is that the PCS puts us at greater risk for long-term problems. Certainly some people never recover from the acute symptoms of PCS, and that is likely due to some unrecognized, but permanent, brain damage.

The greatest concern is that we have developed CTE due to our brain trauma. We now know that CTE is far more widespread than originally believed and that players like Keith or myself are in the highest-risk category. Keith told me, "I know that I've damaged my brain, I don't know what my long-term prognosis is. What does scare me is that when I do begin to deteriorate it's rapid. There's no question that I believe I'm a different person today than I was pre-concussions, from many different fronts. My mannerisms. My personality. My habits. My emotions."

We will likely someday find out if Keith has CTE, as Keith has joined me in pledging to donate his brain to our brain bank when he passes. Most of what we've learned about the long-term effects has come from these families, and the respect and appreciation I have for them is immeasurable. Keith feels the same way, saying, "I applaud the courage of those families who have taken the initiative to donate their loved one's brains to science. It's invaluable, and that's the biggest reason I donated my brain to science… Over the course of time it will make a difference."

Chronic Traumatic Encephalopathy

CTE Research

As of 2014, our understanding of CTE has grown dramatically. The list of unknowns is still much longer than the knowns. We don't yet know how or why it starts, how it progresses, how to diagnose it in living people, or how to treat it.

But we do know what it looks like pathologically, and based on what we have learned there, we are getting close to diagnosing it. The main goal of this research is to find a way to treat it, meaning prevent it, stopping it, slowing it down, or reversing it. Unfortunately it will take many steps to get there.

Thanks to all the brain donors of the past, today we can describe CTE as a progressive degenerative disease of the brain found in athletes and others with a history of repetitive brain trauma. This trauma, which includes multiple concussions and sub-concussive injuries, triggers progressive degeneration of the brain tissue, including the buildup of an abnormal protein called tau.

The tau protein is a structural element of tiny tunnels, called microtubules, in the axon. These tunnels are the transport system of the cell, like a highway or railroad. With diseases like Alzheimer's disease and CTE, we believe that tau malfunctions. It stops functioning normally and the tunnels crumble, meaning nothing that signals or molecules can't get through, and the cell starts malfunctioning. With enough malfunctioning cells, the brain starts behaving differently, and usually in a negative direction. CTE is a visually striking disease. When Dr. McKee stains the tissue using an antibody that turns tau brown, we see the actual remnants of the abnormal tau as strands and clumps of these neurofibrillary tangles.

The knowledge that we have has come from the now over 180 former athletes and veterans whose brains reside at our brain bank. Sports Legacy Institute supports this specific research program by both raising awareness of the program and the breakthrough findings, but also by simply honoring their memories. We call our athletes Legacy Donors, because we believe that with their brain donation they have left a legacy that the sports and medical worlds are only beginning to appreciate. These Legacy Donors are showing us the path to a safer future, and I just hope we listen.

The disease appears to be progressive within the brain, which is correlated with a progression of symptoms. When tau initially starts falling apart and that first tangle forms, the individual won't experience any symptoms. But like Alzheimer's disease, it is believed that once tau begins malfunctioning, it has the ability to transmit itself from cell to cell, spreading throughout the brain. It appears to start around blood vessels and at the depths of the sulci, which are the valleys on the surface of the brain. In football players, tau consistently first appears behind the forehead in the frontal lobes—technically the dorso-lateral prefrontal cortex. From there, it appears to move to adjacent cortices, and eventually to the medial temporal lobes, specifically the hippocampus, which is the area of the brain involved in learning new things, and the amygdala, which is involved in the fight or flight response and emotional regulation.

It is no surprise, then, that the symptoms one tends to see in CTE victims include loss of short-term memory, emotion and impulse control, and executive function disorders. Symptoms of CTE can begin months, years, or even decades after the last concussion or the end of active athletic involvement. Other common symptoms include confusion, impaired judgment, paranoia, aggression, depression, and eventually, progressive dementia.

A recent study by my colleague, Dr. Bob Stern at Boston University, found an interesting pattern while reviewing the clinical symptoms of 36 former football players diagnosed with CTE post-mortem.[148] He found that there appeared to be two distinct patterns to showing symptoms. Of those that appeared to have CTE symptoms, 11 first showed problems with short-term memory, with an average age of onset of 59. Surprisingly, the vast majority, 22 of them, showed behavioral or mood changes before showing memory problems, with their average age of onset at only 36 years old. The behavioral group had a rough experience – 86% were described as depressed, and 68% percent became physically violent.

First called "punch drunk" syndrome and dementia pugilistica, it was first described in 1928 by New Jersey pathologist Harrison Martland in the *Journal of the American Medical Association* in which he noted symptoms such as slowed movement, tremors, confusion, and speech problems typical of the condition. [149] In 1973, a group led by J. A. Corsellis described the typical neuropathological findings of CTE after post-mortem examinations of the brains of fifteen former boxers. The term chronic traumatic encephalopathy appears in the medical literature as early as 1966 and is now the preferred term.

When I started working with Dr. McKee, she decided to search through the medical literature to find all cases of CTE so we could formally wrap our heads around what was already known. Shockingly, through 2009 there were only 49 cases described in all medical literature, 39 of which concerned boxers. [150] Many thought this was a disease exclusive to boxers, although cases have been identified in a battered wife, an epileptic, two mentally challenged individuals with head-banging behavior, and an Australian circus performer who was also involved in what the medical report authors referred to as "dwarf-throwing."

There was so little work done on CTE that we realized the BU CSTE was the world's first research center dedicated to studying the subject. It's a shame that it has taken so long to start looking at sports outside of boxing and distressing how frequently we are finding the disease in athletes who have played a lot of contact sports. 52 of the first 54 former NFL players have been found to be suffering from CTE, along with every former college football player but one. We are four for four in former NHL players. Recently, while publishing the first named rugby and soccer players, we also published the first former Major League Baseball player, Ryan Freel, who had at least ten concussions both in and outside of baseball, and took his own life at 36 years-old.

These are biased samples, but we can't quantify how biased they are. The only random study ever to look at the risk of CTE symptoms in living athletes took a sample of boxers in the United Kingdom between the ages of 30 and 49. They found a correlation between clinical symptoms of CTE and career length. [151]

Years of Experience	% with CTBI
Fewer than 5 years	1%
6 to 10 years	14%
More than 10 years	25%

Other research on boxers found the risk of CTE increases with the number of matches, a history of knockouts (KOs) or technical knockouts (TKOs), punches taken, or simply being a bad boxer. [152] [153] [154] [155]

People have interesting cultural reactions to CTE. Many have dismissed the tragedy of CTE, saying that the athletes knew what they were getting into. I believe that is why CTE has been so poorly studied. People thought of it as a boxers' disease, and that if you punch people in the head all day trying to knock them out as they do the same to you, you should expect brain-related problems.

I don't believe athletes have ever fully understood what they are "getting themselves into." Until 2009, the NFL still told athletes there was no evidence of long-term problems from concussions. We were also putting kids back into sports the same day they had concussions, so it's doubtful that adults really appreciated the consequences. But now at least some athletes are informed of the risk, including the NFL players who have read the poster in the locker room. But this does not include NCAA athletes, as the NCAA has virtually the same poster hanging in locker rooms, except they *removed all language concerning long-term consequences like depression and dementia.*

Now that athletes are informed about CTE, it has changed the moral discussion: it is now a personal choice to play because players have informed consent. It will seem less tragic if in fifty years a former NFL player develops CTE. He will have been fully informed and decided to make a trade of brain cells for money, a trade many adults are willing to make.

We allow adults to do dangerous jobs for a living, and the primary ethical questions are whether or not they understand the risks and whether or not appropriate precautions are taken to make that risk acceptable. We ask police officers to chase criminals with guns; we allow fireman to run into burning buildings; we allow members of the military to go to war; we allow commercial fishermen to work out on the open water and miners to work underground because of informed consent.

Informed consent does not exist for children, however, and that is something we haven't fully wrapped our heads around as a society. By every standard we have, we cannot say children know what they are getting into when they sign up for contact sports. There is no legal construct in the country that assumes a seventeen-year-old child has the same mental capacity as an adult. We now know that an individual's frontal lobes aren't fully mature until one's twenties. We don't let children vote, smoke, own firearms, serve in the military, or be tried for crimes as an adult.

Yet we ask our children what sports they want to play. Then we have them play the same sports as adults, by basically the same rules, even though we now consider those games dangerous for adults. That concerns me, as it has become clear that there is likely no limit to how young CTE can start.

Owen Thomas was born to Reverend Tom Thomas and Reverend Katherine Brearley and grew up in Allentown, Pennsylvania. His father remembers, "When he was born, he came out just screaming and, and so much so that he had two veins that were just standing out. Red hair. The doctor said, 'He's a Viking.'" Owen was from a football family. His father played at the University of Virginia, his grandfather at Millersville, his older brother at East Stroudsburg University.

Owen was invited to play football for the University of Pennsylvania and was elected captain of the football team after his junior spring. Two weeks later he hanged himself in his off-campus apartment. To this day no one understands why. There were no stressors in his life that one could point to. The day before he committed suicide he called his mother to wish her happy birthday, a voice-mail she retains to this day. In the last message Owen left his mother he said, "Hey Mom, it's Owen. Just wanted to wish you a happy birthday, tell you I love you. I'll try back later, hopefully your phone will be turned on. All right Mom, love you, bye!" The next day he was gone.

I reached out to his family to inquire about brain donation, and in this case I felt a special obligation. Owen and I were both defensive linemen in the Ivy League, and it felt as if I had lost one of my own. When I reached his mother she was driving between funeral homes. I asked the question that I hate to ask, and she told me that I wouldn't find anything because Owen never had a diagnosed concussion. I told her that I hoped that was true, because nearly all the brains we had of football players tested positive for CTE. I would love to have a negative brain. Owen's parents agreed, believing that Owen would have wanted to contribute to making the game safer.

I didn't know if Owen's brain would show CTE, but I was confident he'd had concussions in his life but didn't report them. Owen started playing football at age nine, and very few linemen don't get a ding over twelve years. His brother Morgan, who was two years older and played on the same high school team as Owen, confirmed my suspicion, saying, "If we did have like a head ringer, we would not go report that to the trainer. We'd get up and shake it off. And just get back out there and play. We just always wanted to play. And we always wanted to help the team."

Morgan now knows that he's had concussions, although at the time of the interview, after a college football career, he still didn't know the definition. "I've gotten a head ringer. Quote unquote. You get up and like everything's like a different color at first. And then it takes you like a couple minutes to kind of get back in focus. I don't know if that's a concussion. I've never had a concussion where I was pulled out of football."

The test results that came back from Dr. McKee's lab shocked everyone: not only was Owen the second-youngest athlete ever diagnosed with CTE, but he had fifteen or twenty distinct areas of his brain that were already affected and, in essence, rotting away. Owen's case was a big deal, as it was not only that of the first active college football player but also gave us a window into how the disease progresses.

As Dr. McKee studied more and more young brains, it became clear, as she had suspected, that the disease starts in very tiny amounts, and then, for some unknown reason, continues to spread. We haven't found teenage brains that have the widespread tau of older brains, and we have not found elderly athletes with tiny amounts of CTE changes, although there is great variation in the disease. As Dr. McKee theorizes, "If [Owen] had lived longer, the disease gradually would have spread out into the neighboring cortex. Once the fire has started, it just goes on its own without any additional insult."

The question of whether or not CTE contributed to his suicide will forever be unknown. It is impossible to connect the disease to any specific behavior, but that does not mean a connection is out of the question. Owen's mother, Katherine Brearley, remembers, "When the results came through I can't say it was a relief, but it was like, oh my gosh, there is the reason, right there, that Owen would commit suicide. The fact that they found it in the frontal lobe of his brain that controls impulse-control, I think was a very significant factor."

Owen Thomas

The Future of CTE Research

Now that we know our enemy, we are on the attack. Rest assured that our team and many others across North America are now focused on finding a way to diagnose and treat the disease. Dr. Bob Stern recently earned the first-ever grant from the National Institutes of Health for a three-year study to find a biomarker for CTE. Named the DETECT study, we have one hundred former NFL players, ages 40 to 69, traveling to Boston for examination. They will take part in a two-day study that involves multiple types of imaging, neuropsychological tests, spinal fluid assessment, blood work, and more. This group will then be compared to fifty age-matched former college athletes who did not receive brain trauma. We have found interesting differences in our pilot studies, and I'm hopeful that in a few short years we will find a way to diagnose the disease with a high level of sensitivity and specificity.

Positron Emission Tomography (PET) scans may be able to diagnose CTE in living people within a year or two. A few groups have invented radioactive ligands that are injected into the bloodstream and for a limited period of time, will attach to *tau* in the brain, allowing it to "light up" on the PET scan.

Genetics is another important area of research. There are genetic predispositions for every disease and disorder, and CTE is no different. At this time, it appears from our limited research that one gene, APOE IV, may have a role in accelerating CTE, but our population is so small that no one should be making any decisions based on that knowledge. Eventually a day may come where you could give your child a genetic test, and if they had certain genes, you would want to steer them away from contact sports.

Many populations are exposed to repetitive brain trauma, whether voluntarily or involuntarily. One population that we are focused on helping is our veteran population. Many of the athletes we have studied were also veterans, and we have also studied the brains of veterans from Iraq and Afghanistan. We recently

180

published the first-ever case series of four young veterans with CTE, and under a microscope their disease was indistinguishable from the athletes' cases.[156] Considering that some studies estimate 20 percent of veterans are returning with some type of brain injury, we plan to expand our work into the military so that both groups can benefit from the research.

We are trying to find other paths to treatment. We collaborated with Lee Goldstein, MD, PhD, an associate professor of Psychiatry, Neurology, Ophthalmology, Pathology and Laboratory Medicine, and Biomedical Engineering at Boston University, and a prototypical genius scientist, to investigate CTE in the military blast population. Our VA CSTE Brain Bank now has the brains of over fifteen veterans, some of whom were exposed to blasts in the recent wars in Afghanistan and Iraq. Dr. Goldstein and his team developed a breakthrough blast model and were able to give the mice the equivalent of human CTE, which should allow us to test early interventions that may stop the disease before it starts. He is now working on a repetitive brain trauma model to mimic sports.

Finding a treatment is the ultimate goal, and that treatment may come from pharmaceutical and biotechnology companies. To get those companies to invest in treating CTE, we need to find a way to measure the impact of an intervention. Most Alzheimer's disease clinical trials involve measuring the rate of cognitive and functional decline of a patient, with the hope that in the intervention group the decline is slower. The Food and Drug Administration has experience with Alzheimer's disease, and has approved drugs "indicated for the treatment of moderate to severe dementia of the Alzheimer's type." The FDA has no experience with "dementia of the CTE type" and no published criteria to utilize, so our path will be more difficult with the limited funding for CTE research.

In addition, because we cannot diagnose CTE in living people, we have no idea how many actually have the disease. That makes it a risky investment for the drug companies. Unfortunately, until we break the diagnostic barrier, investment into therapies from the private sector will be limited.

The biggest problem with research is that it simply takes time. The change in concussion awareness we've created in sports over the last seven years has been revolutionary, but the research advances have been only evolutionary. I am the kind of person who lacks to the patience to only work on ten or twenty year time horizons. An area where we can make dramatically faster advances is preventing CTE in future athletes. There is a long list of things we should be doing to make sports safer, and at this point we just aren't trying hard enough.

In 2011 we identified a new youngest case of CTE in a seventeen-year-old football player from Kansas named Nathan Stiles. Nathan died of second-impact syndrome. Both SIS and CTE are preventable. I hope we never find another Nathan Stiles again, and in the final section of the book we will focus on how.

Chapter 16: SLI Concussion Checklist

We can prevent nearly all of the bad outcomes that athletes suffer if we apply all of the principles in the SLI Concussion Checklist. The list, and supporting programs, is available at www.ConcussionChecklist.org. We built the checklist to provide a framework through which everyone, including coaches, parents, athletes, administrators, and fans, can identify actions they can take to protect the future.

In 2006, I made a list for the first edition. Much of that game plan has been adopted, so it's time for a new list:

1. Education
2. Prevention
3. Remove from Play
4. Return to Play
5. Return to School
6. Return to Life
7. Medical Infrastructure
8. Equipment
9. Rules & Penalties
10. Playing Surfaces

1. Education

We are not born with a healthy respect for, nor an understanding of, our brain. In ancient Greece, Aristotle thought the brain existed to cool the blood! Aristotle was smarter than your average ten-year-old, so it's important to recognize that education is the first key to solving the concussion crisis. The core groups that need to receive concussion education, initially and on an annual basis, include athletes, coaches, parents, athletic administrators, referees, and medical professionals.

Athletes

Education has to start with athletes. In 2006, the data showed only about 10 percent of concussions were ever diagnosed. Because of greater awareness, concussion rates are starting to creep up, slowly in some places, and faster in others. The football programs at the US Military Academy (Army), the US Naval Academy, and the US Air Force Academy found that concussions *nearly doubled* from 2009–10 to 2010–11.[157] The *Toronto Star* reported that the Canadian women's water polo team was struggling to put together a team for the 2012 Olympics because eight of the twenty athletes suffered concussions in training.[158] We recently took over concussion education and policy for Major League Lacrosse (MLL). I spoke with each team for about 30 minutes during the 2013 season, with the message focused on identifying concussions and how it is in their interest to report them. From 2012 to 2013, concussion jumped 600% in MLL, from 1 to 7.

While we are getting better, we have to be humble and recognize that we rely on athletes to report their own concussions. As observers, we are relatively helpless to see a concussion occur. Look at what happens when you divide the concussions signs and symptoms list from the NFL's concussion definition in the medical journal *Neurosurgery* into things you can easily observe and things you can't.

Easily Observable	Not Easily Observable
loss of consciousness	"ding"
seizure	sensation of being dazed or stunned
loss of balance	sensation of "wooziness" or "fogginess"
syncope	amnesic period
near-syncope	persistent headaches
unsteadiness	vertigo
	light-headedness
	cognitive dysfunction
	memory disturbances
	hearing loss
	tinnitus
	blurred vision
	diplopia (double vision)
	visual loss
	personality change
	drowsiness
	lethargy
	fatigue

Few signs and symptoms can easily be seen by an observer. They cannot see when an athlete has ringing in her ears. A study by Canadian researchers in ice hockey found that this observation gap is extraordinary. Volunteer observers were asked to record and report the details of "head incidents of concern" sustained by their team's players during games. They defined a head incident of concern as a physician-diagnosed concussion or an episode considered seriously indicative of a concussion based on observed signs or symptoms.[159] They found that the observers identified *only one "head incident of concern" for every three times the players said they have symptoms.*

185

The problem is that athletes rarely report their symptoms. We often blame athletes and the "warrior culture" for underreporting of concussions, but when we ask them why they don't report concussions, we consistently find that the number one reason they do not report concussion symptoms has nothing to do with trying to hide it and stay in the game. Building on earlier work by Dr. Mike McCrea[160] and colleagues, my colleague Emily Kroshus decided to ask division one college ice hockey players why they weren't reporting.[161]

Reasons Why Concussions Are Not Reported

Did not think it was serious enough	70%
Did not know it was a concussion	45%
Did not want to leave game	43%
Did not want to let down teammates	29%

NOTE: Players could give more than one reason in this survey.

The third most popular answer was that athlete actively chose not to report to stay in the game. Shockingly, the top two answers had to do with the athlete's lack of education.

The athletes in that survey were in college. Education levels are likely worse globally. I was recently in Dublin for a conference put on by Acquired Brain Injury Ireland (ABIA). A non-profit working hard to raise awareness of sports concussions, they partner with the Gaelic Athletic Association, which governs historically Irish sports like hurling and Gaelic football, which are only played at the amateur level.

Some of the most popular players serve as ABIA ambassadors, where their job is to represent ABIA and take part in concussion education campaigns. The night prior we held a sneak preview of documentary *Head Games: the Global Concussion Crisis*, and the ambassadors attended. On a panel the next day at the conference, one ambassador, who was in his early twenties, admitted that he did not know what a concussion really was until he saw the documentary. And he's supposed to be the most educated on concussions!

The situation is even more dire with children. A recent survey of ten-year-old hockey players found that 64 percent thought they needed to be knocked out to have a concussion, and 45 percent could only name *zero or one* symptoms of concussion.[162]

At Sports Legacy Institute, we launched a program called SLI Community Educators (SLICE), to reach fourth- to twelfth-graders. The program was the brainchild of a Harvard Medical School MD/PhD student, Alex Bagley, and developed by Alex and Boston University School of Medicine MD/PhD student Dan Daneshvar, who launched the program at their respective schools as a student service organization. The college and medical school students learn a curriculum on the latest concussion information, and then they learn to give a thirty-minute interactive and fun presentation to children.

The idea is that we can solve two problems with SLICE. First, we can educate children, and second, we can educate future clinicians, because the reality is that many doctors and medical providers are still not up to speed on the latest changes in concussion policy. It is now at nine universities, including Harvard, Boston University, the University of Southern California, California-Berkeley, University of Miami, De Paul University, the Illinois Eye Institute, Brown University, and Wilfred Laurier University.

Data from our SLICE program found that the average fourteen year-old can name only two to three symptoms of concussion prior to the training session, but can name more than seven after the session. It's amazing how easy it is to teach them, but in most places we still do not provide education for athletes.[163]

After teaching athletes to recognize symptoms, the next, and harder task, is to convince them to report those symptoms to an adult. Player surveys reveal that in 50 percent of concussions, the symptoms last less than two hours, and in 72 percent they last less than one day.[164] My experience is that most

187

athletes will not report concussion symptoms unless they feel them at the immediate moment – an athlete rarely will volunteer that they had a headache yesterday if it went away. This means that athletes have a short window to report how they are feeling, and they have to make that decision to report quickly.

That leads us to another hurdle to reporting: many athletes don't report concussions because they are too concussed to recognize their injury. The tool needed to assess the injury, their brain, is on the fritz. The classic symptom that alerts athletes to injury, pain, doesn't occur with concussions. The brain does not have pain nerves inside of it! So our task is to teach youth athletes how to recognize and care about minor symptoms like a headache or brief blurry vision and train them to recognize these mild symptoms while their already immature brain is malfunctioning. We will never have 100% compliance.

If only we bled out of our eyes, ears, and noses after a concussion! Then we wouldn't have this diagnosis problem.

Dr. Cantu sums it up best: "Unless kids take themselves out of the contests, there's no way to know that they've been mildly impaired. It's only when they're so impaired that they're missing plays, missing assignments, walking into the wrong huddle, et cetera, that outside observers know something is wrong. Obviously, that happens much less often, and nobody is going to miss that."

SLICE does not train children below 4th grade because no one has shown what messaging will work for children below the age of ten. A few years ago we recognized how difficult it will be to teach the youngest athletes about concussion. In a moment of insight I remembered that most boys these days learn the rules of sports, and also about concussion symptoms, through video games. The most popular football video game is the Madden NFL franchise. The Madden NFL games have sold over 90 million copies in twenty-two years, including five million of Madden 11.

The problem with the video games a few years back was that they treated concussions like a cartoon injury. Electronic Arts, the maker of the game, had a poor track record on concussions. In 1992, their NHL game allowed a player that had been checked hard to get knocked unconscious on the ice, with the additional insult creating a growing pool of bright red blood under his head. I was fourteen when that game came out, and played it religiously. Creating that pool of blood was better than scoring a goal!

EA Sports eliminated the blood, but in Madden 11 athletes could still return to the game after suffering a concussion. That sent the wrong message. Eight year-olds were being taught that it was normal to return to the same game after a concussion, just like any other injury.

I had a chance to make a difference in these video games when Isaiah Kacyvenski, who had forged a relationship with someone now senior at EA Sports, set up a conference call in the spring of 2010 to pitch the idea of educating children through the game by handling concussions correctly. I'll never forget the first reaction from EA Sports: "No way the NFL will let us do that."

This conversation happened a few months after the NFL became a concussion advocate, so I was confident they would support a measure so obvious and simple.

A few months later, on April 2, 2011, EA Sports announced that Madden 12 would take a realistic approach to concussions. John Madden told the *New York Times,* "Concussions are such a big thing, it has to be a big thing in the video game. It starts young kids—they start in video games. I think the osmosis is if you get a concussion, that's a serious thing and you shouldn't play. Or leading with the head that you want to eliminate. We want that message to be strong."[165]

NFL spokesperson Greg Aiello said, "We are in the process of working with EA on the precise handling of a concussion injury in the game. We will strive for authenticity and an accurate, responsible depiction."

I could not have been happier. Their responsible depiction included having their writers develop lines for the announcers to say after a player was concussed, like, "Because of the seriousness of concussions... that player will not be returning to the game." It was a home run, and all from a couple of phone calls.

Coaches and Administrators

The need to educate coaches and athletic administrators is obvious. The program in widest use in the United States is the Centers for Disease Control (CDC) Heads Up online educational program. CDC is part of the federal government. It's a thirty-minute program that provides solid information. It is free, it is great, and I was given the honor of providing the voice-over. Over a million coaches have now completed the training.

As terrific as the program is, for some it takes more than 30 minutes to help a coach appreciate that everything they thought about concussions for the past few decades is wrong.

SLI has now been giving *Advanced Concussion Training (ACT)* sessions for five years. A ninety-minute multimedia program that Dr. Cantu and I put together with the advice of the SLI Medical Advisory Board, the our goal is to provide the information coaches need, but also the *inspiration* to change. We have trained over 15,000 coaches in over 150 training sessions around the United States, including mandatory training in programs like the Chicagoland Youth Football League (2,500 coaches), Westport (CT) Police Athletic League, and all across the state of Virginia thanks to the Virginia Department of Health.

It is especially important to get this more comprehensive training to organizations that do not have access to athletic trainers, as coaches may be the only line of defense between a child and second-impact syndrome.

In 2011 we trained over 3,000 coaches and athletic directors in Chicago Public Schools (CPS), the third-largest school district in the nation, and we expanded the program to school nurses and gym teachers in CPS. We now train all the coaches in Arlington (VA) Public Schools, and in 2012 we trained the football coaches in the Los Angeles Unified School District (LAUSD), the second-largest school district in the nation. LAUSD actually cancelled football practice for a day so that a thousand coaches could attend. At the beginning of the training, I asked those thousand football coaches how many had had previous concussion training. Four raised their hands.

Referees

The importance of referee education is only beginning to be recognized, but it is essential. Referees are the closest people to the action—closer than coaches, closer than parents—and the only ones with the authority to stop a game or require an athlete to seek medical attention. Historically, when a concussed athlete walked to the wrong huddle in football, the referee would simply laugh and walk him to the right huddle. During the 2011 NFL season San Diego Chargers guard Kris Dielman hit his head, wobbled, and nearly fell right in front of a referee. The Chargers didn't have any healthy backups left, and Dielman was never evaluated by the team medical staff and kept playing. He had a seizure after the game and retired after the season. The referee may have been able to prevent that but did not.

Medical Professionals

Medical professionals also need to be updated on concussion care, and that includes doctors, nurses, emergency medicine technicians, athletic trainers, and others. Athletic trainers have made concussion education a priority, so I rarely find an athletic trainer who is not up to speed. But they can still be found. I recently had the strangest exchange during Q &A when speaking at a high school in a wealthy suburb of New York City.

191

Nowinski Question & Answer

When I finished my presentation, the head athletic trainer at the school raised his hand and started, "You sure scared a lot of people tonight, okay? You came here and you talked about all these people whose brains are decaying. And what you didn't show is, there's a heck of a lot of people that played ball that don't have problems. Okay? And don't have this post-concussion syndrome. You didn't talk about the hundreds of thousands and millions of people—" I knew where this was going and cut him off. "No, that's right. I didn't talk about all the people who smoke and don't get lung cancer," I rebutted. "I mean...with all due respect, that's a terrible argument when it comes down to people's health and their brain, and the risks that we should be exposing kids to."

But then it went further, and he said, "Well you talk about all these symptoms...my ten-year-old daughter plays soccer and she comes off the field and complains of dizziness and headaches after heading the ball. But that's not a concussion. That's just part of playing the game."

I stood there in shock, and then I got angry. "If your child has concussion symptoms from heading a soccer ball that's a concussion. I cannot believe you asked me that question. I mean, are you serious?!"

He tried to fight back, blubbering, "Have you ever had—"

For his own good I interrupted him, "I don't wanna push too far but I'm worried about your job right now!" We ended the session in dead silence, just staring across the auditorium at each other. Based on the reactions of the parents and other athletic trainers in the audience, I doubt his job can be salvaged.

But I don't want to pick on athletic trainers, as every other experience has been positive. It's the doctors I'm more worried about. Most professionals received their training on concussions prior to 2009, when care was rewritten, and most haven't updated their knowledge. It can be especially bad in emergency rooms. Last year, the twenty-five year-old son of a friend of mine was assaulted and kicked in the head. He went to the emergency room for thirty stitches to his head and told the doctors he didn't remember much of the attack.

The word *concussion* was never spoken, nor was it on his report when he was released. His father, noticing his son's abnormal behavior on the way home, ended up taking him to see me so we could together convince him to see another doctor, as he was abnormally combative. He capitulated, went right back to another doctor, and he received a concussion diagnosis. As a parent, it is important to try to find a concussion specialist, although there is no specific certification for concussion specialists.

In an attempt to help families get to doctors who focus on concussion care, we created a searchable database at www.ConcussionClinics.org with a listing of all the concussion doctors or specialists that we are aware of.

Parents

Parents have a very important role to play. Parents need to know everything a coach knows and more. They need to know their important role in concussion management, coordinating medical care, and closely monitoring return to school. They have to provide social support for the injured athletes. They need to understand life threatening complications of head injury, so they need to know this list of signs or symptoms that require a trip to the emergency room, which, according to the CDC, includes:[166]

Worsening headaches

Slurred speech
Changes in alertness and consciousness
Convulsions (seizures)
Muscle weakness on one or both sides
Persistent confusion
Inability to recognize people or places
Repeated vomiting
Unequal pupils
Unusual eye movements
Walking problems

When in doubt, go to the emergency room. Parents also need to provide the social support that concussed athletes need, especially in those first 72 hours. Remember Austin Trenum.

2. Prevention

Concussion prevention should be a top priority of all sports programs. Prevention should also be a larger topic of conversation in women's sports than it is today, as women appear to be at greater risk for concussion than men.

Dr. Dawn Comstock's injury surveillance program at Ohio State has found that women are diagnosed with more concussions than men in gender equal sports. In basketball, it's three times as many, and in soccer it's nearly twice as many. The research has also shown that women tend to take longer to recover.

There are multiple theories as to why this happens. One theory is that girls may simply be more honest. Another is that hormones may play a role, as there is an ongoing major study on the role of estrogen levels in concussion. Another theory may account for the majority of the difference, which has more to do with biomechanics. Just like females are more likely to tear their anterior cruciate ligament (ACL), they may be more likely to get concussions due to their smaller and weaker necks.

Prevention should be a major focus across all sports and both genders. After all, it is much better to prevent concussions than to manage them and hope for the best. The next section will explore three recommendations for prevention.

Hit Count

Dr. Cantu and I, through SLI, are promoting the idea of a Hit Count®. We wrote a white paper and held a press conference at the Super Bowl in 2012 to launch the campaign. Below are excerpts:

We believe that the fastest and most effective path to safer youth sports is to regulate the amount of brain trauma that a child is allowed to incur in a season and a year. Just as youth baseball has widely adopted a "Pitch Count" to protect the ulnar collateral ligament of the elbow from wear and tear, we urgently call for the development and adoption of a *Hit Count*® to limit the frequency of repetitive brain trauma. Theoretically, a lower *Hit Count*® would reduce the risk of concussion, risk of brain damage from sub-concussive blows, and would theoretically reduce the risk of chronic traumatic encephalopathy (CTE), a degenerative brain disease linked to repetitive brain trauma.

We do not claim ownership of this idea. A *Hit Count*® has been proposed by prominent researchers, many of whom have provided the research evidence to support this policy proposal. Our goal is to make this great idea a reality.

To summarize, we are asking youth sports organizations to change the ways games are played and practiced, with the goal of significantly reducing the number of head hits children incur during sports participation. We hope that leaders of youth sports organizations can see the wisdom of this request.

Scientific evidence exists to support a *Hit Count*®. There are still gaps and unknowns in the research connecting brain trauma to negative outcomes. As with most public health problems, we must make policy decisions before we have absolute knowledge of the issue, as we have with smoking policy. The world now acknowledges smoking is a risk for lung cancer. Has science definitively explained why only 10–20 percent of smokers die of lung cancer? No. Do we allow children to smoke? No.

Referring back to the smoking analogy, smoking as a risk factor for lung cancer becomes even more interesting. Smokers are "only" 15 to 30 times more likely to develop lung cancer than non-smokers.[6] Brain trauma victims are *infinitely* more likely to develop CTE, because no one has ever been diagnosed with CTE who was not exposed to that risk factor.

The hypothesis that CTE is linked more to lifetime brain trauma exposure rather than concussions is admittedly tenuous. Historically, concussions have not been reported—some estimates indicate fewer than 10 percent of concussions end up in a medical report—so it is impossible to know any individual's true concussive and sub-concussive history. Whether or not the cause of CTE is only concussions, sub- concussions, or a combination of both, a *Hit Count®* would limit exposure to either or both types of brain trauma would theoretically reduce one's risk of CTE. Therefore, the science supports limiting an athlete's lifetime exposure to brain trauma.

Due to recent technological advances, we now have a better idea of the frequency and force of brain trauma received by athletes in football. This data, from a limited number of teams and players, reveals the following:

- Football players may receive 2,500 hits to the head exceeding 10 g's [10 times the force of gravity] each season
- The average may be around 1,000 hits per season
- The mean hit is around 20 g's
- There is little difference between mean head acceleration in college, high school football, and youth football

There are a handful of published ice hockey studies that have revealed a hockey player could expect to get nearly 50 percent of the brain trauma of a football player. Due to technology limitations, soccer remains an unknown, although anecdotal evidence suggests that some individuals are involved in thousands of headers per season, mostly in practice.

The decision now is to choose whether or not to establish regulations. The risk of inaction is that we continue to diminish the futures of athletes through unregulated and unnecessary brain trauma. Some experts have stated that we should not act until we know the incidence and prevalence of CTE to ensure we do not overreact.

We believe the true incidence and prevalence of CTE in the population to be irrelevant to this policy decision. What percentage of youth football players with greater than four years of experience, e.g. high school seniors, developing CTE is acceptable in our culture? I challenge anyone to propose a non-zero number. Two players, one 17 and one 18 years old, have already been identified.

There are technological and financial limitations to a universal *Hit Count®*. A *Hit Count®* is not as simple as a pitch count, where coaches only need a pencil and paper.

However, hits to the head can be accurately estimated, and methods can be developed to approximate the brain trauma exposure during games and during practice based on known variables, like position. With these estimations, rule changes and practice guidelines can be provided to ensure few, if any, athletes exceed a proposed limit.

Little League pitch counts are limits on the number of "pitches thrown per day" and mandate up to three days of rest after exposure to elbow trauma to allow the ulnar collateral ligament to recover.

In football, a *Hit Count®* might lead to fewer practices that involve helmets and pads and limits on the use of high-impact drills. In soccer practice, it may mean tracking headers in practice and games. It is expected to be a valuable tool to create individual behavior modification. The players who receive the most hits to their head should be encouraged and taught to change their style.

The white paper was well accepted, and SLI convened six technology companies and a group of experts in October, 2012 to review the research and explore the possibility of developing a single Hit Count® threshold.

The research regarding sub-concussive hits being damaging to the brain is growing. At Purdue University, researcher Tom Talavage and his team have found that high school football players who took a lot of hard hits during the prior week, usually at least 150, and did not suffer a concussion were not performing at normal mental levels. They performed worse on tests of memory, and functional MRIs found that their brains were working abnormally.[167]

At Dartmouth University researcher Tom McAllister and his colleagues found that whereas athletes in contact and non-contact sports performed similarly on neuropsychiatric testing before the season, after the season was a different story. After the season, only 4 percent of non-contact sport players performed significantly worse than their baseline. But a shocking 22 percent of football and hockey players had abnormally worse scores, despite never suffering a diagnosed concussion.[168] Considering these abnormalities appeared to go away by the beginning of each season, it may be evidence that contact sports make you dumber, but only in-season.

Michael Lipton and his team at Albert Einstein College of Medicine recently imaged the brains of adult soccer players who had been playing since they were children using an advanced MRI tool called diffusion tensor imaging (DTI). Heading the ball an average of 885 to 1,550 times in the prior year was associated with white matter changes in the frontal lobes, and more than 1,800 times was associated with poorer memory scores. The relationship was not explained by prior concussion history, indicating subconcussive hits likely played a role[169]

The research makes sense. If I am someone whose concussion threshold on a certain type of hit is 100 g's of force, what happens when I'm hit just under that threshold? Am I fine? I think the most likely scenario is that I am not fine, but I don't know that because I have two things working against me. First, my brain is incredibly powerful and has an innate ability to compensate for damage, so if I have very subtle brain changes, I won't notice. Second, the tools we usually use to assess concussion, which on the sideline is often just question-and-answer and balance testing, are very primitive compared to what we can do in a research lab. I believe that as tests get better, we'll start classifying some sub-concussive hits as concussive hits because we'll be able to measure changes in the brain.

Therefore, we need not only to prevent concussive injuries but also sub-concussive hits. Surprisingly (or not), the number-one way to prevent brain trauma in an athlete is not with a fancy new helmet, but never to hit them in the head in the first place. We have incredible opportunities to do that in sports like football and soccer. For example, in football, the average college and high school football player is recorded taking 500 to 1,000 blows to the head that exceed 10 g's of force per season, yet 60 percent or more of those hits come in practice.[170]

Football is beginning to embrace limiting brain trauma exposure in practice. We have been asking for reductions since 2006, but it wasn't until 2011 that the first rule was made. I played a role in making that happen. When the NFLPA started the Mackey-White Traumatic Brain Injury Committee, the first meeting began with each member getting five minutes to discuss the most important change for which the committee should advocate. I believe I was the only person that focused on reducing hitting in practice.

It was the right room to do it; I remember being able to ask Dr. Kevin Guskiewicz, who led much of the research showing most impacts occur in practice, his opinion on the matter from the podium. Dr. Thom Mayer and Sean Morey immediately advocated for it to be a core part of their negotiations for the new collective bargaining agreement with the NFL. Today, NFL players no longer are allowed to hit twice a day during the preseason and can only have

199

fourteen contact practices during the 18-week season. The toughest guys in football only want to hit less than once a week!

I was able to leverage that victory to get a reduction in hitting as a member of the Ivy League Concussion Committee. Under the strong leadership of executive director Robin Harris, the Ivy League is systematically evaluating every sport as it relates to brain trauma. An early win was the mandatory reduction of hitting days in practice to two days a week, down from the NCAA allowing five. In July 2012, Pop Warner football followed suit and now limits coaches to just three hours of hitting a week. I am so excited to see this happening. Unfortunately, what truly matters is not how many days you practice, but what you do while you practice. That's why the Hit Count® is still so important.

A Hit Count® in soccer could be incredibly effective in reducing trauma to the brain. The studies haven't been done yet, but it is likely that most headers are performed in practice, not in games, and so if we monitor and minimize headers (and attempts at headers, which can cause collisions that cause concussions), then we can minimize exposure. That may have helped Cindy Parlow Cone; most of those times she saw stars were in practice. Learn more www.HitCount.org.

Neck and Core Strength

Another key principal of prevention involves neck strength. There is a growing theory that the strength of the neck can help in concussion prevention by slowing down the movement of the head after impact. The research evidence is growing. One study out of Temple University found that females have 49 percent less isometric strength and 30 percent less neck girth, resulting in 29 percent less neck stiffness. This meant that when the same force was applied to the head of a man versus a woman, the woman suffered 50 percent higher peak head acceleration and 39 percent more head displacement, which in theory makes them more likely to suffer a concussion.[171]

Children likely have a similar disadvantage when it comes to neck strength. Not only do they have less muscle mass and strength than adults, but they have a dramatically different head to body ratio.

According to the Snell Foundation, by age four the size of a child's head (as indicated by head breadth, depth, and circumference) is 90 percent that of an adult. Neck size is 75 percent of full size, and mass is only 20 percent of an adult.

Even by age twelve a child's head is 95 percent of adult size. It is not until age twenty that the bone plates of the skull fully close. The neck is only 85 percent of adult size by age twelve, and the mass is only about 50 percent. [172]

	Age 4	Age 12	Adult
Head Size	90%	95%	100%
Neck Size	75%	85%	100%
Height	53%	76%	100%
Weight	19%	47%	100%

These biomechanical differences have led to an interesting finding. Once upon a time it was thought that youth football players can't hurt each other because they are moving too slowly and hit too softly. Some describe it as looking more like a pillow fight. With the new sensor technology we now know how hard players hit each other. College football average 18 to 22 g's of force per hit. When high school football players were studied, everyone was shocked to discover they hit each other just as hard. Scientists theorized that it was due to their weaker necks and weaker upper bodies, which led to them using their heads more. Stefan Duma, director of the Virginia Tech Center for Injury Biomechanics, was able to get sensors in the helmets of seven- and eight-year-olds, and in 2012 he announced that they were shocked to discover that these little children hit each other just as hard as adults. They recorded hits to the head in excess of 80 g's and found the mean hit was 15 g's, nearly as strong as the college players.[173]

At first it is hard to believe that data, but when you focus not on the size and speed of the striking player, but instead on the struck player, it makes more sense. The g measurement is all about the distance the head travels over time. If you have a giant head, a heavy helmet, and a tiny weak neck, it doesn't take much energy to knock your head into next week. You are defenseless.

The neck strength theory is supported by evidence from Jason Mihalek and colleagues at the University of North Carolina finding that when ice hockey players are able to see a hit coming and brace, which in theory allows them to tense their neck musculature, they are less likely to suffer a concussion.[174]

If we are going to expose children to contact sports, we owe it to them to try to strengthen their necks. I urge you to get a workout program from a professional athletic trainer. For those of you worried that neck exercises might hurt your child's neck development or cause wear and tear, I say this: Why aren't you worried about his brain first?

Core strength follows the same principles. A strong core can slow the movement of the body, neck, and head from impact. I think the best examples come from girls falling backwards. In professional wrestling women appear to have a worse concussion problem than men. Elite men never get a concussion from taking a "back bump," the term for when a wrestler falls backwards onto the mat after taking a move like a clothesline. Wrestlers try to whip their body to the mat as fast as they can so the move looks dynamic, but their head never hits the mat. Male wrestlers might take dozens of back bumps in a match—it's a standard move.

Women wrestlers, however, occasionally get concussions from back bumps because their head sometimes hits the mat. They simply don't have the neck and core strength to prevent their heads from moving too far too fast and slamming into the ground. In my observation the same logic may be a contributing factor to the increased concussions in women's basketball. When men take a charge, their head rarely hits the ground. However, I've seen many tall, skinny women fall backwards and watched their skulls bounce off the wood floor. Strength plays a role, and we need to do more to protect the athletes.

Technique as Prevention

Better technique can contribute to concussion prevention. This is where the quality of coaching plays a role. Football is a great example, and Tom Farrey and ESPN's *Outside the Lines with Bob Ley* recently ran a provocative piece exploring the lack of training coaches get in some sports at the youth level.[175] In some sports, when we do learn techniques that can protect athletes, we often have no way to disseminate that information to the grassroots.

The evidence was provided through the experience of a thirteen-year-old young man who became a quadriplegic after attempting to tackle. He used an incorrect tackling technique by leading with his head.

The player claims that he was taught this technique by his coach, and when he complained that he didn't want to do it because it was too dangerous, he was belittled. A teammate corroborated that story, although the coach denied it. Irrespective of who is most responsible for this tragedy, the story revealed that coaches may be teaching incorrect, head-first tackling techniques all over the country. We can't be sure because most youth football programs have no educational requirement or certification to become a football coach. Pop Warner only required head coaches to take a training course. For assistants it is not mandatory.

Football is in stark contrast to youth ice hockey, where nearly all coaches in America are certified through USA Hockey with regular and robust training.

3. Remove from Play

Return to play has dominated the national discussion for many years, but it may not be the most pressing issue on the concussion front. I believe we are missing the boat on remove from play, meaning that we are doing a terrible job recognizing and diagnosing concussions, and we are not pulling enough athletes off the field.

In 2006 I compiled concussion incidence data in football from multiple sources and made the argument that 90 percent of concussions are not diagnosed. Back then, it was a minority (and unpopular) opinion. Since then, more research has been published to support that reality.

Dr. Cantu worked with Paul Echlin and a number of Canadian researchers in an innovative study that showed we are seeing the tip of the iceberg.[176] They studied sixteen- to twenty-one-year-old ice hockey players in a league that had athletic trainers. They split the league in half. One half did business as usual. For the other half, they put a trained physician in the stands whose job was to watch the game, and if these doctors thought they saw a concussion occur, they had the ability to pull the player off the ice to evaluate them with standard sideline protocols.

The group with the doctor intervening identified *seven times* as many concussions. The business-as-usual group identified concussions in 5 percent of players. The doctor intervention group identified a concussion in over 36 percent of the players. What that means is that if we had the resources to put a trained observer, or "concussion spotter," on every sideline, we'd identify five to ten times as many concussions. Yet we don't do it, and it's not even part of any national discussion!

We know these concussions are happening, but in general we aren't mobilizing to find them. The one organization that continues to innovate to catch every concussion is the NFL. During the 2011 season there were a few obvious concussions that the NFL team medical staffs missed. Colt McCoy, the

204

Cleveland Browns quarterback, looked as though he was briefly knocked unconscious on the field after a hit from James Harrison. The medical team reached him on the field and took him to the sideline, but he was only complaining of his injured hand, not his brain, probably due to the lack of awareness that can follow a concussion. The team medical staff didn't see the hit, so they took him at his word. Three minutes and fifty seconds later, in real time, McCoy was back in the game. He could not have been evaluated for concussion in that time.

Colt's father, a high school football coach, was furious with the treatment, because he and millions of fans around the world saw him get hit in the head and assumed he would be evaluated for a concussion, which would have taken at least 15 minutes. He told the *Cleveland Plain Dealer*, "He was basically out [cold] after the hit. You could tell by the rigidity of his body as he was lying there. There were a lot of easy symptoms that should've told them he had a concussion. He was nauseated and he didn't know who he was. From what I could see, they didn't test him for a concussion on the sidelines. They looked at his [left] hand."[177]

This wasn't the only time during the 2011 season that players with obvious concussions were not evaluated, and every time it happened, the team claimed the medical staff did not see the impact or see the obvious symptoms that the rest of the world saw on television. The NFL quickly announced a new rule; they would put an athletic trainer in the skybox whose job was to watch the television feed to identify concussions that the medical staff might miss. They have a hotline to the sideline, and they are expected to use it.

The most interesting thing about this new rule is not what it says about the NFL, but what it says about youth sports. The first barrier to diagnosing a concussion during the game is recognizing symptoms of the injury. Through this rule the NFL has admitted that concussions are so difficult to spot that they need to hire someone just to look for the concussions missed by a large medical staff.

In comparison, a youth football team has no medical staff whatsoever and coaches who may never have been trained on concussions (or anything related to football). What chance do they have to recognize every concussion?

On top of our current difficulty in recognizing concussions, we also have limited options once an athlete gets to the sideline with a suspected concussion. Last year the NFL rolled out a very comprehensive sideline concussion assessment test that only an athletic trainer or doctor could possibly conduct. The most commonly used sideline test is called a SCAT3, which is a hodgepodge of tests with around a twenty-minute duration. The irony of the SCAT3 is that it consists of a number of individual tests, like the SAC and the Murdock Test, that have never, on their own, been very good at diagnosing concussions on the milder end of the spectrum, and together have never been validated to be any better.[178] The second barrier to concussion diagnosis, after struggling to recognize the injury, then, is our lack of a fast and effective sideline tests for medical professionals.

I suspect that one reason why we aren't liberally pulling athletes off the field for concussion evaluations is that each one takes at least fifteen minutes, and who wants to lose a player for fifteen minutes? If we had an effective 30-second test, I expect that we would be willing to employ it much more frequently, and we'd therefore diagnose more concussions.

The third barrier to concussion in-game concussion diagnosis is that the vast majority of athletes don't have access during a game to any medical professional. Athletic trainers are the first people that programs hire for the sideline, and they only work at 42 percent of high schools. In addition, they have to cover multiple sports in multiple locations. Athletic trainers below the high school level are rare. So not only do we not have a test that medical staff can be confident in, we do not have a test simple enough to be given by a person who is not a medical professional, like a coach.

Therefore, most athletes, especially youth athletes, exist in a system where their coaches are hesitant to pull them off the field for a suspected concussion because once a coach admits suspicion of a concussion, that athlete cannot return again until they see an appropriate medical professional. In the vast majority of sports programs, a proper evaluation cannot happen on the sideline, and may not happen during the week if the parent cannot get an appointment with a specialist.

What this means is that until we find a fast test that can be given by a coach on the sideline, we will forever be putting young athletes in a risky situation that we'd never allow for adult professional athletes. Human nature and a lack of education will make youth coaches act conservatively with "suspecting" concussions, and children will continue to be allowed to play through the "dings."

One test that may fit that bill is the King-Devick (K-D) Test.[*] It is an interesting test with a surprising history. It was invented decades ago and is still utilized as a screen for dyslexia and eye movement dysfunction related to reading, and when concussions hit the news, the inventor, Dr. Steve Devick, decided to see if might also work for concussions. It is called a "rapid number naming test" and consists of a series of three test cards that have numbers spaced across the page. The idea is to read the numbers out loud, in order, without

---

[*] Disclosure: The author has separate business relationships with the inventor and principal owner of the King-Devick Test, Steve Devick. He began his career as an optometrist, and became a serial entrepreneur. He was the CEO/founder of Platinum Entertainment (NASDAQ:PTET), and a founding Director/investor in Platinum Technology (NASDAQ:PLAT) and Blue Rhino (NASDAQ:RINO) Steve owns several businesses including a movie company. In 2011 Steve and other investors licensed my book as the basis for a documentary film of the same name, *Head Games* He hired Steve James, the acclaimed director of *Hoop Dreams* and *The Interrupters*, and I had no creative control over the film. The King-Devick Test does not appear in the film per Steve Devick's request. Steve Devick is also the person who convinced me to write a second edition of *Head Games* and his group published the book, although he has no editorial control.

mistakes, as quickly as possible. The timed test can be completed in less than a minute. Athletes establish their own baselines, and then if they are suspected of injury, they re-take the test. Studies have shown concussed athletes are usually slower or make errors on this retest.

King Devick Test

Scientists that have evaluated the test were interested in it because testing vision is an efficient way to test brain function. Dr. Steve Galetta, Chairman of Neurology at New York University's Langone Medical Center, who has published on the King-Devick Test, said, "About 50 percent of the brain is dedicated to vision, and the circuits are widely distributed all over the brain—in the cortex, in the brain stem, in the coordination center, the cerebellum." The publications on concussions have shown the test to be effective.

A recent publication focused on New Zealand rugby players. The study planned to assess players during the game who showed symptoms, but also give the K-D to every player after the game in the locker room, which was possible because the test is so fast. Among of group of 37 players with an average age of 22, five had "witnessed" concussions, where they were removed from the contest and evaluated on the sideline. However, another 17 had "unwitnessed" concussions, meaning that they failed the K-D test, and by confirming with additional tests as well as player self-report, were found to have had suffered an unrecognized concussion during the game.. The players never reported symptoms during the games, and they never exhibited signs of concussion, yet they were found to have a significantly delayed K-D score that remained for days.[179] These concussed athletes would have continued to play the next practice or game with great risk had the test not been used.

Similar results were found in a study of high school hockey players in which the K-D test was helpful in detecting subclinical concussion in athletes without obvious head injury.[180] The King-Devick Test must be studied further before it can be used on every sideline in America, but the interesting thing is that it is one of the only tests in development that theoretically could be used on every sideline in America. Growing evidence is showing that coaches and parents can likely give the test as effectively as a medical professional. In addition, at its core it is a low-tech, low-cost test (although there is an iPad version), so it's affordable. Many tests in development are aiming at $10,000 price points, and therefore only serving colleges. So few seem to be interested in a practical solution serving seven-year-olds.

Research investigating the King-Devick test is continually on-going, especially to further validate that the test works as well for children as it does for adults, but I'm surprised more people aren't excited about it, and I'm shocked it hasn't been adopted or widely trialed at the college and professional levels. I have not heard discussions about adding the one-minute test to the existing SCAT3, despite the fact that there are already more studies validating King-Devick than have ever been published on SCAT3. A recent study has shown that as a stand-alone test, the one-minute K-D test is more effective than the 15 minute SCAT3. In a study of college football, women's soccer, and women's lacrosse players at the University of Florida, the K-D score correctly identified 79% of concussions, while the SCAT3 only identified 52%. Used together, they identified 89% of concussions.[181] Yet the K-D test is not yet incorporated into any professional sideline assessment except for Major League Lacrosse, and only because Dr. Cantu wrote the guideline. It's amazing that many of the doctors calling for "evidence-based" CTE research are the same ones developing

209

sideline protocols and ignoring the fact that the K-D, according to the available evidence, appears to be the most effective minute in a sideline test.

4. Return to Play

Allowing the brain to recover after concussion has become a cornerstone of concussion management. Trying to tough out concussions leads to negative consequences we are only beginning to understand. One of the more interesting potential examples is Lou Gehrig. The former New York Yankee was nicknamed the "Iron Horse" for his toughness – for decades he held the record for consecutive games played in Major League Baseball with 2,130 straight.

Lou Gehrig is also remembered as the face of Amyotrophic Lateral Sclerosis in the United States – the disease is often called Lou Gehrig's disease. As discussed earlier, Dr. Ann McKee connected a subtype of ALS to CTE and brain trauma in 2010. If we believe that playing through concussions might increase one's risk of CTE, Gehrig may be a tale of warning.

Gehrig was incredibly unlucky in baseball, and suffered numerous high-profile concussions as a Yankee. According to the Alan Schwarz of the *New York Times* and newspaper reports at the time, Gehrig had numerous concussions. [182] In 1930 Gehrig was knocked out by a ground ball to the face. In 1935 he was knocked out by a runner. In 1924 he was knocked out when he swung at Ty Cobb during a post-game brawl, missed, and hit his head on concrete. Finally, Gehrig was once knocked out for five minutes from a beanball directly to the forehead (hard batting helmets had yet to be invented). Although he had a headache and his head was so swollen he had to borrow one of Babe Ruth's larger baseball caps, against a doctor's orders he played the next day. Lou Gehrig *always* played the next day.

Knowing what we know now, it is interesting to think that it was Gehrig's toughness, specifically playing through concussion that could have triggered or accelerated CTE + MND—if he in fact had it. I believe there is a good chance

210

he did, because on top of his baseball concussions, Gehrig was a high school football player and went on to play halfback at Columbia University. If Gehrig had CTE + MND, the irony of his toughness being the cause for his demise is something every athlete should ponder.

The greatest changes in concussion care in the past five years have come in the form of return-to-play rules and regulations. At the 2008 Zurich consensus meeting in Switzerland, the experts finally came to a consensus that athletes should no longer be allowed to return to the same game after suffering a concussion.

It is now standard that we never allow athletes to return to play the same day they have suffered a concussion, and it is law in most states in the US. It has been firmly established that it is impossible to recover from a concussion in minutes or hours. It is now also law in most states that athletes cannot return until they have been cleared by an appropriate health care professional.

The treating doctor performs a number of tests to evaluate when it is safe to return. The first thing a parent should understand is that our tests for determining when an athlete's brain has "recovered" are relatively primitive. There is no straightforward objective test for when a concussion exists or when a concussion has healed, so we currently return athletes with our fingers crossed, hoping it's not too soon. Most clinicians use some combination of a medical exam, neurological exam, symptom checklist, balance test, and cognitive test. Athletes are not supposed to return until all tests are normal, and then they are supposed to begin a return-to-play progression.

Doctors perform cognitive, balance, and other tests because they are looking for indirect evidence that the brain is not operating normally, which, after trauma, is assumed to be from the concussion. One problem is that no single test can evaluate all the possible domains that could be malfunctioning. The current model tries to evaluate multiple domains of functioning using multiple tests to

211

see if one is abnormal. Cognitive domains and balance domains are emphasized in the current model as they've shown to be sensitive to concussion.

Cognitive baseline testing has become very popular, and can be a useful tool in a doctor's toolbox, but it is quite amazing how it is misunderstood and misused. In a computerized neuropsychological baseline test system, a player takes a 20- to 30-minute test that establishes their "baseline" cognitive function, which includes evaluating things like short-term memory and reaction time.

When an injury occurs, the theory is that athletes have abnormal cognitive function, and this test is an easy way to confirm functional changes and to evaluate how long they last. In practice, an athlete is not supposed to return until he has recovered to his personal baseline function. The test is valuable because athletes cannot always tell that their brains are impaired. Athletes who are asymptomatic after a concussion can still have subtle cognitive deficits that indicate it's not safe to return, and this test can sometimes pick up those deficits.

It is important to recognize that the test is not perfect (no test is). Therefore, the value of the test can be completely eliminated if the test is not used correctly. First, there is a risk that an athlete's baseline is not valid. The problem with this sort of test is that everyone, but especially young people, have natural variability in their day-to-day cognition, which can be caused by an endless list of factors like sleep, diet, stress, illness, and more.[183] A computerized neuropsychological test may not be able to pick up that variability during a onetime baseline test. The younger an athlete is, the more likely he is to perform inconsistently and the faster he outgrows his baseline.

A study by Stephen Broglio and colleagues in 2007 found that computerized tests had low test-retest reliability, meaning that your baseline score today may not be your baseline score a week later.[184] Twenty to 40 percent, depending on the test, of study participants were classified as impaired on at least one domain of their follow-up test 45 days later, although none had a concussion or any other medical change. Jacob Resch claims that one computerized program misclassified 29 percent of healthy participants.[185] Many sports organizations require that an athlete must "return to baseline" before he or she can return to play. In light of this evidence, that doesn't make any sense.

In addition, some athletes are purposefully "tanking" their baseline test, performing more poorly so they set a lower bar for a "normal" post-concussion retest, allowing them to return more quickly if they are injured. When I speak to students I often ask for a show of hands for who tanked their baseline, and there is always an unapologetic minority that proudly raise their hands. What's worse, athletic trainers administering the baselines frequently don't check a score index to identify the tankers.[186]

All of this data points to the fact that a multifaceted approach is best and that often the most reliable indicator of a persisting concussion is a symptom checklist and an honest athlete. Unfortunately, because not all athletes are honest, and because some symptoms are subtle, we do need external tests, and we need to continue to improve them, as growing evidence suggests that brain dysfunction extends beyond the limit of our current tests.

According to published studies, computerized neuropsychological testing remains abnormal for more than ten days for about 50 percent of athletes, and is abnormal more than 21 days for about 15 percent of athletes.[187]

Researcher Lester Mayer explored how long athletes should be taken out of their sport after having more sophisticated tests. He wrote that if we test athletes after a concussion with more powerful tests, the "window of vulnerability" doesn't extend for just a week or two, but instead always lasts *longer than a month.*[188]

Dr. Mayer extrapolated data using tests that evaluate electrical brain wave activity, evoked-responses using transcranial magnetic stimulation, attention span/executive functioning while doing two simultaneous activities, cerebral glucose metabolic rate, and diffusion tensor imaging. All the data points to the concept that if we utilized more expensive and longer tests, we'd be holding

213

athletes out longer after each concussion, and nearly all of them longer than a month. Due to financial pressures, it will be some time before these tests are widely utilized.

Having observed the "average" number of days lost to concussion consistently creep up over the last decade, I don't doubt that we will be holding out athletes longer in the future. The hard question for a parent becomes: do I hold my child out until she is cleared by a doctor utilizing today's primitive tools, or do I buck the trend and hold her out even longer than what the doctor recommends? There is no simple answer, but I don't think any parent should feel guilty about being conservative with their child's return to play.

Once an athlete has been cleared by a doctor, he should then begin a graduated return-to-play. That means that once an athlete is cleared by a doctor, they are not yet cleared to return to games. They should follow the six-stage protocol below, and take 24 hours between stages. [189] If any stage causes symptoms to reappear, the athlete moves back to stage 1. This system works as an additional safety net as we know our concussion tests are not perfect.

Rehabilitation Stage	Functional Exercise	Objective
1. No activity	Complete physical and congitive rest	Recovery
2. Light aerobic activity	Walking, swimming, stationary cycling. Mild intensity	Increase HR
3. Sport-specific activity	Running or skating drills. No head impact activities	Add movement
4. Non-contact training drills	Progression to more complex training drills	Exercise, coordination, cognitive load
5. Full contact practice	Following medical clearance. Normal training activities	Restore confidence, assessment of functional skills by coaching staff
6. Return to play	Normal game play	

5. Return to School

Since the dawn of sports concussions, the focus has always been on return to play. When can we get them back on the field? We need him for the big game! We have forgotten about the more important part, which is return to school and return to life. We know that sports, exercise, and trauma are bad for a recovering brain, but we now recognize that simply thinking and concentrating can be just as damaging to those fragile neurons and axons, and we now need to better monitor a child's return to daily living.

Returning a child to school requires a coordinated effort among school professionals, including teachers, nurses, and guidance counselors, health care professionals, the parent, and the student. The CDC recommends allowing post-concussed students to: [190]

- Take rest breaks as needed
- Spend fewer hours at school
- Be given more time to take tests or complete assignments
- Receive help with schoolwork
- Reduce time spent on the computer, reading, or writing

To help these students recover, it's important to remember that their brains are not functioning normally for a period of time, and asking them to keep up with schoolwork can be very stressful and therefore very damaging to their brain.

Parents should beware of the problem of standardized college entrance exams. Too frequently I hear about high school students who had the SAT or ACT scheduled for a Saturday morning during the sports season. Sometimes they get a concussion on a Friday night. With the pressure of entrance exams, and the risk of looking bad by not showing up to a test, many athletes have chosen to go ahead and take the test. Not only do they often score poorly, but the mental stress of a 6 hour exam has often sparked long-term post-concussion symptoms.

6. Return to Life

Return to life is another important cornerstone of the SLI Concussion Checklist. Austin Trenum is an example of someone who was not given the right advice to return to life. Austin played linebacker for the Brentsville District High School football team in northern Virginia. A wonderful, well-adjusted young man, he was in the top 10 percent of his senior class and planned to study chemical engineering in college.

Austin sustained a concussion on September 24, 2010. His teammates alerted the athletic trainer that he was "out of it," and he was then assessed on the sideline. The athletic trainer found Austin dazed and slurring his words and he could not name where he was or the opposing team. He was sent to the emergency room at his local hospital.[191]

By the time he got to the hospital he seemed fine, even flirting with the nurses. He was offered Tylenol for his headache and declined, saying, "I don't have a headache. Except for my normal football headache. I get them after every game."

Austin was advised not to return to sports until seeing a doctor, and his parents were told to limit him to "quiet activities" for 24 hours. His father, Gil, to this day has no idea what "quiet activities" really means.

On Saturday morning Austin watched the game film with his teammates, went fishing in the afternoon, and went to a Sugarland concert with his girlfriend in the evening. Sunday morning he played video games. Sunday afternoon his mother scolded him for falling behind in school. He hadn't turned in two papers, and Michelle Trenum was worried he would become a senior slacker. Austin appeared to become angry and went upstairs, presumably to do his homework. Minutes later Gil went up to check on him and found him dead, hanging from a rope around his neck. Less than 48 hours later I called the Trenum family to ask if we could study Austin's brain, and they agreed. Dr. McKee found that Austin had multi-focal axonal injury—physical damage to the white matter of his brain that changed the way his brain worked. It's a pattern she is starting to recognize, as our brain bank now has a wing of teenagers and twenty-somethings that have committed suicide within weeks or months of a concussion. This is not unexpected, as a population study found that people who were diagnosed with a concussion in a hospital were three times more likely to commit suicide than the normal population.[192] Dr. McKee told a reporter, "It's the same pattern. They have disordered thinking and electrical impulses in the brain. They have a minor irritation. And they just want to end it. It's like having a fly in your room and deciding to blow up your house."

I hope we learn from Austin's story. SLI has used it to draw attention to how vulnerable young people are after a concussion. A concussion changes the way your brain functions, and usually in negative ways. Austin is a worst-case example, but much can go wrong when we don't handle brain trauma correctly.

It is important to limit neurological stimulation at home. Dr. Cantu recommends no texting, video games, or television, as interpreting visual stimulation requires a lot of hard work for the brain. Other types of stimulation should be avoided, like sex (most parents and medical professionals are too prudish to tell them that, but they need to know), loud music at concerts or parties, crowds, and bright or flashing lights. If Austin Trenum's family could do it over again, he would not have attended a concert the day after his concussion, and he wouldn't have played video games the next day. That might have made all the difference.

7. Equipment

Equipment is an important piece of the puzzle as we work to make sports safer for the brain. Helmets are frequently the first piece of equipment that people think of when they want to prevent concussions. They are important, but it's important to understand their history and their limitations.

217

One of the first sports to add helmets was American football. When Princeton and Rutgers played the first football game on November 6, 1869, the players wore nothing on their heads, and their football game was more like a game of rugby. The only protection the players had for their heads was their long hair.[193] Although I wasn't there to watch that game, I can imagine from my experiences playing street football that head-to-head contact was probably avoided at all costs. But players still occasionally bashed skulls, leading to dire consequences. This led Rutgers University to invent the leather football helmet in 1896.[194] Whatever the effect that leather helmets had on injuries, it wasn't enough, and deaths and catastrophic injuries mounted.

In the early 1900s, the main causes of death from head injuries in football were due to skull fractures and bleeding on the brain. So, when the technology became available, someone created a stronger helmet surface to protect the brain. In 1917, the first hard-shelled, plastic helmet was introduced. This helmet didn't become standard until the NCAA mandated protective headgear in 1939.[195] These early helmets were suspended above the scalp by a webbing and were successful in reducing serious injury. Dr. Cantu explained, "Helmets have reduced the instance of subdural hematomas [bleeding on the brain] by about 70 percent, the most life-threatening injury in football."

Naturally I thought that plastic shells would make athletes safer. Not necessarily. Jerry Seinfeld had it all figured out when he joked that a sign of human stupidity was inventing the helmet. We created it because we were involved in activities that were cracking our skulls. Instead of avoiding the activity, we created a device to allow us to "continue enjoying our head cracking lifestyle."

While the hard-shelled helmets were eventually preferred to their leather predecessors, they still didn't prevent facial injuries—especially to the eyes, mouth, and nose. Arguably, the biggest impact that the plastic helmet had on the way the game was played wasn't due to the helmet itself, but what could be attached to it. The hard plastic provided a solid anchoring point for plastic bars to be positioned across a player's face, allowing for the widespread adoption of the facemask. Over time, facemasks have evolved from one bar to two bars to today's grills, which allow players to lead with their faces with little fear of having an eye poked or their teeth knocked out.

Surprisingly, though the hard-shelled helmet and facemask each made sense, the combination of the two proved deadly. Football deaths have been recorded since 1931. As the use of facemasks grew, and the facemask became more protective, catastrophic injuries swelled. They peaked in 1968, when thirty-six players died from football injuries and thirty men were permanently paralyzed.[196]

Football Head Related Fatalities by Decade

Years	Head-Related Fatalities
1945–1954	87
1955–1964	115
1965–1974	162

Frederick Mueller, a leading authority on football-related head injuries, explained what happened: "The increase in fatal head injuries that began in the early 1960s and continued into the early 1970s can be directly related to the skills of tackling and blocking that were being taught during those years."[197]

This period in football became known for tactics such as spearing, butt blocking, face to the numbers, and face in the chest. Players were being taught to make initial contact with the head and face into the opponent's chest.

219

The problem was partially one of design. The helmet was designed to protect the skull alone—there was little knowledge of the physics of concussions back then—and the helmet's effect on the brain was an afterthought. Merill Hoge captured this concept: "No helmet can eliminate trauma. To do that, you'd have to put a little helmet inside the skull, because the brain floats inside there. People need to understand that the helmet is there to protect the skull. It's not there to protect the brain, because that's impossible."

Players started using helmets as a weapon, and they were effective. A study was performed at Virginia Tech University that recorded hits from actual games. They found that half of all the hits measure greater than 30 g's, and the hardest hits are more than 130 g's. Stefan Duma, director of the Virginia Tech (VT) Center for Injury Biomechanics and an author of that study said, "An impact of 120 g's would be like a severe car accident, which you could survive if you were wearing a seatbelt."[198] Mike Goforth, VT's head athletic trainer, said, "We were surprised. That's like running your head into a brick wall."[199]

Most of the big hits were caused by helmet-to-helmet contact, so we should make that illegal. Except it has already been illegal for years. High schools made butt blocking and face tackling illegal in 1976. It's just a question of whether we enforce the rules we have.

We have been making progress with improving helmet design to reduce risk of concussion. There is a consensus that newer models in all sports are better than older ones, although it is pointless to discuss which helmet might be better than another, as the helmet companies cannot even agree on how we should properly test a helmet.

The most important thing to know is that helmets can only do so much to protect the brain, and the more important thing is to do whatever it takes to avoid hitting athletes in the head in the first place. There are two forces involved in a hit to the head—linear and rotational. Linear forces knock the brain forward or backward in a straight line. Rotational forces twist the head, like a boxer taking a hook to the chin.

Helmets do a terrific job of preventing linear forces from reaching the brain, but they do a terrible job of limiting rotational forces. Researcher David Halstead reports, "Many of the remaining head injuries that occur on the field today may have rotational acceleration as the primary injury mechanism. Helmets would not prevent these injuries."[35] If we assume that rotational forces are the primary culprit for concussions, or even play a significant role, then we cannot prevent concussions. Dr. Halstead emphasized, "The helmet was not designed, and cannot be designed in the current state of the art . . . to prevent injuries to the brain which result from rotational acceleration."

Halstead isn't the only expert to say this.[200] In his article "Birth and Evolution of the Football Helmet," published in the journal *Neurosurgery*, Michael Levy, MD, PhD, writes, "The American football helmet was and is designed to protect the areas of the player's head directly covered by the helmet from direct linear impact only. The helmet was not and cannot be designed to prevent . . . injuries to the brain that result from rotational acceleration."[201]

Taking this logic even further, if any improvement we make in helmets only serves to reduce linear forces, and that each improvement makes players more likely to make contact with the head and/or allows them to deliver more punishing hits, "improving" helmets could paradoxically increase the strength of the rotational forces that reach the brain, increasing the severity of rotational injuries, and possibly make the player less safe overall.

Increasing the potential for strong rotational forces in impacts is especially dangerous because research has shown that brain injuries caused by rotational forces tend to be more severe than those caused by linear forces. As Dr. Cantu explained, "Animal work was done by Ayub Ommaya and Thomas Gennarelli years ago. They found that when they injured these animals by blows that were to the side of the head, the animals had more horrific injuries than they did by blows that were straight to the front, or straight to the back. They thought that was due to the fact that the brain stem was more likely angulated by those kinds of blows. So there is some animal work to suggest that if you take a shot to the ear, it may have a greater effect on you than a shot to the forehead would."[202]

Mouthpieces have been getting attention from the media as reducing risk of concussion. Today there is no controlled study has ever found that a mouthpiece significantly reduces concussions.[203]

8. Medical Infrastructure

Increasing our medical infrastructure is another way we can better protect athletes. The NFL is becoming the gold standard for medical personnel. They have multiple athletic trainers at every practice and games, multiple specialists on the sideline on game day, including neurological specialist, and even the eye in the skybox watching the television feed for missed injuries. If these NFL athletes deserve all of that safety, what does your child deserve? Would you send your child to a pool without a lifeguard?

In the Remove from Play section, we explored the data on athletic trainers. Fewer than half of high schools have them, and below high school, athletic trainers are almost non-existent. In a perfect world, should children have the most medical professionals on the sideline to help them or the fewest?

As you think about that, let's consider the disadvantages that children have versus adults when it comes to brain trauma.

1. **Children's brains are still developing**. They have a lack of myelination of the axons, which in theory is protective against axonal injury.

2. **Children's brains are more sensitive** to the excitotoxic shock of concussion.

3. **Children have weak necks** that don't distribute force to the body well.

4. **Children have weak torsos** that don't keep the head from hitting the ground.

5. **Children have a poor head to body ratio** when compared to adults. They are the equivalent of human bobblehead dolls.

6. **Children often have poor equipment.** Did you know that football helmets for children are not studied as thoroughly as adult helmets?

7. **Children lack the cognitive development** to recognize the subtle symptoms of concussion.

8. **Children lack the language development** to alert coaches or parents to concussion symptoms or explain them appropriately, especially if they occurred in the past.

9. **Children have poor access to medical resources.** No athletic trainer. No team doctor.

10. **Children's coaches may lack appropriate training.** USA Hockey requires extensive training for youth hockey coaches, including concussion training, and most hockey coaches are required to take the training. In youth football, training is up to the league, and most require no training at all.

11. **Children cannot provide informed consent.**

Children vs. Adults

Informed consent is one of the more important issues as we work to solve the concussion crisis. I worry less about the future of professional sports than I do that of youth sports. The NFL and NHL are allowed to be dangerous because we allow adults to perform dangerous jobs in America. The key issue is the concept of informed consent—are they aware of the risks involved? Before the NFL began actively warning players in 2010, it was hard to make the case that anyone understood the risks of playing. That's one of the major reasons why I wrote *Head Games: Football's Concussion Crisis* in 2006, because everyone deserved to choose whether they wanted to take the risks.

Children, however, cannot provide informed consent before the age of eighteen. Think of all the things we don't let them do, because we don't believe they can understand the consequences; we don't let them vote, drink, serve in the military, or sign contracts. If they break the law, we have a special court system for juveniles. We don't let them smoke cigarettes, and we don't even let cigarette companies advertise on television anymore, lest they be tempted. Why are we asking them what sport they want to play, and letting them choose whether they want to risk CTE?

The connection between smoking and lung cancer is probably most analogous to brain trauma and CTE. It's a behavior that can start young, and you won't notice the effects for years, if not decades. Both are likely a dose-response relationship, meaning that the more you smoke or the more you get hit in the head, the higher your risk of problems.

But because there is little initial evidence that either activity is dangerous, we were unaware of the consequences until a lot of research was conducted. When we did connect the dots between smoking and lung cancer, we banned smoking from just about every public aspect of life, and it's against the law to smoke or buy cigarettes if you are under eighteen.

What has been our reaction to brain trauma? We don't limit how frequently or how hard they are hit. Not quite the same. We don't set age limits for when a child may begin receiving brain trauma in sports. We ban teaching boys in baseball to throw a curveball until the age of twelve because we know that it might be dangerous for their elbow ligament. And yet as soon as a kid is old enough to run, it's open season on his brain. Thanks to pitch counts, America is the safest country for a young boy or girl to grow up with an elbow. Thanks to the absence of hit counts, it's also the most dangerous country for a boy or girl to have a brain.

One way to combat the greater risks for children is to invest in a greater medical infrastructure – more personnel, technology, and training. The reality is that we do not, and children are at the greatest risk to suffer preventable brain damage. Because of this information and his decades of clinical experience, Dr. Cantu, in his book *Concussions and Our Kids*, advocates no repetitive brain trauma for children under the age of fourteen, partially because we don't do enough to protect them. How do you argue with that?

9. Rules & Penalties

In light of everything we now know about the brain, sports need to get comfortable and aggressive with *reform*. Everything needs to be in play, down to the building blocks of the game. Let's remember that a sport is not static. When someone says a new rule proposal will mean "That's not football anymore," they are forgetting their history. American football looks nothing like it did in the 1800s. Imagine how much people fought against the forward pass.

225

Throwing a football? That's crazy! Banning the flying wedge? How dare you! Remember that the National Basketball Association didn't have a three-point line or a shot clock in *my lifetime*.

Health and safety is a better reason to reform a game for children than is entertainment or increased scoring, so let's stop complaining and get to work. USA Hockey was a leader in this reform, raising the age in which they introduce checking from eleven to thirteen. Many fought the change, saying that children need to "learn how to get hit," and if they don't learn until thirteen, the players are so much faster and stronger that the outcome will be worse.

Though a logical theory, the evidence didn't support it. A study was performed tracking concussions in leagues children learned to check at eleven and at thirteen. They found that players who were in their first year of checking at thirteen suffered no more concussions than the players in their third year of checking.[204] Because checking increases concussions, the net effect was that by waiting until thirteen it would save the players tens of thousands of concussions. The reality is that every child learns how to brace for a hit *the second time*. That first time, look out!

The Ivy League created the Ivy League Multi-Sport Concussion Committee to review every sport, top to bottom, to identify ways to make the games safer. No other college conference has gone that far yet. The NFL has been severely penalizing intentional hits to the head. The result? There were fewer top players, especially quarterbacks and receivers, getting injured, as well as more passing touchdowns.

The NHL did a tremendous job in making hockey safer through rules, rule enforcement, and penalties in 2011–12. Brendan Shanahan, the future Hall of Famer, is now the Senior Vice President for Player Safety for the NHL. If a player intentionally hits another player in the head, that player is no longer given a 2-minute penalty, but a 25-game suspension. That is the right and fair thing to do. Think about it strategically. If the penalty for going after the head was a 2-

minute penalty or one-game suspension, in big game or seven-game playoff series why wouldn't you try to concuss the opponent's best players? With the strength and speed of modern athletes, it's not that hard to knock someone out, so in a game with lax enforcement, it was a great trade. Today, with the threat of major suspensions, fines, and more, cheap shots to the head are on their way out of the game.

I have to applaud the NHL's effort on this, because not only are they enforcing new rules, but they are teaching with them. Brendan Shanahan makes videos that are posted on YouTube every time he suspends someone. They explain everything step by step:

> *Brendan Shanahan: Wednesday night in Chicago, an incident occurred during the game between the Chicago Blackhawks and the Detroit Red Wings. At 5:26 of the third period Detroit defenseman Brendan Smith delivered an illegal hit to the head of Chicago forward Ben Smith causing him to lose consciousness. I have suspended him for the remainder of the preseason plus 5 regular season games.*

I anticipate that this strict enforcement of safety rules will also have an impact on fighting. Fighting in hockey is one of those curious phenomena that prove that the NHL is more sports-entertainment than pure sports. But considering I used to jump through tables and take chair shots to the head for my WWE career, I have to fall back on the idea that adults can do dangerous jobs if they understand the risks. Now that we at BU CSTE are telling them about the risks, including publicizing that former enforcers Reggie Fleming, Bob Probert, and Derek Boogaard all had CTE when they died, it's up to the players and the league to figure out the future of fighting. With stiff penalties for cheap shots, however, Shanahan might be right when he said, "Here at the NHL, I'm the new enforcer."

All of the rule changes need to eventually get us to a place where the head is off-limits, and under no circumstances should we accept hits to the head as a normal part of the game. We can accept accidents, but we cannot be complacent with repetitive brain trauma. Former NFL player and coach Herm Edwards was recently on ESPN's *Outside the Lines* talking about youth football, and in defense of youth football, said that concussions can happen in any aspect of life, and a child can hurt his head getting hit by a car walking out his front door.

What Herm and everyone is missing is that that same child may get hit by a car once, but he will not be hit by a car 500 times (unless he lives on a *very* dangerous street). He will get hit in the head at car-crash type forces over and over again in football. That is what we need to be thinking about.

Changing substitution rules, especially in sports like soccer and rugby, are an obvious place to make gains, as was discussed earlier.

Cindy Parlow Cone, who is still coaching soccer, has seen how the current international substitution limit of three puts players at risk. She told me, "A lot of times people will reserve one of those subs in case someone gets hurt late. So, you're really looking at 2 subs and maybe a late sub. And so to have to sub someone out early in the game is either a huge tactical move or a move that you just don't want to make unless you absolutely have to." The net effect is that soccer players are asked to keep playing through concussion. In a 2012 match between the U.S. Women's Soccer Olympic team and New Zealand, the New Zealand goalie was very clearly knocked unconscious by a collision. She continued playing and finished the game, and no one said much about it.[205]

I also recommend that parents become advocates for rule changes. One of my favorite parent moments came in an ice hockey game. Gina O'Toole was watching her sixteen-year-old son Mark's team play near Boston when a fight broke out. Fighting is illegal in youth hockey, but the referee refused to break it up. He just stood on the periphery, occasionally blowing his whistle. She watched the players punching each other in the head for over a minute before she'd had enough.[206] She walked out onto the ice and started screaming at the referee. Caught on tape, the video of her wagging her finger at the lazy referee went viral and Gina was soon on *Good Morning America.*

She said, "I've seen fights usually between one or two children and the refs usually step in immediately and break it up. That didn't happen. I just found myself opening the gate and walking onto the ice and saying, 'Hey, you need to get control of this game. What are you doing?'

"The ref turned around and he yelled at me and told me to get off the ice and I said, 'You need to do your job!' What concerned me was the feeling of the blows to the back of the head and a child going down the ice of maybe a potential head injury."

When I read that she went on the ice to prevent a head injury, I tracked her down and gave her a call to tell her she was my new hero. I hope more parents feel confident enough to intervene when something stupid is going on. The public embarrassment will last minutes, but the consequences of a head injury to a child can last forever.

10. Playing Surfaces

The last area that every sports program needs to review is the impact that playing surfaces have on the risk of brain injuries. I often hear former NFL players complain about the original Astroturf fields, as they felt like—and in some places may have been—carpet on concrete. That probably wasn't helpful for concussions. The boards in hockey have definitely been a source of concussion, as not every brand has been flexible enough to absorb energy from an impact. The goalposts in soccer have caused injury. In football, the goalposts used to be at the front of the end zone, which caused one of John Mackey's concussions.

Only recently have we started thinking about how those surfaces might affect the brain, and I'm certain improvements can be made. Think about this unique

229

problem in ice hockey: when a player gets knocked out colliding with another player or the boards, they fall and take a second blow from the hard ice surface. The same thing doesn't happen in football, as they fall on soft grass and dirt or turf. One of my next goals is to invent a type of ice that is softer to prevent concussions. Okay, I'm only kidding about that, but you get the idea.

What to Do With Your Child

I've thrown a lot of data and information at you, when many of you just want to know how to keep your child safe and if, when, and what you let him or her play. There is no simple answer, and I've watched a lot of good parents struggle with this question.

Keith Primeau's daughter asked him if she should play hockey. He answered, "Well that's your decision, you don't have to play if you don't want to, but there's no guarantee in life. You could be walking down the street and get hit by a car, or a bus, or stand up in the kitchen and hit your head on the kitchen cabinet and suffer a concussion. I suppose you don't have to play, but we're a competitive family and we enjoy sport."

Keith told me, "She understood, and I think that's the right answer. I'm not 100 percent sure. Some people might sit there and think that I'm not concerned about my kids' health or well-being, but I am. But I don't live in fear of them getting hurt playing sport. It's the enjoyment I see in their faces when they're doing it and that's enough for me."

Dr. Tina Master struggles as well. A pediatrician, she knows how devastating concussions can be from work and also from raising her son Nathan. At twelve, Nathan already has three diagnosed concussions. Knowing what she knows, she was asked why she didn't move him out of ice hockey and into golf.

She answered, "I think it's really difficult because he loves to play hockey, we love that he loves to play hockey and we love watching him play hockey. It's probably something that's hard to understand if you're not in that, so at the point

230

where we find ourselves, we're willing to take a little bit more of a risk. I think there are a lot of families out there where this internal dilemma will resonate. Of loving a sport that has so much risk to it."

Tina Master, MD

I can't advise you on what to do with your child. Everyone's situation is different. Sometimes contact sports have fewer risks than the alternative. Latanya Thomas has a boy playing tackle football on the South Side of Chicago. She told me, "I love the program. It keeps the kids off the street. I mean, they get out of school 2:30, they (go to) practice until eight. You can't do nothing but come home and do homework, and that's how I like it."

Latanya Thomas

Her son's coach agreed, saying, "Football is an alternative to the streets. If our organization didn't get them, then those organizations that we don't want to have them will."

Latanya summed it up, saying, "I believe you have to protect them as much as you can and pray."

I can advise you to be careful with your choice, and very careful with the information you base that decision on. Be skeptical of all sources of information out there, including this book, because there is a battle for the revenue that can be made off of your child. Throughout 2013, the NFL has been on the road running a program called "Football Safety Clinic for Moms." At one in Chicago, NFL Commissioner Roger Goodell's wife, former Fox News reporter Jane Skinner, told mothers while moderating a panel that, "Kids are more likely to get injured riding their bike on the way to (football) practice than at practice."[207]

That, of course, is not true. The statement is based on a talking point that NFL leaders have used, that more children suffer concussions from riding bikes than playing football. From a gross perspective, that may be true, but multiple times more children ride bikes than play football, and when reduced to injuries per hour, football is certainly more dangerous. But as pithy quotes go, Jane Skinner's sounds believable. But it's not true.

I hope this book gives you the information you need to make an informed decision, and I hope you appreciate how much we just don't know about brain trauma at this point in time. There are some simply guidelines to think about, and keep up with our rapidly changing knowledge and recommendations at www.ConcussionChecklist.org.

Giving advice to those not yet damaged by brain trauma is easy. What is harder is giving advice to those whose lives have already been affected by brain trauma. Right now, there is not a lot of good advice I can give you, but I can give you hope. Now that awareness of concussions, TBIs, and CTE has exploded, there are exponentially more scientists working on solving the problem and exponentially more resources to conduct the research with.

If you or someone you love might be affected by CTE, I invite you to join our team as we work to develop a treatment and a cure. I'm in this for the long haul.

If I don't have CTE, I am certain that people I care about do; and I'm not going to rest until we can fix what we've done.

I look forward to hearing from you at <u>nowinski@post.harvard.edu</u>.

Acknowledgements

Head Games: The Global Concussion Crisis is now a third edition, and I have to thank everyone who has been involved for the last decade. First and foremost, I would like to thank my wife, Nicole, for her steadfast support.

I am grateful for the friendships of those who brought their own unique talent and perspectives to the development of this book. Thank you to Steve Devick for inspiring me to update the original book and for turning Head Games into two fantastic documentaries. I'd like to thank the brilliant director Steve James, producer Bruce Sheridan, Billy Corgan for providing his epic music, as well as everyone else involved in the making of films. Thank you to Dr. Cantu, the Board of Directors, Advisory Board members, staff and supporters of the Sports Legacy Institute. I'd like to acknowledge Ann McKee, Bob Stern, Lee Goldstein, and the researchers, funders, graduate students and collaborators involved in the ongoing CTE collaborations at Boston University School of Medicine and the U.S. Department of Veteran Affairs. Thank you to all of our SLI Legacy Donor families who have generously donated the brain of loved ones to research, as well as those who participate in our on-going research to cure CTE.

Thank you to my agent, Kim Zayotti, and her team at Blue Sky for their guidance and hard work. Thank you to Sandy Tennant and his team for their invaluable strategic guidance and hustle. Thank you to every administrator, coach, parent and concerned citizen who opened their door to facilitate our educational efforts.

I'd like to thank my editors, Pam Liflander and Erin Clermont, as well as Danielle Leong and my mother Brenda – the first reader of every major manuscript. I'd like to thank all of the researchers who provided the studies cited in this book and for inspiring me and taking the time to teach me, including Dr. David Hovda, Dr. Kevin Guskiewicz, Dr. Heechin Chae and so many others. Thank you to Alan Schwarz for his Pulitzer-worthy work with The New York Times and all involved in the media who have worked so hard to raise awareness. Thank you to all the advocates on behalf of the brain injured and all who participated in interviews for the making of this book including: Isaiah Kacyvenski, Ted Johnson, Keith Primeau, Cindy Parlow-Cone, Gene Atkins, and the families of Owen Thomas and Patrick Grange – thank you for sharing your stories.

I would like to thank all of my new international friends who have help spread our new awareness to all corners of the globe, including Willie Stewart, Barry O'Driscoll, James Dobson, Peter FitzSimons, and the family of Tizza Taylor.

I'd like to thank the contributors to the original book *Head Games: Football's Concussion Crisis,* many who were instrumental in the 2012 and 2014 editions. I'm grateful to my former attorney and agent, Barbara Jones, for her tireless efforts and now for her service on the board of SLI. To John Corcoran, Dave Fitzhenry, and everyone at Trinity Partners, thank you for teaching me to perform this type of medical research, and then giving me the professional freedom to do it. Thank you Gordon Laws, my original editor.

I'm also thankful for the help and support of everyone at WWE who did not pressure me to return and did not cut me loose, but instead provided a new opportunity that helped get me through the worst years. To Head Coach Tim Murphy and everyone involved with the Harvard football program, thank you for the opportunity to play for the Crimson. This work should in no way reflect negatively on either the football program or the medical staff, both of which I hold in the highest regard.

I interviewed dozens of athletes and their families for this book, and I'd like to express my appreciation to every person that appears in the text and those who

235

do not. It took courage to share their personal experiences, thoughts, and doubts. I'd like to single out the following people who do not fit into one of the above categories for their counsel, assistance, or encouragement: Governor Jesse Ventura, Mick Foley, Walter Norton Jr, Melissa Panchuck, Billy Fairweather, Sal Paolantonio, Jeremy Schaap, Ruben Millor, Tina Cantu, Julius Bishop, Charles Wells, Sue Wells, Anthony Loscalzo, Jen Savage, Kate Taylor-Steeves, Barbara MacNeill, Aron Valevich, Tim Warner, Brian Daigle, Nick Fisher, Leslie Sandberg, SHAD, David Byer, Amy Matthews, Artie Clifford, Jennifer Phillips, and Beth Adams. If I forgot anyone, and I'm sure I did, I conveniently blame my concussions. Finally, I'd like to thank my family, who taught me to stand up for those who cannot stand up for themselves. Thanks for your unconditional support. It was reassuring to know that I always had somewhere to go if I never bounced back from my concussions.

A sincere thank you to you all.

About the Author

Chris Nowinski the co-founder and executive director of the Sports Legacy Institute, a non-profit organization dedicated to solving the sports concussion crisis, and co-founder and co-director of the Center for the Study of Traumatic Encephalopathy at Boston University School of Medicine. A former Harvard football player and WWE professional wrestler, Mr. Nowinski was forced to retire in 2003 from a series of concussions. He now serves on the National Football League Players Association Mackey-White Traumatic Brain Injury Committee, the Ivy League Multi-Sport Concussion Committee, and as an advisor to Major League Lacrosse. Named a 2011 Eisenhower Fellow, Mr. Nowinski now travels the world trying to make sports safer and accelerating the quest for a treatment for CTE. He lives in Boston, Massachusetts with his wife Nicole. To learn more, visit www.chrisnowinski.com.

References

[1] John Seabrook, "Tackling the Competition," The New Yorker, August 18, 1997.

[2] Ken Leiker, with Mark Vancil, *WWE Unscripted* (New York: Simon and Schuster, 2003.

[3] ibid.

[4] Quality Standards Subcommittee, American Academy of Neurology, "Practice parameter: The management of concussion in sports," *Neurobiology* 48 (1997): 1–5.

[5] E. J. Pellman, D. C. Viano, A. M. Tucker et al., "Concussion in professional football: Reconstruction of game impacts and injuries," *Neurosurgery* 53/4 (October 2003): 799–812.

[6] C.G. Giza, D. A. Hovda, "The neurometabolic cascade of concussion," *Journal of Athletic Training* 36/3 (2001): 228–35.

[7] R. C. Cantu, M. Lovell, J. Norwig et al., "Cerebral concussion in athletes: Evaluation and neuropsychological testing," *Neurosurgery* 47/3 (September 2000): 659.

[8] K. M. Guskiewicz et al., "Epidemiology of concussion in collegiate and high school football players," *Am J Sports Medicine* 28 (2000): 643–50.

[9] S. G. Gerberich, J. D. Priest, J. R. Boen et al., "Concussion incidences and severity in secondary school varsity football players," *Am J Public Health* 73 (1983): 1370–75.

[10] E. D. Zemper, "Two-year prospective study of relative risk of a second cerebral concussion, " *American Journal of Physical Medicine and Rehabilitation* 82 (2003): 653–59.

[11] M. W. Collins, M.R. Lovell, G.L. Iverson et al., "Cumulative effects of concussion in high school athletes," *Neurosurgery* 51/5 (2002): 1175–81.

[12] Gerberich et al., "Concussion incidences and severity in secondary school varsity football players."

[13] B. Vastag, "Football brain injuries draw increased scrutiny," *JAMA* 287/4 (January 23/30, 2002): 437–39, citing A. H. Moore, C.L. Osteen, A. F. Chatziioannou et al., "Quantitative assessment of longitudinal metabolic changes *in vivo* after traumatic brain injury in the adult rat using FDG-MicroPET," *J Cerebral Blood Flow & Metabolism* 20 (2000): 1492–1501.

[14] R. C. Cantu, "Second-Impact Syndrome: What Is It?" http://www.teamsofangels.org/research/head_injury_info_second_impact_syndrome.shtml.

[15] Lisa Dillman and Mai Tran, " Blows to head likely caused Colby's death," *Los Angeles Times*, December 7, 2001.

[16] Ann Moore, "Head injuries grim reality of athletics." WTVW, Evansville, IN, http://www.wtvw.com/.

[17] Brandon Schultz news release, "High school football player who sustained catastrophic brain injury settles lawsuit with school district," http://www.firmani.com/SIS-case/release.htm.

[18] Christopher Dabe, "Arrowhead linebacker clinging to hope," *Milwaukee Journal Sentinel,* September 22, 2005.

[19] Lee Filas, "Coaches, players vow youth football season to go on: Parents of 12-year-old who died are in favor, league says," *Daily Herald* (IL), October 1, 2003.

[20] Brooke De Lench, "To nineteen athletes dying young," Mom's Team Media, http://www.momsteam.com/alpha/features/editorial/ seventeen_athletes.shtml.

[21] Ed Koch, "Player's death stuns school, community." *Las Vegas Sun,* November 24, 2003.

[22] ABC News, Denver, "Teen took two blows before fatal football game: Doctors say Snakenberg died from closed head injury," September 22, 2004, http://www.thedenverchannel.com/news/3751851/detail.html.

[23] Tanya Schevitz, "Student dies day after football-field accident. *San Francisco Chronicle,*" November 8, 2004, http://www.SFGate.com/.

[24] Guskiewicz et al., "Epidemiology of concussion in collegiate and high school football players."

[25] J. T. Barth, W. M. Alves, T. V. Ryan et al., "Mild head injury in sports: Neuropsychological sequelae and recovery of function," in *Mild Head Injury,* ed. H . S . Levin, H. M. Eisenberg, A. L. Benton (New York: Oxford University Press, 1989). 257–75.

[26] K. M. Guskiewicz et al., "Cumulative effects associated with recurrent concussion in collegiate football players: The NCAA concussion study," *JAMA* 290/19 (November 19, 2003): 2549–55.

[27] Zemper, "Two-year prospective study of relative risk of a second cerebral concussion.

[28] M. McCrea, J.P. Kelly, J. Kluge et al., "Standardized assessment of concussion in football players," *Neurology* 48 (1997): 586–88.

[29] J. Powell, K. Barber-Foss, "Traumatic brain injury in high school athletes," *JAMA* 282 (1999): 958–63.

[30] W. Langburt, B. Cohen B, N. Akhthar et al., "Incidence of concussion in high school football players of Ohio and Pennsylvania." *Journal of Child Neurology* 16/2 (February 2001): 83–85.

[31] J. S. Delaney, V. J. Lacroix, S. Leclerc et al., "Concussion among university football and soccer players," *Clin J Sport Med* 12/6 (November 2002): 331–38

[32] J. S. Delaney, V. J. Lacroix, S. Leclerc et al., "Concussions during the 1997 Canadian Football League season," *Clin J Sport Med* 10/1 (January 2000): 9–14.

[33] Bruce Jancin, "College football players often underreport head injury symptoms to coaches and trainers." Larik Woronzoff-Dashkoff, MD. *Family Practice News,* May 15, 2001.

[34] Gerberich et al., "Concussion incidences and severity in secondary school varsity football players."

[35] M. McCrea, T. Hammeke, G. Olsen et al., "Unreported concussion in high school football players: Implications for prevention," *Clin J Sport Med* 14/1 (January 2004): 13–17.

[36] J.M. Sefton, K. Pirog, A. Capitao et al., "An examination of factors that influence knowledge and reporting of mild brain injuries in collegiate football," *Journal of Athletic Training* 39/2. (June 2004).

[37] M. W. Collins, S. H. Grindel, M. R. Lovell et al., "Relationship between concussion and neuropsychological performance in college football players," *JAMA* 282/10 (Sept 8, 1999): 964–70.

[38] Delaney et al., "Concussion among university football and soccer players."

[39] Guskiewicz KM, Marshall SW, Bailes JB, et al. Association between recurrent concussion and late-life cognitive impairment in retired professional football players *Neurosurgery* 57:4 (2005): 719–726.

[40] Molgaard CA, Stanford EP, Morton DJ, et al. Epidemiology of head trauma and neurocognitive impairment in a multi-ethnic population. *Neuroepidemiology* 190:9 (1990): 233–242.

[41] Molgaard CA, Stanford EP, Morton DJ, et al. Epidemiology of head trauma and neurocognitive impairment in a multi-ethnic population. *Neuroepidemiology* 190:9 (1990): 233–242.

[42] Associated Press. October 3, 2002. ESPN.com. http://espn.go.com/classic/obit/s/2002/0924/1435977.html.

[43] Garber, Greg. A tormented soul. ESPN.com. January 24–28, 2005.

[44] Omalu BI, DeKosky ST, Minster RL, et al. Chronic traumatic encephalopathy in a National Football League player. *Neurosurgery* 57:1 (July 2005): 128–134.

[45] Roberts AH. *Brain Damage in Boxers*. London: Pitman Medical Scientific Publishing Co., 1969.

[46] Hamberger A, Huang YL, Zhu H, et al. Redistribution of neurofilaments and accumulation of beta-amyloid protein after brain injury by rotational acceleration of the head. *J Neurotrauma* 20:2 (February 2003): 169–178.

[47] Chen XH, Siman R, Iwata A, et al. Long-term accumulation of amyloid-secretase, presenilin-1, and caspase-3 in damaged axons following brain trauma. *American Journal of Pathology*, 165:2 (August 2004): 357–371.

[48] Roberts GW, Allsop D, Bruton C. The occult aftermath of boxing. *J Neurol Neurosurg Psychiatry* 53 (1990): 373–378.

[49] Casson IR, Pellman EJ, Viano DC. Correspondence. *Neurosurgery*. 58:5. May, 2006.

[50] LaRussa, Tony. Ex-Steeler Long drank antifreeze. *Pittsburgh Tribune- Review*, January 27, 2006.

[51] Associated Press. September 13, 2005. http://msn.foxsports.com/nfl/story/4867722.

[52] Greenwood, Jill King. Terry Long's death tied to football injuries. *Pittsburgh Tribune-Review*, September 14, 2005.

[53] Bouchette, Ed. Surgeon disagrees with Wecht that football killed Long. *Pittsburgh Post-Gazette*, September 15, 2005.

[54] Milbank, Dana. Nobody sings in this 5th Amendment stretch. *Washington Post*, March 18, 2005.

[55] McKinley, James C. Jr. A perplexing foe takes an awful toll. *New York Times*, May 11, 2000.

[56] Pellman, Elliott. Interviewed by *Inside the NFL*, HBO Sports, December 10, 2003.

[57] Seel RT, Kreutzer JS. Depression assessment after traumatic brain injury: An empirically based classification method. *Arch Phys Med Rehabil* 84:11 (November 2003): 1621–1628.

[58] Glenn MB, et al. Depression amongst outpatients with traumatic brain injury. *Brain Inj* 15:9 (Sep 2001): 811–818.

[59] Mathias JL, Coats JL. Emotional and cognitive sequelae to mild traumatic brain injury. *J Clin Exp Neuropsychol* 21:2 (April 1999): 200–215.

[60] Pellman, EJ. Background on the National Football League's research on concussion in professional football. *Neurosurgery* 53:4 (October 2003).

[61] Pellman, EJ. Background on the National Football League's research on concussion in professional football. *Neurosurgery* 53:4 (October 2003).

[62] Borzi, Pat. Favre's concussion adds to the Packer's woes. *The New York Times*, October 4, 2004.

[63] Reuters. NFL notebook. *Taipei Times*, September 14, 2003. http://www.taipeitimes.com/News/sport/archives/2003/09/14/2003067882/print.

[64] Goheen, Kevin. Associated Press. Victory Sunday is crucial. *Cincinnati Post*, November 30, 2004. http://www.cincypost.com/2004/11/30/ bengnotes11–30–2004.html.

[65] Goheen, Kevin. Associated Press. Victory Sunday is crucial. *Cincinnati Post*, November 30, 2004. http://www.cincypost.com/2004/11/30/ bengnotes11–30–2004.html.

[66] Pittsburgh Steelers press conference. October 5, 2004. www.steelers.com.

[67] Gerheim, Tim. Audibles at the line: Week 11. November 21, 2005. www.footballoutsiders.com.

[68] Trotter, Jim. A softer, gentler Schottenheimer? *The San Diego Union- Tribune*, November 1, 2004.

[69] Sullivan, Tim. Long-term health of Drew Brees more important than the next game. *The San Diego Union-Tribune*, September 20, 2004.

[70] Associated Press. Brees expects to start despite concussion. September 20, 2004.

[71] Pellman EJ, Viano DC, Casson IR. Concussion in professional football: Injuries involving 7 or more days out. Part 5. *Neurosurgery* 55:5 (November 2004): 1100–1119.

[72] Associated Press. Brees expects to start despite concussion. September 20, 2004.

[73] Sullivan, Tim. Long-term health of Drew Brees more important than the next game. *The San Diego Union-Tribune*, September 20, 2004.

[74] Associated Press. Jets lost Chrebet for the rest of season. http://www.msnbc.com/news/992827.asp?cp1=1. November 12, 2003.

[75] Jets Confidential Staff. New York Jets team report, November 6, 2003. http://jets.theinsiders.com/2/198360.html.

[76] Jets Confidential Staff. New York Jets team report, November 6, 2003. http://jets.theinsiders.com/2/198360.html.

[77] Associated Press. Jets lost Chrebet for the rest of season. http://www.msnbc.com/news/992827.asp?cp1=1. November 12, 2003.

[78] Associated Press. Chrebet out for season with post-concussion syndrome. November 13, 2003. *Boston Herald*. http://patriots.bostonherald.com/otherNFL/otherNFL.bg?articleid=129&format=text.

[79] Giza CG, Hovda DA. The neurometabolic cascade of concussion.*Journal of Athletic Training* 36:3 (2001): 228–235.

[80] Jets Confidential Staff. New York Jets team report, November 15, 2003. http://jets.theinsiders.com/2/201923.html.

[81] Cimini, Rich. Chrebet a real head case. *New York Daily News*, November 6, 2003. http://www.nydailynews.com/sports/football/ v-pfriendly/story/134137p-119550c.html.

[82] Jets Confidential Staff. New York Jets team report, November 15, 2003. http://jets.theinsiders.com/2/201923.html.

[83] Cimini, Rich. Chrebet a real head case. *New York Daily News*, November 6, 2003. http://www.nydailynews.com/sports/football/ v-pfriendly/story/134137p-119550c.html.

[84] Pellman EJ, Viano DC, Casson IR. Concussion in professional football: Injuries involving 7 or more days out. Part 5. *Neurosurgery* 55:5 (November 2004): 1100–1119.

[85] Associated Press. Injured New York Jets receiver Wayne Chrebet uncertain about future. December 16, 2003.

[86] Cimini, Rich. Jets give Chrebet concussion clause. *New York Daily News*, March 31, 2004.

[87] Berger, Ken. Knockout blow for Chrebet. *Newsday*, November 8, 2005.

[88] Adelson, Andrea. Jets receiver Wayne Chrebet retires. *Associated Press*. Forbes.com. June 2, 2006.

[89] Pennington, Bill. A sports turnaround: The team doctors now pay the team. *New York Times*, May 18, 2004.

[90] Calandrillo, Steve P. Sports medicine conflicts: Team physicians vs. athlete patients. *St Louis U. L.J.* 50 (2006) 185–210. http://www.law.washington.edu/Faculty/Calandrillo/Publications/Sports%20Medicine%20Conflicts%20(PDF).pdf.

[91] Duff. M.L.B. medical adviser falsifies resume. *The New York Times*, March 29, 2005.

[92] ESPN.com. ESPN.com's steroid hearing scorecard. March 17, 2005.

[93] Wilson, Duff. M.L.B. medical adviser falsifies resume. *New York Times*, March 29, 2005.

[94] Quoted from William Sherman, Growing nightmare of steroid abuse: Athletes' cocktail big in nation's gyms. New York *Daily News*, July 28, 2002. In McCloskey, John and Julian Bailes, M.D. *When Winning Costs Too Much: Steroids, Supplements, and Scandal in Today's Sports.* Lanham, MD: Taylor Trade Publishing, 2005: 38.

[95] Wilson, Duff. M.L.B. medical adviser falsifies resume. *The New York Times*, March 29, 2005.

[96] Wilson, Duff. M.L.B. medical adviser falsifies resume. *The New York Times*, March 29, 2005.

[97] Thomsen, Sara. Favre's concussion raises awareness in school athletes. WBAY TV, October 5, 2004

[98] Pellman EJ, Viano DC, Casson IR. Concussion in professional football: Repeat injuries—Part 4. *Neurosurgery* 55:4 (October 2004): 860–876.

[99] Pellman EJ, Lovell MR, Viano DC. Concussion in professional football: Neuropsychological testing—Part 6. *Neurosurgery* 55:6 (December 2004): 1290–1305.

[100] Pellman EJ, Viano DC, Casson IR, Arfken C, Powell J. Concussion in professional football: injuries involving 7 or more days out--Part 5.Neurosurgery. 2004 Nov;55(5):1100-19.

[101] "NFL introduces new way for kids to play," *Christian Science Monitor*,May 3, 2000.

[102] ibid.

[103] Leigh De Armas, "Catch 'em young." *Orlando Weekly*, June 2, 2005, http://www.orlandoweekly.com/features/story.asp?id=4756.

[104] ibid.

[105] Peter Keating, " NFL Won't Bite on Dentist's Concussion Device," *ESPN The Magazine*, February 13, 2006.

[106] ibid.

[107] Union-Tribune News Services, November 21, 2006.

[108] Dave Caldwell, "NFL Gladiators Have Less Than Total Recall," Knight-Ridder, November 16, 1994

[109] Alan Schwarz, "Expert Ties Ex-Player's Suicide to Brain Damage," *New York Times,* January 18, 2007

[110] Kevin Mulligan, *Philadelphia Daily News*, November 12, 1990

[111] Brian Biggane, "Head Hits," *Palm Beach Post*, November 2, 1994.

[112] ibid.

[113] Caldwell, "NFL Gladiators Have Less Than Total Recall."

[114] Personal interview, 2007

[115] ibid.

[116] William C. Rhoden, "In the N.F.L., Violence Sells, But at What Cost?" *New York Times,* January 20, 2007.

[117] Ken Murray, "NFL Looks at Effects of Head Injuries," *Baltimore Sun,* March 8, 2007.

[118] Alan Schwarz, "Concussion Panel Has Shakeup as Data Is Questioned," *New York Times,* March 1, 2007.

[119] See http://www.kffl.com/player/10454/NFL#ixzz22benO5TY.

[120] Denise Koch, "WJZ Investigates: Brain Injuries and NFL Player," http://wjz.com/topstories/local_story_113164344.html.

[121] Carroll, Linda and David Rosner. The Concussion Crisis: Anatomy of a Silent Epidemic. Simon & Schuster, 2012.

[122] Omalu, Bennet. Play Hard, Die Young. Neo-forenxis Books. 2008.

[123] Personal interview, 2007.

[124] AP, "Strzelczyk Was Fleeing After Hit-and-Run," October 1, 2004

[125] NFL Media, "Goodell Talks Concussions, Health Care". June 26, 2007 [AU: URL?]

[126] Alan Schwarz, Sixth N.F.L. Player's Brain Is Found to Have Damage," *New York Times*, January 29, 2009.

[127] Alan Schwarz, "Dementia Risk Seen in Players in N.F.L. Study," *New York Times,* September 30, 2009.

[128] Alan Schwarz, "N.F.L. Acknowledges Long-Term Concussion Effects," *New York Times,* December 20, 2009.

[129] Alan Schwarz, "N.F.L. Scolded Over Injuries to Its Players," *New York Times.* October 28, 2009.

[130] Howard Fendrich, AP, "NFL Partners With Critics at BU for Study, Encourages Players to Donate Brains," *Minnesota Star-Tribune*, December 21, 2009. .

[131] Bull, Andy. Death of a schoolboy: why concussion is rugby union's dirty secret. The Guardian. December 13, 2013. http://www.theguardian.com/sport/2013/dec/13/death-of-a-schoolboy-ben-robinson-concussion-rugby-union. Accessed Dec. 24, 2013.

[132] Fitzsimons, Peter. Sideline concussion test a disgrace. Sydney Morning Herald. July 11, 2013. http://www.smh.com.au/rugby-union/union-news/sideline-concussion-test-a-disgrace-20130710-2pqhg.html#ixzz2oOllCH9a. Accessed Dec 24, 2013.

[133] Peters, Sam, and Dan Schofield. Rugby's ticking timebomb! Fears grow as evidence links brain damage and dementia to increasing number of serious head injuries suffered by top players. The Daily Mail. August 31, 2013. http://www.dailymail.co.uk/sport/rugbyunion/article-2408067/Rugbys-ticking-timebomb-Fears-grow-evidence-links-brain-damage-dementia-increasing-number-head-injuries-suffered-players.html#ixzz2oUgh5peR. Accessed Dec. 24, 2013.

[134] Peters, Sam, and Dan Schofield. Rugby's ticking timebomb! Fears grow as evidence links brain damage and dementia to increasing number of serious head injuries suffered by top players. The Daily Mail. August 31, 2013. http://www.dailymail.co.uk/sport/rugbyunion/article-2408067/Rugbys-ticking-timebomb-Fears-grow-evidence-links-brain-damage-dementia-increasing-number-head-injuries-suffered-players.html#ixzz2oUgh5peR. Accessed Dec. 24, 2013.

[135] Raftery, Martin. *British Journal of Sports Medicine.* Concussion and chronic traumatic encephalopathy: International Rugby Board's response. Published online first: October 4, 2013.

[136] Osnato, Michael; and Giliberti, Vincent: Postconcussion Neurosis Traumatic Encephalitis, Arch. Neurol. & Psychiat. 18: 181-211 (Aug.) 1927 cited in Martland, H. Punch Drunk. JAMA. 91:15 1103-1107. October 15, 1928.

[137] Peters, Sam. Victory! Rugby facing up to truth as IRB admits 'potential link' of concussion and dementia. *Daily Mail.* November 16, 2013. Accessed December 25, 2013. http://www.dailymail.co.uk/sport/article-2508468/Victory-Rugby-facing-truth-IRB-admits-potential-link-concussion-dementia.html#ixzz2oWGTX8a6

[138] Kunz, Mattias. Big Count. FIFA Magazine. July, 2007. 10-15.

[139] BBC. Tottenham 'irresponsible' over Hugo Lloris head injury. November 4, 2013. Accessed December 25, 2013. http://www.bbc.com/sport/0/football/24797343

[140] Jack Gaughan, Laurie Whitwell, Dominic King and Martyn Ziegler, Press Association. Spurs claim Lloris WAS fit to continue after Everton KO, despite FIFA's top doc insisting AVB should have subbed the keeper (who had a '99% chance' of concussion). Daily Mail. November 3, 2013. http://www.dailymail.co.uk/sport/football/article-2486571/Tottenham-claim-Hugo-Lloris-fit-play-despite-FIFA-guidelines-concussion.html#ixzz2oddwl5ta.

[141] Delaney JS, Lacroix VJ, Leclerc S, et al. Concussions among university football and soccer players. Clin J Sport Med . 2002;12:331–338.

[142] Geddes JF, Vowles GH, Nicoll JA, et al. Neuronal cytoskeletal changes are an early consequence of repetitive head injury. Acta Neuropathol 1999;98:171–78.

[143] Morris, Stephen. Heading the ball killed striker. The Guardian. Nov 11, 2002.

[144] Aspinall, Adam. West Brom star Jeff Astle's widow in blistering attack on FA bosses. Birmingham Mail. Debember 4, 2011.

[145] Pupillo E, Messina P, Logroscino G, Zoccolella S, Chiò A, Calvo A, Corbo M, Lunetta C, Micheli A, Millul A, Vitelli E, Beghi E; EURALS Consortium. Trauma and amyotrophic lateral sclerosis: a case-control study from a population-based registry. Eur J Neurol. 2012 Apr 27.

[146] Lehman EJ, Hein MJ, Baron SL, Gersic CM. Neurodegenerative causes of death among retired National Football League players. *Neurology* 79, November 6, 2012.

[147] Keith Primeau interview Sunday, October 16th, 2011- Voorhees, N

[148] Stern, R.A., Daneshvar, D.H., Baugh, C.M., Seichepine, D.R., Montenigro, P.H., Riley, D.O., Fritts, N.G., Stamm, J.M., Robbins, C.A., McHale, L., Simkin, I., Stein, T.D., Alvarez, V., Goldstein, L.E., Budson, A.E., Kowall, N.W., Nowinski, C.J., Cantu, R.C., & McKee, A.C. Clinical presentation of Chronic Traumatic Encephalopathy. Neurology. 2013 August 21; 81: 1122-1129

[149] Martland HS: Punch drunk. JAMA 91:1103–1107, 1928"

[150] McKee AC, Cantu RC, Nowinski CJ, Hedley-Whyte ET, Gavett BE, Budson AE, Santini VE, Lee H-Y, Kubilus CA, Stern RA. Chronic Traumatic Encephalopathy in Athletes: Progressive Tauopathy following Repetitive Head Injury. J Neuropath Exp Neurol, 2009; 68(7): 709–35.

[151] Jordan BD. Chronic traumatic brain injury. In *Sports-Related Concussion*, Bailes JE, Lovell MR, and Maroon JC, eds. St. Louis: Quality Medical Publishing, 1999.

[152] Roberts AH. *Brain Damage in Boxers*. London: Pitman Medical Scientific Publishing Co., 1969.

[153] Critchley M. Medical aspects of boxing, particularly from a neurological standpoint. *Br Med J* 51:5015 (February 16, 1957): 357–362.

[154] Jordan BD, Matser E, Zimmerman RD, et al. Sparring and cognitive function in professional boxers. *Physician Sports Med* 24 (1996): 87–98.

[155] Jordan BD, Jahre C, Hauser WA, et al. CT of 338 active professional boxers. *Radiology* 2 (1992): 181–185.

[156] Goldstein LE, Fisher AM, Tagge CA, Zhang XL, Velisek L, Sullivan JA, Upreti C, Kracht JM, Ericsson M, Wojnarowicz MW, Goletiani CJ, Maglakelidze GM, Casey N, Moncaster JA, Minaeva O, Moir RD, Nowinski CJ, Stern RA, Cantu RC, Geiling J, Blusztajn JK, Wolozin BL, Ikezu T, Stein TD, Budson AE, Kowall NW, Chargin D, Sharon A, Saman S, Hall GF, Moss WC, Cleveland RO, Tanzi RE, Stanton PK, McKee AC. Chronic traumatic encephalopathy in blast-

exposed military veterans and a blast neurotrauma mouse model. Sci Transl Med, 2012; 4(134ra60): 1-40.

[157] Science Daily. Concussions Affect College Players at High Rates Too. http://www.sciencedaily.com/releases/2012/07/120712092230.htm July 12, 2012

[158] Starkman, Randy. Concussion epidemic hits women's water polo team before Olympic qualifier. *Toronto Star.* April 2, 2012.

[159] Williams IJS, Goodman D. Converging evidence for the under-reporting of concussions in youth ice hockey Br J Sports Med 2006;40:128–132.

[160] McCrea M, Hammeke T, Olsen G, Leo P, Guskiewicz K. Unreported concussion in high school football players: Implications for prevention. *Clin J Sport Med* 14:1 (Jan 2004): 13–17

[161] Kroshus E Daneshvar DH, Baugh CM, Nowinski CJ, Cantu RC. NCAA concussion education in ice hockey: an ineffective mandate. BJSM. 2013 Aug 20. E-publication.

[162] Cusimano MD. Canadian minor hockey participants' knowledge about concussion. Can J Neurol Sci. 2009 May;36(3):315-20

[163] Bagley AF, Daneshvar DH, Schanker BD, Zurakowski D, d'Hemecourt CA, Nowinski CJ, Cantu RC, Goulet K. Effectiveness of the SLICE program for youth concussion education. Clin J Sport Med. 2012 Sep;22(5):385-9.

[164] Delaney JS, Lacroix VJ, Leclerc S, et al. Concussions among university football and soccer players. Clin J Sport Med . 2002;12:331–338.

[165] Schwarz, Alan. Madden Puts Concussions in New Light in His Game. *New York Times.* April 2, 2011.

[166] Acute Concussion Evaluation (ACE) http://www.cdc.gov/concussion/headsup/pdf/ace-a.pdf

[167] Biomechanical Correlates of Symptomatic and Asymptomatic Neurophysiological Impairment in High School Football. Evan L. Breedlove, Meghan Robinson, Thomas M. Talavage, Katherine E. Morigaki, Umit Yoruk, Kyle O'Keefe, Jeff King, Larry J. Leverenz, Jeffrey W. Gilger, Eric A. Nauman, *Journal of Biomechanics*, vol. 45, no. 7, pp. 1265-1272, Apr 2012.

[168] Pittman, Generva. Minor, repeat head blows may impair athletes' learning. Reuters. May 16, 2002 http://articles.chicagotribune.com/2012-05-16/sports/sns-rt-us-athletesbre84f19f-20120516_1_multiple-concussions-head-impacts-athletes

[169] Lipton ML, Kim N, Zimmerman ME, Kim M, Stewart WF, Branch CA, Lipton RB. Soccer heading is associated with white matter microstructural and cognitive abnormalities. Radiology. 2013 Sep;268(3):850-7. doi: 10.1148/radiol.13130545. Epub 2013 Jun 11.

[170] Guskiewicz KM, Mihalik JP, Shankar V, Marshall SW, Crowell DH, Oliaro SM, Ciocca MF, Hooker DN.Measurement of head impacts in collegiate football players: relationship between head

impact biomechanics and acute clinical outcome after concussion. Neurosurgery. 2007 Dec;61(6):1244-52; discussion 1252-3.

[171] Tierney RT, Sitler MR, Swanik CB et. al. Gender Differences in Head-Neck Segment Dynamic Stabilization during Head Acceleration. *Medicine & Science in Sport & Exercise.* 2005 Feb;37(2):272-9

[172] Arbogast, KB et. al. editors. Review of Pediatric Head and Neck Injury: Implications for Helmet Standards. Snell Memorial Foundation, 2003.

[173] Daniel, R. W., S. Rowson, and S. M. Duma. Head impact exposure in youth football. Ann. Biomed. Eng. 40(4):976–981, 2012.

[174] Mihalik JP, Guskiewicz KM, Marshall SW, Greenwald RM, Blackburn JT, Cantu RC. Does cervical muscle strength in youth ice hockey players affect head impact biomechanics? Clin J Sport Med. 2011 Sep;21(5):416-21.

[175] Farrey, Tom. Football at a Crossroads: Safe Youth Football? *ESPN Outside the Lines.* August 27, 2012.

[176] Echlin PS, Tator CH, Cusimano MD, Cantu RC, Taunton JE, Upshur RE, Hall CR, Johnson AM, Forwell LA, Skopelja EN. A prospective study of physician-observed concussions during junior ice: implications for incidence rates. Neurosurg Focus. 2010 Nov;29(5):E4.

[177] ESPN News Services. Browns say Colt McCoy seemed OK. December 10, 2011. http://espn.go.com/nfl/story/_/id/7336211/colt-mccoy-cleveland-browns-diagnosed-concussion

[178] Dziemianowicz MS, Kirschen MP, Pukenas BA, Laudano E, Balcer LJ, Galetta SL. Sports-Related Concussion Tests. Curr Neurol Neurosci Rep. 2012 Oct;12(5):547-59.

[179] King D et al. Concussions in amateur rugby union identified with the use of a rapid visual screening tool. J Neurol Sci. 2013; 326(1-2):59-63. (Dr. Doug King has no relation to the King-Devick test)

[180] Dhawan P et al. King-Devick Test Identifies Symptomatic Concussion in Real-time and asymptomatic concussion over time. American Academy of Neurology, 2014.

[181] Marinides Z et al. Vision Testing is Additive to the Sideline Assessment of Sports-Related Concussion. Neurol Clin Pract. 2013.

[182] Schwarz, Alan. Study Says Brain Trauma Can Mimic A.L.S. *New York Times.* August 17, 2010.

[183] Mihalik JP, Lengas E, Register-Mihalik JK, Oyama S, Begalle RL, Guskiewicz KM. The effects of sleep quality and sleep quantity on concussion baseline assessment. Clin J Sport Med. 2013 Sep;23(5):343-8.

[184] Broglio SP, Ferrara MS, Macciocchi SN et al. Test-Retest Reliability of Computerized Concussion Assessment Programs. Journal of Athletic Training. 2007;42(4):509–514

[185] Resch J, Driscoll A, McCaffrey N, Brown C, Ferrara MS, Macciocchi S, Baumgartner T, Walpert K. J. ImPact test-retest reliability: reliably unreliable? Athl Train. 2013 Jul-Aug;48(4):506-11. Epub 2013 May 31.

[186] Covassin T, Elbin R, Stiller-Ostrowski J, Kontos AP. Immediate Post-Concussion Assessment and Cognitive Testing (ImPACT) Practices of Sports Medicine Professionals. J Athl Train. 2009 Nov-Dec; 44(6): 639–644.

[187] Collins M, Lovell MR, Iverson GL, Ide T, Maroon J. Examining concussion rates and return to play in high school football players wearing newer helmet technology: a three-year prospective cohort study. Neurosurgery. 2006 Feb;58(2):275-86; discussion 275-86.

[188] Mayers, L. Return-to-Play Criteria After Athletic Concussion: A need for revision. *Arch Neurol.* 2008; 65(9):1158-1161

[189] Adapted from McCrory, W., Meeuwisse, W., Dvorak, J., Aubry, M., Molloy, M. & Cantu, R. (2009). Consensus statement on concussion in sport- The 3rd International Conference on concussion in sport. Journal of Clinical Neuroscience, 16, 755-763.

[190] Centers for Disease Control. TBI Factsheet for Nurses http://www.cdc.gov/concussion/pdf/tbi_factsheet_nurse-508-a.pdf

[191] Personal correspondence; Patrick Hruby, "Did Football Kill Austin Trenum?" *Washingtonian.* August 2012.

[192] Teasdale TW, Engberg AW.J Neurol Neurosurg Psychiatry. 2001 Oct;71(4):436-40. Suicide after traumatic brain injury: a population study.

[193] Halstead PD, Alexander CF, Cook EM, Drew RC. Historical evolution of football headgear. Unpublished, given to author through personal correspondence.

[194] www.helmethut.com.

[195] Halstead PD, Alexander CF, Cook EM, Drew RC. Historical evolution of football headgear. Unpublished, given to author through personal correspondence.

[196] National Center for Catastrophic Sport Injury Research. *Annual Survey of Football Injury Research.* 1931–2002.

[197] Mueller, O. Catastrophic head injuries in high school and collegiate sports. *Journal of Athletic Training* 36:3 (2001): 312–315.

[198] Kahn, Chris. Football hits, car crashes have similar impacts on skull. *The Ithaca Journal,* January 5, 2004. www.theithacajournal.com/news/ stories/20040105/localnews/166892.html.

[199] Garber, Greg. NFL players in harm's way. ESPN.com. January 25, 2004. http://sports.espn.go.com/espn/print?id=1718306&type =story.

[200] Halstead PD, Alexander CF, Cook EM, Drew RC. Historical evolution of football headgear. Unpublished, given to author through personal correspondence.

[201] Levy ML, Ozgur BM, Berry CB, et al. Birth and evolution of the football helmet. *Neurosurgery* 55:3 (September 2004): 656–652.

[202] Ommaya AK, Gennarelli TA. Cerebral concussion and traumatic unconsciousness: Correlation of experimental and clinical observations on blunt head injuries. *Brain* 97 (1974): 633–654.

[203] Levy ML, Ozgur BM, Berry CB, et al. Birth and evolution of the football helmet. *Neurosurgery* 55:3 (September 2004): 656–652.

[204] Emery CA ET al. Risk of injury associated with body checking among youth ice hockey players. JAMA. 2010 Jun 9;303(22):2265-72.

[205] http://theconcussionblog.com/2012/08/06/reflection-on-the-weekend/

[206] Kindelan, Kate. Hockey Mom Reveals Why She Stormed the Ice Mid-Fight. ABC News. June 18, 2012. http://abcnews.go.com/blogs/headlines/2012/06/hockey-mom-reveals-why-she-stormed-ice-mid-fight/

[207] Farrey, Tom. Preps at greater concussion risk. ESPN.com. October 31, 2013. http://espn.go.com/espn/story/_/id/9902116/report-details-concussion-risks-high-school-athletes. Accessed December 29, 2013.

DATE DUE

PRINTED IN U.S.A.